CW01081427

DEFIANCE!
WITHSTANDING THE
KAISERSCHLACHT

DEFIANCE!
WITHSTANDING THE KAISERSCHLACHT

G.H.F. NICHOLS

Pen & Sword
MILITARY

This edition published in 2015 by

Pen & Sword Military
An imprint of
Pen & Sword Books Ltd.
47 Church Street
Barnsley
South Yorkshire
S70 2AS

This book was first published as 'Pushed and the Return Push'
by William Blackwood & Sons, Edinburgh & London, 1919.

Copyright © Coda Publishing Ltd. 2015.
Published under licence by Pen & Sword Books Ltd.

ISBN: 9781473833562

A CIP catalogue record for this book is available from the British Library.

All rights reserved. No part of this book may be reproduced or transmitted in any form or by any means, electronic or mechanical including photocopying, recording or by any information storage and retrieval system, without permission from the Publisher in writing.

Printed and bound in England
By CPI Group (UK) Ltd., Croydon, CR0 4YY

Pen & Sword Books Ltd. incorporates the imprints of Pen & Sword Aviation, Pen & Sword Family History, Pen & Sword Maritime, Pen & Sword Military, Pen & Sword Discovery, Pen & Sword Politics, Pen & Sword Atlas, Pen & Sword Archaeology, Wharncliffe Local History, Wharncliffe True Crime, Wharncliffe Transport, Pen & Sword Select, Pen & Sword Military Classics, Leo Cooper, The Praetorian Press, Claymore Press, Remember When, Seaforth Publishing and Frontline Publishing

For a complete list of Pen & Sword titles please contact
PEN & SWORD BOOKS LIMITED
47 Church Street, Barnsley, South Yorkshire, S70 2AS, England
E-mail: enquiries@pen-and-sword.co.uk
Website: www.pen-and-sword.co.uk

CONTENTS

PUSHED

THE RETURN PUSH

PUSHED

CHAPTER I

BEFORE THE ATTACK

BY MEANS OF a lorry lift from railhead, and a horse borrowed from the Divisional Ammunition Column, I found Brigade Headquarters in a village that the Germans had occupied before their retreat in the spring of 1917.

The huge, red-faced, grey-haired adjutant, best of ex-ranker officers, welcomed me on the farmhouse steps with a hard handshake and a bellowing "Cheerio!" followed by, "Now that you're back, I can go on leave."

In the mess the colonel gave me kindly greeting, and told me something of the Brigade's ups and downs since I had left France in August 1917, wounded at Zillebeke: how all the old and well-tried battery commanders became casualties before 1917 was out, but how, under young, keen, and patiently selected leaders, the batteries were working up towards real efficiency again. Then old "Swiffy," the veterinary officer, came in, and the new American doctor, who appeared armed with two copies of the 'Saturday Evening Post.' It was all very pleasant; and the feeling that men who had got to know you properly in the filthy turmoil and strain of Flanders were genuinely pleased to see you again, produced a glow of real happiness. I had, of course, to go out and inspect the adjutant's new charger - a big rattling chestnut, conceded to him by an A.S.C. major. A mystery gift, if ever there was one: for he was a handsome beast, and chargers are getting very rare in France. "They say he bucks," explained the adjutant. "He'll go for weeks as quiet as a lamb, and then put it across you when you don't expect it. I'm going to put him under treatment."

"Where's my groom?" he roared. Following which there was elaborate preparation of a weighted saddle - not up to the adjutant's 15 stone 5, but enough to make the horse realise he was carrying something; then an improvised lunging-rope was fashioned, and for twenty minutes the new charger had to do a circus trot and canter, with the adjutant as a critical and hopeful ringmaster. In the end the adjutant mounted and rode off, shouting that he would be back in half an hour to report on the mystery horse's preliminary behaviour.

Then the regimental sergeant-major manoeuvred me towards the horse lines to look at the newly made-up telephone cart team.

"You remember the doctor's fat mare, sir - the wheeler, you used to call her? Well, she is a wheeler now, and a splendid worker too. We got the hand-wheeler from B Battery, and they make a perfect pair. And you remember the little horse who strayed into our lines at Thiepval - 'Punch' we used to call him - as fat as butter, and didn't like his head touched? Well, he's in the lead; and another bay, a twin to him, that the adjutant got from the ——th Division. Changed 'Rabbits' for him. You remember 'Rabbits,' sir? - nice-looking horse, but inclined to stumble. All bays now, and not a better-looking telephone team in France."

And then an anxious moment. Nearest the wall in the shed which sheltered the officers' horses stood my own horse - dear old Silvertail, always a gentleman among horses, but marked in his likes and dislikes. Would he know me after my six months' absence? The grey ears went back as I approached, but my voice seemed to awake recognition. Before long a silver-grey nose was nozzling in the old confiding way from the fourth button towards the jacket pocket where the biscuits used to be kept. All was well with the world.

A rataplan on a side-drum feebly played in the street outside! - the village crier announcing that a calf had committed hari-kari on one of the flag-poles put up to warn horsemen that they mustn't take short cuts over sown land. The aged crier, in the brown velveteen and the stained white corduroys, took a fresh breath and went on to warn the half-dozen villagers who had come to their doorways that uprooting the red flags would be in defiance of the express orders of Monsieur le Maire (who owned many fields in the neighbourhood). The veal resulting from the accident would be shared out among the villagers that evening.

My camp-bed was put up in a room occupied by the adjutant; and during and after dinner there was much talk about the programme of intensive training with which the Brigade was going to occupy itself while out at rest. For the morrow the colonel had arranged a scheme - defence and counter-attack - which meant that skeleton batteries would have to be brought up to upset and demolish the remorseless plans of an imaginary German host; and there was diligent studying of F.A.T. and the latest pamphlets on Battery Staff Training, and other points of knowledge rusted by too much trench warfare.

It was exactly 2 P.M. on the morrow. We were mounted and moving off to participate in this theoretical battle, when the "chug-chug-chug" of a motor-cycle caused us to look towards the hill at the end of the village street: a despatch-rider, wearing the blue-and-white band of the Signal Service. The envelope he drew from his leather wallet was marked "urgent."

"It's real war, gentlemen," said the colonel quietly, having read the contents; "we move at once. Corps say that the enemy are massing for an attack."

Then he gave quick, very definite orders in the alert confident manner so well known to all his officers and men.

"Send a cycle orderly to stop Fentiman bringing up his teams! You can be ready to march by 3 P.M.... Stone. Townsend, you'd better send off your groom to warn your battery! Times and order of march will be sent out by the adjutant within a quarter of an hour! One hundred yards' distance between every six vehicles on the march! No motor-lorries for us this time, so all extra kit and things you can't carry will have to be dumped, and a guard left behind!"

A clatter of horsemen spreading the news followed.

I stood at the door of the village's one café and watched two of our batteries pass. The good woman who kept it asked if I thought the Germans would come there again. "They took my husband with them a prisoner when they went a year ago," she said slowly. My trust in our strength as

I had seen it six months before helped me to reassure her; but to change the subject, I turned to the penny-in-the-slot music machine inside, the biggest, most gaudily painted musical box I've ever seen. "Did the Boches ever try this?" I asked. "No, only once," she replied, brightening. "They had a mess in the next room, and never came in here."

"Well, I'll have a pen'orth for luck," said I, and avoiding "Norma" and "Poet and Peasant," moved the pointer towards a chansonette, something about a good time coming. Such a monstrous wheezing and gurgling, such a deafening clang of cracked cymbals, such a Puck-like concatenation of flat notes and sudden thuds that told of broken strings! And so much of it for a ten-centime piece. When the tumult began a third time I made off. No wonder the Germans only tried the instrument once!

By 8 P.M. we found ourselves in a sort of junction village, its two main roads alive with long lines of moving batteries and lorries and transport waggons. Inky blackness everywhere, for the Hun bombed the place nightly, and "No lights" was a standing order. Odd shouts and curses from drivers in difficulties with their steeds; the continuous cry of "Keep to the right!" from the military police; from a garden close by, the howl of an abandoned dog; and from some dilapidated house Cockney voices harmonising: "It's a Long, Long Trail." There would be no moon that night, and a moaning wind was rising.

A halt had been called in front of our column, and there was talk of the batteries watering their horses before completing the further three miles to their roadside encampments. The Headquarters party had resigned themselves to a good hour's wait, when I heard the adjutant's voice calling my name.

"Headquarters will go up to Rouez to-night, and we shall mess with the General," he shouted at me from out of the darkness. "Traffic isn't supposed to go this way to the right; but you come with me, and we'll talk to the A.P., at the Corps Commandant's office. They ought to let our little lot through."

Headquarters mess cart and G.S. waggon, Maltese cart and telephone waggon did indeed get through, and by 9.15 P.M. the horses were watered and fed, the men housed, and we ourselves were at dinner in the cottage that had become Divisional R.A. Headquarters.

A cheerful dinner with plenty of talk. It wasn't believed now that the Hun would attack next morning; but, in any case, we were going up to relieve a R.H.A. unit. The brigade-major was very comforting about the conveniences of our new positions. Then some one carried the conversation away and beyond, and, quoting an "Ole Luk-Oie" story, submitted that the higher realms of generalship should include the closer study of the personal history and characteristics - mental and moral - of enemy commanders. Some one else noted that the supposed speciality of the General immediately opposite us was that of making fierce attacks across impassable marshes. "Good," put in a third some one. "Let's puzzle the German staff by persuading him that we have an Etonian General in this part of the line, a very celebrated 'wet-bob.'" Which sprightly suggestion made the Brigadier-General smile. But it was my good fortune to go one better. I had to partner him at bridge, and brought off a grand slam.

Next morning snow; and the colonel, the adjutant, and myself had a seven-miles' ride before us. The Germans had not attacked, but the general move-up of fresh divisions was continuing, and our brigade had to take over the part of the line we were told off to defend by 5 P.M.

All the talk on the way up was of the beautiful quietude of the area we were riding through: no weed-choked houses with the windows all blown in; no sound of guns, no line of filled-up ambulances; few lorries on the main thoroughfares; only the khaki-clad road-repairers and the "Gas Alert" notice-boards to remind us we were in a British area. As we reached the quarry that was to become Brigade Headquarters, we marvelled still more. A veritable quarry *de luxe*. A mess fashioned out of stone-blocks hewn from the quarry, perfectly cut and perfectly laid. Six-inch girders to support the concrete roof, and an underground passage as a funk-hole from bombs, shells, and gas. Separate strong-room bedrooms for the officers; and some one had had time to paint on the doors, "O.C., R.F.A. Brigade," "Adjutant," "Intelligence Officer, R.F.A.," and "Signal Officer, R.F.A.," with proper professional skill.

Electric light laid on to all these quarters, and to the Brigade office and the signallers' underground chamber. Aladdin didn't enjoy a more gorgeous eye-opener on his first tour of his palace.

"Never seen such headquarters," grinned the adjutant. "Wonder why there's no place for the Divisional Band."

I shall never forget the content of the next week. The way from Brigade H.Q., past the batteries and up to the front line, was over a wide rolling country of ploughed and fallow lands, of the first wild flowers, of budding hedgerows, of woods in which birds lilted their spring songs. The atmosphere was fresh and redolent of clean earth; odd shell-holes you came across were, miracle of miracles, grass-grown - a sight for eyes tired with the drab stinking desolation of Flanders. A more than spring warmth quickened growing things. White tendrils of fluff floated strangely in the air, and spread thousands of soft clinging threads over telephone-wires, tree-tops, and across miles of growing fields - the curious output of myriads of spinning-spiders. There were quaintly restful visits to the front line. The Boche was a mile away at least; and when you were weary of staring through binoculars, trying to spot enemy movement, you could sit and lounge, and hum the rag-time "Wait and See the Ducks go by," with a new and very thorough meaning. The signal officer was away doing a course, and I took on his duties: plenty of long walks and a good deal of labelling to do, but the task was not onerous. "We've only had one wire down through shell-fire since we've been here," the signalling officer of the outgoing brigade had told me: and indeed, until March 21, the telephone-wires to batteries and "O.P.'s" remained as undisturbed as if they had skirted Devonshire fields and lanes. The colonel was quite happy, spending two or three hours a day at O.P.'s, watching our guns register, or do a bit of sniping on the very very rare occasions when a Hun was spotted.

"I can see how the subalterns shoot on a big open front like this - and teach them something," he said. "This is an admirable part of the line for instruction purposes."

Whether the Boche would attack in force on our part of the front was argued upon and considered from every point of view. There were certain natural features that made such an attempt exceedingly improbable. Nevertheless infantry and artillery kept hard at it, strengthening our means of defence. One day I did a tour with the machine-gun commander in order to know the exact whereabouts of the machine-gun posts. They were superlatively well hidden, and the major-general himself had to laugh when one battalion commander, saying, "There's one just about here, sir," was startled by a corporal's voice near his very boot-toes calling out, "Yes, sir, it's here, sir." Gunners had the rare experience of circling their battery positions with barbed wire, and siting machine-guns for hand-to-hand protection of the 18 pdrs. and 4·5 hows.; and special instruction in musketry and Lewis-gun manipulation was given by infantry instructors. There was memorable jubilation one morning at our Brigade Headquarters, when one of the orderlies, a Manchester man who fired with his left hand, and held the rifle-butt to his left shoulder, beat the infantry crack shot who came to instruct the H.Q. staff.

Camouflaging is now, of course, a studied science, and our colonel, who issued special guiding notes to his batteries, had a few sharp words to say one afternoon. The British soldier, old and new, is always happy when he is demolishing something; and a sergeant sent to prepare a pit for a forward gun had collected wood and corrugated iron for it by pulling to pieces a near-by dummy gun, placed specially to draw enemy fire. "Bad as some Pioneers I noticed yesterday," said the colonel tersely. "They shifted a couple of trees to a place where there had been no trees before and thought that that was camouflage."

Happy confident days! The doctor, noting the almost summery heat that had set in, talked of the mosquito headquarters that would develop in the pond near our quarry. "I'll oil that pond," he gave forth, and prepared accordingly. Each mail brought him additional copies of the 'Saturday Evening Post,' which he devoured every moment he was off duty.

I made the joyful discovery that the thick stone blocks kept the mess so dry and at such an even temperature that the hundred decent-quality cigars I had brought from England could be kept in condition as perfect as if they were at the Stores. The adjutant learnt that his new steed could indeed buck; but as the afternoon which saw him take a toss preceded the day on which he left for leave to England, he forgot to be furious, and went off promising to bring back all sorts of things for the mess.

Our companion infantry battalion were as gorgeously housed as ourselves in an adjoining quarry, and at the dinner parties arranged between their mess and ours reminiscences of Thiepval and Schwaben Redoubt, and July 1st, 1916, and St Pierre Divion and the Hindenburg Line, brought out many a new and many an old story.

On the night of March 19th our chief guest was the youthful lieutenant-colonel who a very few weeks before had succeeded to the command of the ——. Tall, properly handsome, with his crisp curling hair and his chin that was firm but not markedly so; eyes that were reflective rather than compelling; earnest to the point of an absorbed seriousness - we did right to note him well. He was destined to win great glory in the vortex of flame and smoke and agony and panic into which we were to be swept within the next thirty-six hours. My chief recollection of him that night was of his careful attentiveness to everything said by our own colonel on the science of present-day war - the understanding deference paid by a splendid young leader to the knowledge and grasp and fine character of a very complete gunner.

CHAPTER II

"THE BOCHE IS THROUGH!"

A T 5.10 P.M. on March 20 I was in the mess, casting an appraising eye upon the coloured study of a girl in pink - dark-haired, hazel-eyed, *très soignée*, but not too sophisticated, one would say; her beauty of the kind that glows and tells of abundant vitality and a fresh happy mind. The little American doctor had sacrificed the cover of one of his beloved 'Saturday Evening Posts' for this portrait, and with extreme neatness had scissored it out and fastened it on the wall - a pleasant change from the cocaine and chocolate-box suggestiveness of the languorous Kirchner type that in 1916 and 1917 lent a pinchbeck Montmartre atmosphere to so many English messes in France and Flanders.

The day had been hot and peaceful, the only sound of gun-fire a six-inch how. registering, and, during a morning tour with the second lieutenant who had come from one of the batteries to act as temporary signalling officer, I remembered noting again a weather-beaten civilian boot and a decayed bowler hat that for weeks had lain neglected and undisturbed in one of the rough tracks leading to the front line - typical of the unchanging restfulness of this part of the front.

Suddenly the door opened, to admit Colonel ——, C.O. of the Infantry Battalion who were our near neighbours in the quarry.

"Have you had the 'PREPARE FOR ATTACK'?" he asked abruptly as we held ourselves to attention.

"No, sir," I replied, and moved to the telephone to ring up Divisional Artillery Headquarters.

"Just come in," he said; and even as I asked exchange to put me through to "D.A.," the brigade clerk came in with the telephoned warning that we had talked about, expected, or refused to believe in ever since the alarm order to move into the line a fortnight before.

The formal intimation was sent by wire to the batteries, and I telephoned to find which battery the colonel was visiting and gave him the news, which, according to our precise and well-thought-out scheme of defence, was a preliminary warning not intended to interfere with any work in hand.

Then the doctor and myself and the Divisional Artillery gas officer, who had called in while on an inspecting tour, settled down to tea, jam, and water-cress.

That night our dinner guest was the former captain of our 4·5 how. battery, now in command of a heavy battery that had come into action within a quarter of a mile of our H.Q. The "MAN BATTLE POSITIONS," the order succeeding "PREPARE FOR ATTACK" in the defence programme, was not expected that night, and we gossiped and talked war and new gunnery devices much as usual. No story goes so well at mess as the account of some fatuous muddle brought about by the administrative bewilderments that are apparently inevitable in the monster armies of to-day. This was one told with quiet relish by our guest that night:-

"You remember the —— show?" he said. "A lot of stores were, of course, lost in the scramble; and, soon after I joined my present battery, I had to sit on an inquiry into the mysterious loss of six waggons belonging to a 60-pounder battery. Two courts of inquiry had already sat on the matter, and failed to trace the whereabouts of the waggons, which had been reported in all sorts of places. At the third inquiry a witness stated that the last place the waggons were seen at before getting lost was such and such a place. A member of the court asked casually whether any one had since visited the spot; and as it was near lunch-time some one else suggested that the court adjourn while an officer motor-cycled over and made inquiries. And I'm hanged," concluded the teller of the story, "if the officer didn't come back and report that the waggons were still there, had been there all the time, and were in good condition and under a guard. Piles of official correspondence had been written over the matter, and the investigation had drifted through all sorts of channels."

Midnight: I had sent out the night-firing orders to our four batteries, checked watches over the telephone, and put in a twenty minutes' wrestle with the brain-racking Army Form B. 213. The doctor and signalling officer had slipped away to bed, and the colonel was writing his nightly letter home. I smoked a final cigarette and turned in at 12.30 A.M.

3.30 A.M.: The telephone bell above my head was tinkling. It was the brigade-major's voice that spoke. "Will you put your batteries on some extra bursts of fire between 3.45 and 4.10 - at places where the enemy, if they are going to attack, are likely to be forming up? Right! - that gives you a quarter of an hour to arrange with the batteries. Good-night!"

My marked map with registered targets for the various batteries was by the bedside, and I was able, without getting up, to carry out the brigade-major's instructions. One battery was slow in answering, and as time began to press I complained with some force, when the captain - his battery commander was away on a course - at last got on the telephone. Poor Dawson. He was very apologetic. I never spoke to him again. He was a dead man within nine hours.

I suppose I had been asleep again about twenty minutes when a rolling boom, the scream of approaching shells, and regular cracking bursts to right and left woke me up. Now and again one heard the swish and the "plop" of gas-shells. A hostile bombardment, without a doubt. I looked at my watch - 4.33 A.M.

It was hours afterwards before I realised that this was the opening bombardment of perhaps the mightiest, most overpowering assault in military history. Had not the "PREPARE FOR ATTACK" warning come in I should have been in pyjamas, and might possibly have lain in bed for two or three minutes, listening quietly and comfortably while estimating the extent and intensity of the barrage. But this occasion was different, and I was up and about a couple of minutes after waking. Opening my door, I encountered the not unpleasant smell of lachrymatory gas. The Infantry Battalion headquarters' staff were already moving out of the quarry to their forward station. By 4.40 A.M. our colonel had talked over the telephone with two of the battery commanders. Their reports were quite optimistic. "A Battery were wise in shifting from their old position three days ago," he remarked cheerfully. "The old position is getting a lot of shelling; there's nothing falling where they are now. Lots of gas-shelling apparently. It's lucky the batteries had that daily drill serving the guns with gas-masks on."

The doctor and the acting signal officer came into the mess from their quarters farther along the quarry. "If this gas-shelling goes on, I guess we shall all have to have lessons in the deaf-and-dumb talk," puffed the doctor, pulling off his gas helmet. "Keep that door closed!"

"D Battery's line gone, sir," rang up the sergeant-signaller. "M'Quillan and Black have gone out on it."

"Keep Corporal Mann and Sapper Winter on the telephone board to-day," I advised Bliss, the youngster who had come to headquarters the day before to do signal officer. "The colonel will be doing a lot of telephoning, and they know his methods. Be sure to keep all the Scotsmen off the board. The colonel says Scotsmen ought never to be allowed to be telephonists. Impossible to understand what they say."

By 5 A.M. one of the two officers who overnight had manned the forward O.P.'s had spoken to us. He was 2000 yards in front of the most forward battery, but a still small voice sounded confident and cheery, "A few shells have dropped to the right of the O.P., but there's no sign of any infantry attack," was his message. We heard nothing more of him until six weeks afterwards, when his uncle wrote and told the colonel he was safe, but a prisoner in Germany.

5.15 A.M.: The cook was handing round early morning tea. D Battery were through again, and we learned that a sergeant had been killed and one gunner wounded by a 4·2 that had pitched on the edge of the gun-pit. Two other batteries were cut off from headquarters; however, we gathered from the battery connected by the buried cable - that a week before had kept 500 men busy digging for three days - that, as far as they could see, all our batteries were shooting merrily and according to programme.

By 6 A.M. the Brigadier-General, C.R.A., had told the colonel that the situation to left and right was the same as on our immediate front: enemy bombardment very heavy and continuing, but no infantry attack. "We'll shave and have breakfast," the colonel said. "Looks as if the actual attack must be farther north."

By 8 A.M. the shelling near us had died down. It was going to be a lovely spring day, but there was a curiously heavy, clinging mist. "Want to be careful of the gas shell-holes when the sun warms up," said the doctor.

Fresh ammunition was coming up from the waggon lines, and our guns continued to fire on arranged targets. The only additional casualty was that of an officer of A Battery, who had had a piece of his ear chipped off by a splinter, and had gone to a dressing station. The news from B Battery aroused much more interest. An 8-inch shell had landed right on top of their dug-out mess. No one was inside at the time, but three officers, who were wont to sleep there, had had every article of kit destroyed. One subaltern who, in spite of the PREPARE FOR ATTACK notification, had put on pyjamas, was left with exactly what he stood up in - viz., pyjamas, British warm, and gum-boots.

11 A.M.: The colonel had spoken more than once about the latest situation to the brigade-major of the Infantry Brigade we were covering, and to our own brigade-major. The staff captain had rung me up about the return of dirty underclothing of men visiting the Divisional Baths; there was a base paymaster's query regarding the Imprest Account which I had answered; a batch of Corps and Divisional routine orders had come in, notifying the next visits of the field cashier, emphasising the need for saving dripping, and demanding information as to the alleged damage done to the bark of certain trees by our more frolicsome horses. Another official envelope I opened showed that Records were worrying whether a particular regimental sergeant-major was an acting or a temporary sergeant-major.

The doctor and the signalling officer had gone forward to visit the batteries. Hostile shelling seemed to have died out. The mist was denser than ever - a weather phenomenon that continued to puzzle.

The telephone bell tinkled again; the colonel turned from the big map-board on the wall and took up the receiver. "Col. —— speaking! - Yes! - Have they? - Sorry to hear that! - Umph! - No! no signs of an attack on our front. Let me know any further developments - Good-bye!"

He looked towards me and said briefly, "The Boche infantry have got over on our left! Came through the mist! I'm afraid the ——rd (our companion Field Artillery Brigade) have caught it badly. Two of their batteries have lost all their guns. Get me the brigade-major of the —— Brigade" - turning to the telephone again.

He told the brigade-major of the Infantry we were covering the news of the break on the left. No, our infantry had not yet been attacked; but up in the front it was difficult to see anything in the mist.

The colonel studied his wall-map with intentness, and put a forefinger on the ——rd Brigade gun positions. "If he's through there we can expect him in —— (naming a village of great strategical importance) in a couple of hours."

A runner came in from C Battery, with whom we had had no communication for nearly two hours. The Huns seemed to know their position, and had put over a regular fusilade of 4·2's and 5·9's and gas-shells. The duck-board running outside the dug-outs behind the guns had had six direct hits, and two of the dug-outs were blown in, also No. 2 gun had had its off-wheel smashed by a splinter; two men rather badly wounded.

For an hour there was no further news, and, assisted by my two clerks, I proceeded peacefully with the ordinary routine work of the adjutant's department. The doctor came back and said that A Battery were all right, but could not get communication with their F.O.O., not even by lamp. The 8-inch shell had made very short work of B Battery's mess. "Poor old Drake," went on the doctor, "he'd got a new pair of cavalry twill breeches, cost him £5, 10s., and he'd never even worn them. They came by parcel yesterday, and the fools at the waggon line sent them up last night." Bliss, he added, had stayed with B Battery, and was trying to get the line through between A and B, so that Headquarters could speak to A.

I strolled over to the other side of the quarry where the colonel's, the doctor's, and my horses were under cover, and found they had not been troubled by the gas. The men were at dinner; we were to lunch at 1.15 P.M.

12.40 P.M.: The colonel was again speaking to the Infantry brigade-major. Still no signs of the German infantry in our front line.

Then in one swift moment the whole situation changed. A sweating, staggering gunner blundered into the doorway. He made no pretence at saluting, but called out with all his strength: "The Boche is through."

"Who is that man?" demanded the colonel, whipping round like lightning, and frowning. "Bring him here! Who do you belong to?"

The man had calmed; but before he could reply there was another interruption. A strained voice outside shouted, "Is the colonel there? Is the adjutant there?" Hurrying through the doorway, I saw a tall, perspiring, hatless young subaltern, cursing because he had got entangled in the guy-ropes of some camouflage netting posts. It was Hetherton of C Battery.

The colonel came outside. "The Huns came on us in the mist, sir," panted Hetherton, "out of the wood. They've killed Dawson, sir." His voice broke - "and some of the others. There were only four of us got away. I came on to tell you." He stopped and breathed hard.

The colonel looked stern, but his voice was smooth and collected. "That's all right," he said, almost soothingly. "You cut off with your party and report to the retiring position."

The young man looked dazed, but saluted, and was moving off when the colonel caught him by the arm. "Come and have a drink, Hetherton, before going on," he said; "it'll do you good."

"No, thank you, sir," replied Hetherton, and this time he saluted with body as erect and arm as taut as if on parade. In another second he had vanished.

There was tense silence as the colonel seized the telephone.

"Put me through to B Battery," he said. Turning towards me, he added: "Turn out all the men not on telephone duty to take post on the top of the quarry."

I slipped out and passed the order to the sergeant in charge of the signallers, roused up the servants, and saw that each man had his rifle.

"Now, Duncombe," I said to the left-handed orderly who had beaten the infantry crack shot a few days before, "you may have a chance to see if your eye is in to-day."

When I got back to the mess, I learned that the infantry had news that the Boche was coming over the crest towards our battle positions. The major commanding B Battery had told the colonel that his battery and A had the enemy in full view, and were firing with open sights. "We are killing hundreds of 'em, sir," he had reported with delightful insouciance.

One sharp outburst from the colonel. As he came outside to see if our twenty-odd men were placed in the best positions for defending the quarry, he looked across and noted that the officers' chargers were saddled up, and that the grooms were leading them on to the road above.

"Stop those horses!" he called out angrily. "Who gave orders for them to leave? Have my horses unsaddled at once. There's always some damn fellow who does a stupid thing like that and puts the wind up people."

The situation was really saved by the adjutant's new charger, which, startled by an overcoat the groom had flung over him, began the best exhibition of bucking he had given since he joined us. As he was in the lead, and access to the road was by a narrow closed-in track, no one could get by him.

The grooms in a shamefaced way protested that some one had passed the "Saddle-up" order, and had a few hectic stinging words addressed to them. Apparently a mounted orderly, galloping past with a message, had shouted out something about the enemy being close behind.

The incident being closed, the colonel and myself strapped on belts and revolvers. The colonel glanced swiftly at the map position of the battery that the approaching Huns had scuppered, and then said quickly -

"Whatever happens, we shall have time for something to eat. Tell Manning to bring in lunch."

CHAPTER III

THE END OF A BATTERY

W E NONE OF us exactly enjoyed that lunch. It was a nice
lunch, too: the steak cut thin, like steak *à la minute*, and not
overdone, with crisp onion sprigs - "bristled onions" the cook always
called them; and, wonder of wonders! a pudding made by cribbing our
bread allowance, with plum jam and a few strips of macaroni to spice
it up. But the thought that the Boche had scuppered C Battery not a
thousand yards away, and was coming on, did *not* improve the appetite.
And news of what was really happening was so scant and so indefinite!
The colonel commented once on the tenderness of the steak, and then
looked thoughtful; the doctor remained dumb; for myself, I felt keyed
up to the state that seems to clear the mind and to make one doubly
alert in execution, but my hand did perhaps shake a trifle, and I drank
two whiskies instead of my usual one. I thought of one or two things I
ought to have done and had left undone. I remember feeling distinctly
annoyed because a particular hair lotion on its way from England might
not be delivered. I made sure that a certain discoloured Edward and
Alexandra Coronation medal - given me for luck - was secure in my
pocket-book, and stuffed my breast-pockets with all the cigars they
would hold.

Lunch was finished in about eight minutes, and the imperturbable
Manning cleared away.

"What about these Defence File papers and the maps on the wall,
sir?" I asked the colonel, my mind harking back to newspaper accounts
of German strategic documents captured by us in some of our advances.

"Tear them up and put them on the fire. We won't destroy this map"

- pointing to a neat and graphic piece of coloured draughtsmanship showing infantry and artillery dispositions - "until we have to."

I got to work, and the fire crackled joyously. "Don't say we shall have to leave these to the Hun, doctor!" I said in shocked tones, picking up four copies of his adored 'Saturday Evening Post.'

The doctor smiled vaguely, but answered nothing.

Hostile shelling had ceased in our neighbourhood. The sound our ears waited for was the "putt - puttr - putt" of machine-guns, always the indication of a near infantry attack. I went out and made sure that the look-outs at both ends of the quarry were doing their work, and found our little Headquarters army, twenty-five men all told, quiet and steady, and ready for the moment, should it come.

Half an hour slipped by. We spoke on the telephone to D Battery, who were on high ground. No, they could see no wave of German infantry approaching; but Bullivant, B Battery's major, who for the time being was commanding C Battery's rear uncaptured guns as well as his own rear and forward 18-pounders, said Huns were coming up *en masse* from the south-west. "My guns are firing at them, and A's forward guns are shootin' as well," he went on. "No! I have seen nothing of our infantry, but observation is still bad; pockets of mist still about. About Bliss" (the signalling officer who had gone out in the morning and not returned). "Oh! he stayed some time at our forward position and then said he was going to get over to A Battery to see why they were cut off from communication. A lot of 4·2's were coming over at the time, and there were snipers about. He had to duck three or four times on the way and then disappeared from view."

Dumble, captain of A Battery, who had come up from the waggon line, dropped in and hurried off, saying he was going forward to see if he could get anywhere near the Battery.

3 P.M.: No further developments. "I'm going over to see General ———," announced the colonel, naming the brigadier-general commanding the Infantry Brigade we were covering.

Five minutes later the adjutant of an infantry battalion on our left rang through and told me that large numbers of Germans were over the crest and advancing towards what the map showed me was our A Battery's forward positions. I put A Battery's rear position guns to fire on them by the map, and guessed that the Battery's forward guns would be hard at it already.

The colonel came back from the Infantry Brigade, quiet and self-possessed as ever. "Defence in depth means forces more scattered, and greater difficulty in keeping up communication," he remarked, taking a chair and lighting a cigarette. "As far as can be gathered, the situation is this: The Boche got through in force on our left and the ——th Division gave way. That bared our own Division's left flank, and is the reason why the ——rd Brigade had such a bad time and lost so many guns. The enemy is still coming on; and he's doing too well, also against the ——th Division on our right. Our own people say he has worked past their outposts, but that so far as is known they are holding out. The main battle positions are still safe, and a counter-attack is being arranged. No news at all of what is happening farther north!" This was the longest speech the colonel made on that 21st of March.

4 p.m.: I telephoned to the regimental sergeant-major and told him to come up with the mess cart and the G.S. waggon for remaining kit, and ordered the servants to pack up. Twenty minutes later Dumble returned, dusty and dispirited.

"Well, Dumble, what news?" inquired the colonel quickly.

"I couldn't get to the Battery, sir - the enemy are round it, between it and our infantry," began Dumble in cut-up tones.

"The nearest I got was in a trench held by the 7th Westshires. An officer told me that an advanced party of the enemy came over the crest about 12.30. They fired Very lights in response to a Hun contact plane that flew towards the switch-trench leading N.E. towards the battery. By 2 o'clock more enemy infantry were coming from the south, apparently to join up with the advanced party who had sat tight. Both A and B Batteries fired on this new body, and they seemed to me dispersed. But by half-past three, while I was there, Germans in small parties were crawling through the wire in front of A Battery, and getting into our trenches."

He paused and wiped his streaming face with his handkerchief.

"What were our infantry doing?" the colonel interrogated.

"There were only small parties of them, sir, and very scattered," went on Dumble. "The officer and myself, with a dozen men, got along a trench to within thirty yards of some Huns and fired on them. But another party, from almost behind us, came along and bombed us back. We had two killed and brought one wounded man back with us. Another lot came up on our left and we had to move farther back."

"Was the battery still firing when you came away?" demanded the colonel.

"Yes, sir, firing well, but mostly on fresh parties of Boche eight hundred yards away."

A knock at the door, and the entrance of a quick-eyed dapper bombardier from the very battery talked of prevented Dumble continuing.

"From Major Harville, sir," he said, saluting.

Just a slip from an Army Book 136, in Harville's neat cramped handwriting. And the message itself was formal enough: a plain bald statement of a situation that contained heroism, drama, a fight against odds - despair, probably, were the truth known; but despair crowned with the halo of glory and self-sacrifice. The message ran -

"I have fired 2200 rounds, and have only 200 rounds left. My S.A.A. for Lewis guns and rifles is also running short. Can more ammunition be sent up immediately, please?

"The enemy has got through the wire in front of the battery, and is now on two sides of us. If the infantry can assist we can hold out until dark, when I will retire to rear position."

The note was timed 3.40 P.M. It was now 4.30 P.M. The colonel was never more collected or more rapid in acting than at this moment. In two minutes he had spoken to the Infantry brigadier, and asked whether immediate assistance could not be sent. Then he wrote this note to Major Harville -

"Your message timed 3.40 P.M. received at 4.30 P.M.

"Hold on: you are doing splendidly, and counter-attacks are being organised.

"Teams with limbers to withdraw your guns to rear position by 8 P.M. are being sent for."

"I hope the counter-attack is in time," he said to me with a certain sad thoughtfulness before handing the note to the bombardier. "Do you think you can get back to the battery, bombardier?" he added. "I'm afraid you'll find more Boche there now."

"I'll try, sir," replied the bombardier stoutly.

"Off you go then, but be careful!"

In the period of waiting that followed we seemed to have forgotten that three hours ago we were expecting every minute to have to turn out and face the Boche with rifle and revolver. Save for the colonel and two or three of the signallers and a couple of servants, none of us were experienced soldiers; all our previous experience had been in attack; it was something new this feeling that a powerful, energetic, determined foe was beating down our opposition and getting nearer and nearer. Yet, whatever they may have felt, not one of our little band showed signs of depression or nervous excitement. The signalling-sergeant was cursing the sanitary orderly for not having cleared up a particular litter of tins and empty cigarette packets; the officers' cook was peeling potatoes for dinner, and I heard the old wheeler singing softly to himself some stupid, old-time, music-hall ditty.

In the mess no one spoke a word, but each of us knew that our one thought was whether A battery would be able to hold out.

5.30 P.M.: The answer, a grim and saddening one. A sergeant came hurrying in.

"They've captured the battery, sir," he said bluntly, "and Major Harville is killed. I came to report, sir. I was the only one to get away."

I think sometimes of famous cases of tragedy and passion I have heard unfolded at the Old Bailey and the Law Courts, and the intense, almost theatrical atmosphere surrounding them, and compare it to the simple setting of this story, told in matter-of-fact tones by a sergeant standing to attention. "We finished all our ammunition, sir," he began, addressing the colonel, "and took our rifles. Major Harville was shot by a machine-gun while he was detailing us to defend the two gun-pits farthest from the place where the enemy had got past our wire. He fell into my gun-pit, sir, shot in the head. Mr. Dawes, who took command, said we would keep on with rifles, and Bombardier Clidstone was doing fine work with his Lewis gun. The Huns didn't seem inclined to come close, and after a conference in my gun-pit with Mr. Bliss, Mr. Dawes asked for a volunteer to try and find the nearest infantry, and to tell them we'd hold on if they could engage the enemy and prevent him rushing us. I said I would try, and crawled on my belly, sir, through the grass to an empty trench. The battery fired several fine volleys; I heard them for a long time. It was slow work crawling away without being seen, and when I had got 600 yards and was trying to get my bearing - I don't know what time it was.

"Then I noticed that no firing came from the battery. There was no sound at all for over ten minutes. Then about a hundred Germans rushed forward and started bombing the gun-pits, and some of our men came up. I saw about a dozen of them marched off as prisoners."

"You are quite sure Major Harville was killed?" asked the colonel quietly.

"Yes, sir; he fell right in my gun-pit."

We all stood silent, looking on the ground. Poor Harville! The phrase that kept running in my mind was, "One of the best," but with a different meaning to that in which generally it is used. A gallant upright soul. The very best type of the civilian soldier who fought this war for England. Before the war a professional man who had given no thought to fighting: when he became a soldier it was because he understood thoroughly, and believed in completely, all that for which he was ready to give his life.

A clean-living, truly religious man too, who loathed loose talk and swearing, and lived up to his ideals even amid the slime and filth of war. And his bravery was that of the honest man who fears and yet faces danger, not the bull-headed heroism of the "man who knows no fear." Poor Harville!

The sergeant spoke again.

"Before I came back here, sir, after the enemy had marched off our men, B Battery turned their guns on the Germans in A Battery's position."

"Did they?" said the colonel, his face lighting up. "Splendid!"

"Yes, sir; they fired well, a hundred rounds, I should think. They scattered all the Germans, sir: they ran like mad."

We had given up hope of ever hearing again of the two sniping guns sited just behind the original front line, C's 18-pdr. and D's 4·5 how. They were at least 2000 yards in front of the ill-fated A Battery, and must have been captured. What was our surprise then to note the arrival, at a slow easy walk, of the sergeant of D Battery who had been in charge of the 4·5 howitzer. He reported that the detachments had come away safely at 5.45 P.M., and before doing so had "spiked" both guns, and so left their enemy useless booty. It was such an orderly account of action, taken strictly according to drill-book procedure, that I have pieced it together in this form:-

2.30 A.M. A few shells falling.

4.30 A.M. Intense hostile bombardment begun. Officer at O.P. ordered detachments to man guns.

4.32 A.M. Fired on two targets on orders from O.P.

Noon. Communication with O.P. broke down.

12.30 P.M. Attempt to mend O.P. wire failed, as it was too badly cut by shell fire.

1 P.M. The sergeant of D Battery went away to try and discover the situation and to obtain orders.

2 P.M. The sergeant found the men in neighbourhood of O.P. Officer obviously killed or a prisoner. Enemy troops also along road leading to battery positions where officers could be found. Returned to "sniping" howitzer.

4.30 P.M. The sergeant then endeavoured to get in touch with the infantry, and to obtain orders from them. He found none of our own infantry, but a machine-gun officer directed him to hold on as long as he could. He returned again, and discovering Germans close to the 18-pdr. and the 4·5 howitzer, ordered the detachments to open fire on them with rifles. The enemy were dispersed after ten minutes' shooting.

5.45 P.M. The two detachments came away, first blowing up the 4·5 how. and removing the breech mechanism, dial sight, and sight clinometer of the 18-pdr. As soon as he had vacated the position the sergeant reported to the machine-gun officer and then to his battery's rear position.

"That's the way to carry on war," exclaimed the colonel when the sergeant had saluted and departed: "A stout fellow that!"

The reports from Divisional Artillery and from the Infantry Brigade with whom we were in liaison showed that the Hun was still coming on to the left and the right of us. Directly in front of us he seemed quiescent, but our orders were to get over the canal after nightfall. The colonel dictated orders for the batteries to me, and then said -

"I want you to get a telephone line out from here over the canal. The batteries will come into action behind the railway embankment." He indicated the positions on the map. "I'm going to keep an officer at B Battery's rear O.P. until the last moment, and the line must run from him to here and thence over the canal to the batteries in their new positions. You quite understand? I shall stay with General —— (the infantry brigadier) and cross the canal with him. Leave me one telephonist. We'll have dinner and get the kit and the mess cart back to the waggon lines; and you'd better get your line out immediately after dinner."

These orders were clear enough. We dined comfortably, and by 8 P.M. all the waggons, save the mess cart, were ready to move out of the quarry.

As I stepped out of the mess to see that arrangements were complete the regimental sergeant-major approached me, saying: "They say the strong point at —— (about 600 yards away) has fallen, sir. We're quite ready to move, sir!"

A voice behind me, the colonel's: "Put a stop at once to such a ridiculous, panicky rumour. The next man who repeats it is to be put under arrest."

Nevertheless, when the telephone bell rang and I went inside the mess to answer it, the infantry brigade-major's high-pitched voice said in quick sharp tones: "The strong point has just been carried by the enemy. You'd better be clearing out of your quarry."

CHAPTER IV

THE NIGHT OF MARCH 21

SOMETHING THAT AROUSED anger, recrimination, and some amusement occurred during our night evacuation of the quarry. Officers' and men's kit, the signalling outfit, the doctor's medical stores, and the cook's stove and kitchen utensils, had been packed. The sergeant-major had a final hunt round, and then gave the order "Walk march!" The G.S. waggon, drawn by six D.A.C. mules, set off at regulation pace, the mess cart drawn by Minnie, the fat roan, followed with due sedateness; and then, hang me! if the pole of the Maltese cart didn't snap in two. Old-soldier resource and much hard swearing failed to make it a workable vehicle. Worse still, it was this cart that contained the officers' kit, including the colonel's. It was pitch-dark, and the advancing enemy not more than a thousand yards away.

I wasn't there at that exact moment, but I believe the sergeant-major blamed the size of our "on leave" adjutant's spare kit for the breakdown. "A valise and a half, two bags and a portmanteau - enough for three people," he growled. An attempt was made to get our kit away by adding to the load on the G.S. waggon, but that made it altogether too top-heavy; and after ten minutes of sweating and shouting the sergeant-major told the drivers to move off, leaving the wrecked Maltese cart and the officers' kit behind. That was how I found it - on the ground - when, having received final instructions from the colonel for linking up the batteries by telephone as soon as they took up new positions on the other side of the canal, I came out of the mess. The colonel's servant stood by, looking angrily at the abandoned kit; and the sergeant-major, now on his horse, was saying he would try to borrow a cart from one of the batteries and get the stuff over the canal at any rate.

"Get away as soon as you can," I interrupted, "and bring back the first cart you unload at the waggon lines. You've got to get the Maltese cart away as well. Two of the servants will stay behind to help load up when you return. And look sharp if you don't want the Boche to be here first."

A squadron of Yeomanry, with picks and shovels, were lining up in front of the quarry as I came away with three of the signallers. It was extremely dark, there was a dampness in the air that suggested rain, some Boche howitzers were firing over our heads across the canal, and a steady "putt-puttr-putt-putt" in the direction of the strong point, that less than half an hour ago had fallen, told of a machine-gun duel in progress. It was not an inspiriting moment; and over us, like a pall, lay an atmosphere of doubt and apprehension, that lack of knowledge of what was really happening only added to.

But at such moments there's nothing so steadying to mind and senses as something definite to do. Earlier on I had noted marked on a Corps signalling-map a test-box between the quarry and the canal and another one along the railway embankment, not far from the retiring positions assigned to the batteries. If we could find them the labour of laying an overland telephone wire from the quarry to the opposite side of the canal would be saved. We set out, got off the roadway, and did a good deal of floundering about in hedge-bottoms and over waste lands; but the important thing was that we found both test-boxes, and that the buried cables we hoped for were there.

10.30 P.M.: I had reeled out my lines alongside the railway from the test-box to D Battery and to C and A, who, because of the nine guns the brigade had lost in the morning, had become a composite battery. They had crossed the canal in comparative quiet and were now laying out lines of fire by compass bearings. B Battery were coming along to a spot near the railway farther north, and my signallers were waiting to connect them up. Things were indeed getting ship-shape again. I had spoken through to the colonel and put him in touch with his battery commanders, and to the F.O.O. left at the rearmost O.P. on the eastern side of the canal. The colonel had issued a night-firing programme just as if we were in settled positions, and with fresh ammunition arriving from the original waggon lines the batteries began "pooping off" with brisk enthusiasm, their object being, of course, to cover the retirement of our infantry.

Every one of us had turned out that morning immediately the Hun bombardment started. No sleep could be looked for that night either; but there was the morrow, March 22nd, to be reckoned with - it might entail even more wear and tear than the day which was ending; so I sent back to the waggon lines all but six of the signallers, the brigade clerks, the two wireless operators, who had nothing whatever to do, and most of the servants, telling them to get as much sleep as possible. The colonel's servant was still in the quarry guarding our castaway kit; my own servant I had stationed on the canal bridge so that he could report to me as soon as the sergeant-major and the rescuing waggon hove in sight.

Our discovery of the buried cable running under the canal had a sequel equally welcome. One of the telephone linemen said he believed there was another "bury" on the far side of the railway cutting, and that it connected with the back areas. The signalling-sergeant and myself set out on another hunt, and, joy! we discovered, after patient test calls with a D.III. telephone, that by speaking through two exchanges we could communicate with our own Divisional H.Q. It was six hundred yards from the railway cutting, but I could now keep in touch with the colonel in front, the batteries to right and left of me along the railway, and the brigadier-general and the brigade-major in rear.

1 A.M.: My work for the moment was complete and I could take it easy. I stood outside the test-box that had become a sort of Brigade H.Q. and listened to the waspish crack of our 18-pdrs. sending defiance to the enemy. The six signallers - plus a terrier - had crowded into the tiny sandbag shelter that protected the test-box. One of them, receiver to ear, waited for calls, a candle stuck on an inverted mess-tin shedding sufficient light for the pencilling of messages. The others sprawled in cramped positions, snuggled one against another for warmth, and

sought sleep. The doings of the Boche seemed more puzzling than ever. What was happening on the other side of the canal? Five hours ago he had captured a strong post within 1800 yards of the spot on which I now stood, and we had no reserve lines of infantry in front of him. Why this strange quiescence? And then my mind took another turn. What had become of the sergeant-major with the waggon that was to gather up our left kit? Why did he take such a long time? I thought bitterly of my field boots, and the British warm I was beginning to want, and the new jacket and breeches, all in my valise. Why hadn't I put on my best pair of leggings to come away in? The Boche would have been welcome to the older ones I was wearing; besides, they didn't fit so well as the pair left in the quarry.

The little American doctor suddenly nipped my elbow. I had missed him during the last two hours. "Say, son," he said, "come and take a walk along the line: I've happened on a hut down along there with a fire in it. Belongs to some sappers. Come and take a warm."

"Can't," I replied, shaking my head; "I'd like to, but I shall have to be like the Boy who stood on the Burning Deck to-night. I must stop on this spot until the colonel comes across."

The doctor toddled off, and I got the telephonist to ring through to the colonel. "The enemy seems to be waiting. He's not troubling our infantry," he informed me, and then added, "Has the kit been got away from the quarry yet?"

I made sure that the telephonist was ringing up each battery every ten minutes to see that the lines were in working order, and then climbed up the railway bank and walked over to inquire if the brigade-major had any news. He hadn't. "And try and keep in touch with us on this line," he added. "It's the only way we have at the moment of speaking to your Brigade."

2 a.m.: The best news of the night. The sergeant-major had crossed the bridge. Our precious kit would be borne to safety! At 3.15 a.m. he passed again, triumphant, the Maltese cart in tow as well. Hurrah! Let the war now proceed!

At 4.30 the colonel telephoned that the infantry brigadier and himself were about to cross the canal. The telephone wire could be cut, and I was to meet him at the railway bridge in twenty minutes' time.

"The infantry are crossing the canal at six o'clock," he said when he rode up and called my name through the mist. "Batteries will start to withdraw to their next positions at 6.30. Each battery will withdraw a section (two guns) at a time; and the last section must not pull out until the preceding section is in action at the new position." He gave me the map co-ordinates of the new positions, and rode off to visit the battery commanders.

6 A.M.: Extraordinary, it was to be another rainless hazy morning. How the weather always assists the Boche! In the grey gloom on top of the embankment I could see forms moving - our own infantry, marching steadily, neither cheerful nor depressed, just moving, impersonal forms. "What's happened?" I asked a subaltern, keeping time with him as he marched.

"We're going back to Rouez Wood," he answered. "The Westshires are lining up now behind the canal."

"Are they going to hold it?" I asked.

"Don't know," was the reply; "only know our orders."

"Had many casualties?" I asked again.

"No! only a few from snipers. We weren't in the counter-attack."

They swung round and passed over the railway bridge, making west. On the bridge stood a keen-eyed, small-featured sapper major. I talked to him.

"No!" he informed me, "there's no intention of making a stand here. We've blown up all the canal bridges except one." A muffled boom! "Ah, there goes the last one. All our infantry are over by now."

A few German 4·2's were coming over now, mostly on the western side of the railway cutting. They helped to put a bit of ginger into the withdrawal of the guns. A section of each battery had now pulled out; the teams "walked out," crossing the bridge and heading down the road. There was no trotting. The batteries went out heads high.

7 A.M.: On the telephone I learned that the last two sections were waiting the arrival of mounted orderlies to tell them to pull out. Right! I

disconnected the wires, told the signallers to report to B Battery where I would pick them up, and not to waste time getting there. Then I sought a copse on the other side of the bridge, where I knew my horses would be waiting.

The sentry and the sappers who waited to blow up the bridge remained at their posts silent and still. Forty yards after passing them I was alone. I stopped in the road and turned to look back. The sun was breaking through the mist, but it was a mournful landscape - dull, soulless. All at once I felt chilled and tired, and for the first time my thoughts turned seriously and intently towards what the newly-arrived day had in store for myself, for the Brigade, for England.

From the other side of the canal the "putt-puttr-putt" of machine-guns! I turned westwards and went in search of my horses.

CHAPTER V

A GUNNER'S V.C.

NOT EVEN ON this twenty-second of March did we realise fully the vast conception and the extent of the German swoop, and that our Brigade was as jetsam and as flotsam carried along on the mightiest part of the storm flood.

7.30 A.M.: The last sections of our batteries to pull out from behind the railway embankment passed me on the road, the horses walking grandly, the men tired but in high enough spirits. The enemy long-range guns were waking up now and playing a damnable tattoo on the main routes leading west. I saw one limber-waggon belonging to the Engineers blown sky-high, and three maimed horses had to be shot.

At the cross-roads east of the wood behind which the batteries were retiring I came upon the colonel, his overcoat buttoned up, his face pallid with sleeplessness; but his mood was one for overriding difficulties. He rode beside me awhile, and then pulled up, exclaiming, "Let's have a cup of tea to start the day with. Laneridge" - to his groom - "bring my Thermos flask."

"The first thing for you to do," he went on, as we drank tea and munched ration biscuits, a few of which wise folk always slip into their pockets when things are a-doing out here, "is to get wires out to the batteries again. Headquarters will be at Rouez. Division have gone back to where —— Corps were yesterday, and we take over their quarters."

"What's the view of things at Infantry Headquarters, sir?" I asked as we mounted again.

"Well, they blame the mist for the enemy getting past the outposts. Most of the machine-guns they camouflaged with so much trouble never came into the picture. But for some reason or other the Boche didn't follow up. Perhaps he was waiting for reserves, or perhaps he got suspicious. Our infantry didn't suffer many casualties, and I'm sure the enemy didn't. We retired according to schedule time, and things were quite quiet when I crossed the canal at four o'clock this morning.

"Extraordinary attitude of mind some of the men out here nowadays have," he proceeded. "Last night they brought in one of the ——'s, who was captured by the Boche in the morning but escaped and got back to the battalion. He said that the enemy set prisoners bringing ammunition up to their front line. When he was asked how he escaped, he said that a shell killed 'the man-in-charge' of the party and he got away. 'The man-in-charge,'" repeated the colonel. "He spoke as if the Boche N.C.O. were a sort of foreman, and as if bringing up ammunition which was to be shot at your own countrymen was the most ordinary thing in the world."

Two high-velocity shells whizzed above our heads, and the colonel's mare plunged excitedly. The enemy were evidently "stoking up" for a fresh effort. We trotted on and toured the batteries, the colonel inspecting the O.P.'s from which our fire was to be directed, and ascertaining whether there was difficulty in keeping ammunition supply up to 300 rounds per gun. When we reached the Brigade Headquarters horse lines, I instructed the sergeant-major to turn out the telephone waggon in readiness to lay lines to the new battery positions. Then breakfast - steaming tea and sizzling fried eggs and bacon cooked to the minute. Nothing like being out all night for galvanising the breakfast appetite. And no time for lingering afterwards. A canter along the roadside to catch up the telephone cart; then, while the signalling-sergeant, a good fellow who could read a map, reeled out lines through the wood to the batteries, I undertook a tussle with the terminal boards in the huge and elaborate dug-out telephone exchange, that up to 5 A.M. had been the chief exchange of the whole Division. Now that Divisional Headquarters had been established where Corps Headquarters had been the day before, four miles back, there had to be a re-allotment of lines to Infantry, Artillery, Engineers, A.S.C., and the other units that work out the will of the Divisional Commander.

"I'll get young Bushman down from B Battery to do signalling-officer to-morrow. It will be difficult for you to do adjutant and signalling-officer as well," remarked the colonel two hours later, as he bent over his maps.

3 p.m.: A R.H.A. brigade had put in a claim for the quarters destined for us. Three days ago this would have resulted in polite recrimination and telephoned appeals to higher authorities, but to-day, such is the effect of mobile warfare, we all managed to dig in somehow. A decent hut for the colonel had been found, and there was a room in a bomb-mauled cottage, where the doctor, "Swiffy," the veterinary officer, and myself hoped to spread our camp-beds. We had shaved and washed and lunched, and looked and felt respectable again. The C.R.A. and the brigade-major had called and gone off with the colonel to see the batteries shoot. I had forwarded by despatch-rider the Brigade return of casualties to the staff captain, so that reinforcements might be applied for forthwith. A French pointer of confiding disposition, who came into the mess from nowhere in particular, seemed quite to have made up his mind that we were come to stay.

The telephone bell! The brigade-major of our companion Infantry Brigade, with the latest news! "He's not crossed the canal on our front yet, and your guns are doing good work keeping him back. But he's got farther forward than we expected north of us. It's from the south that we want more news. There's a report that we have been pushed out of Tergnier. That's very bad, if true."

A quarter of an hour later he rang up again. "There's a report that enemy infantry are massing in Z 23 d 5.8. Can you turn your guns on to 'em?" I looked at the map co-ordinates he had given, and rang through to the batteries.

4.30 p.m.: Pretty definite signs now that the enemy was coming on. A 5.9 had made a hole a hundred yards from where Headquarter horse lines had been staked out. Another had crashed among the trees that sheltered our mess, and a branch, after being jerked yards high in the air, had fallen plunk through the cook's bed. And they were not long-range shells either. Also, there had been seven shots from the most wicked, the most unsettling weapon in the Hun armoury - the 4.2 high-velocity gun, that you don't hear until it is past you, so to speak. One shell grazed the top of the office in which the doctor and myself were sitting; another snapped off a tree-trunk like - well, as a 4·2 does snap off a tree-trunk. Most ominous sign of all - when the seven shots had been fired, three ugly-looking holes ringed themselves round the colonel's hut. Next, a Hun aeroplane, with irritating sauciness, circled above our camp, not more than five hundred feet up. Our "Archies" made a lot of noise, and enjoyed their customary success: the Hun airman sailed calmly back to his own lines.

6 P.M.: The adjutant of the R.H.A. Brigade came in to tell me that the enemy were getting closer, and that the break-through on our right admitted of no doubt. I despatched written orders to the battery waggon lines for gun teams and limbers to be brought up to within a thousand yards of the guns.

7 P.M.: The colonel was back. A battery that had only reached France three days before had been put under his command, to compensate for the loss of seven guns from A and C batteries. It was getting dark, but the officers at the O.P.'s in front of the wood were still able to pick up moving targets, and many Germans were being accounted for.

The colonel found time to mention more episodes of the March Twenty-first fighting. "Every bridge over the canal was blown up by 6.30 this morning," he said; "but, do you know that D Battery's cook, who had got left behind last night, and seems to have wandered about a good deal, did not come over until nine o'clock this morning? No wonder we retired in comfort."

The brigadier had told him more of what had happened to the ———rd, our companion Divisional Artillery Brigade. "Their C Battery put up a wonderful fight - got infantry and trench mortars to help, and didn't come away until 10 P.M., after putting their guns out of action. One gunner did extraordinarily stout work. Unaided, and with a rifle, he held up a Boche machine-gun party that had worked round on the battery's left flank, and later, with three others, captured the machine-gun. One Boche, who broke through, he chased over half the country apparently, and shot him down. The amusing thing is that when he had killed the Boche he searched his pockets, and found a cake, addressed to a bombardier in another battery. The Huns had scuppered this battery and ransacked their dug-outs. The bombardier was somewhat surprised last night when the gunner handed him his lost cake."

This was a gunner who eventually was awarded the highest honour a soldier can win.

8 P.M.: A dinner much disturbed by German artillery. They started a tremendous shelling of the wood in which we were encamped. Salvos of 5·9's made deafening crashes among the trees, and the earth was shaken by the heavier, more awe-inspiring "crump" of the 8-inch how. There was now, too, a steady bombardment of Villequier Aumont, the village, a mile and a half behind, in which the battery waggon lines had been installed.

The colonel came to a rapid decision. "They'll make Villequier Aumont and the wood too hot for waggon lines to-night," he remarked. "We'll move them at once to the other side of Villequier Aumont. Dump them on the roadside. You'd better go and see it carried out. Leave me two cycle orderlies, and I'll stay with the Infantry Brigade. They have a mined dug-out here."

So, for the second time in twenty-four hours, we did a night retirement. Infantry were coming back along the road, and big shells were falling at regular intervals.

Any amount of retreating traffic on the other side of Villequier Aumont, but no signs of panic or confusion. A block caused by supply lorries coming from the opposite direction threatened to hold up some ambulance cars, but it was only momentary. Our little American doctor did good work here, galloping off to halt the supply lorries and raising Cain until the traffic sorted itself out.

I selected a field near the roadside for Headquarter waggon lines. A stream ran conveniently by. The horses were watered and fed; our Headquarter notice-board was duly affixed to a roadside tree; and the doctor added to his previous achievement by tying a tarpaulin to the side of the mess cart, so that "Swiffy," the doctor himself, and myself had shelter when we lay down.

The moon rose glorious, serene; there was no need for candles to light us to bed. We slept heavily, too tired to worry about the morrow, or the menacing drone of Hun 'planes overhead.

CHAPTER VI

BEHIND VILLEQUIER AUMONT

I HAVE TRIED to explain how "this flood-burst of moving war, such as the world had never before seen," affected one unit of the R.F.A., and one unimportant civilian soldier who was doing adjutant; how the immensity and swift thoroughness of the German effort must have been realised by the casual newspaper reader in England more quickly than by the average officer or man who had to fight against it.

5.30 A.M.: That six hours' sleep under a tarpaulin did me all the good in the world, and by 5 A.M. I was out seeing that our Headquarter horses were being groomed and fed and got ready for immediate action.

The guns were particularly quiet, and I remember thinking: we have retreated eight miles in forty-eight hours - it's about time we stopped. Something is sure to be doing farther north, where we are so much stronger.

Breakfast and a shave; then a move forward to find the colonel, and to learn whether he wanted the waggon lines brought up again. It was a lovely morning. A beautiful stretch of meadowland skirted the road leading back to Villequier Aumont, and my horse cantered as if the buoyancy of spring possessed him also. I caught up Fentiman of D Battery, who said he was shifting his waggon lines back to Villequier Aumont. "The water and the standings are so much better there," he said.

I found the colonel standing in the square at Villequier Aumont, watching the departure by car of the three American ladies who for a month past had dispensed tea and cakes in the gaily-painted maisonette at the top of the village. They had been the first harbingers of the approaching brotherhood between the British and American Armies in this part of the Front: brave hospitable women, they had made many friends.

The colonel was not in such good mood this morning. He had remained through the night with the infantry brigadier in the wood from which our horse lines had withdrawn the previous evening. The dug-out was none too large, and his only rest had been a cramped four hours trying to sleep on the floor. With no rest at all the night before, no wonder he looked fagged. But immediately there were orders to give, he became his usual alert, clear-headed self. "It is most important this morning that we should keep communication with our Divisional Artillery Headquarters," he began. "Bring the telephone cart back to the wood at once, and put a couple of telephonists into the dug-out. They'll be safe there until the last possible moment. It's uncertain yet whether we're going to hold the enemy up there or not."

I galloped back and brought the telephone cart along at a trot. The two wheelers, particularly "the doctor's mare," stepped out in most refreshing style. "The old cart's never had such a day since it's been to France," grinned the signalling-sergeant when we pulled up. Odd 5·9's were falling in the wood; our batteries had shifted in the early morning from the eastern side of the wood to positions more north-west, and two Horse Artillery batteries were moving up behind the rise that protected our right flank. But what was this? Coming up at a steady march, bayonets glinting, a long column of blue-grey wound into view. French infantry! The thin line of khaki was at last to receive support!

7 a.m.: The Infantry battle was now developing sharply two thousand yards in front of us. Shells crashed persistently into the wood; the "putt-puttr-putt" of machine-guns rattled out ceaselessly…. Whimsically I recalled quieter days on the Somme, when our machine-gunners used to loose off seven rounds in such a way as to give a very passable imitation of that popular comic-song tag, "Umtiddy-om-pom-Pom-pom!" After three attempts we had given up trying to keep telephone touch with the batteries, and I had detailed mounted orderlies to be in readiness. One line I kept going, though, between the hut where the infantry brigadier

and his brigade-major and the colonel received messages describing the progress of the fighting, and the telephone dug-out, whence the colonel could be switched on to the artillery brigadier. There was bad news of the battery just out from England that had come under the colonel's command the evening before. Three of their guns had been smashed by direct hits, and they had lost horses as well. The Boche were swarming over the canal now, and our A and C and B Batteries were firing over open sights and cutting up Germans as they surged towards our trenches.

11 A.M.: Orders from our own brigadier to pull out the guns and retire to a crest behind Villequier Aumont. I heard the news come along the telephone wire, and went through the wood to seek further directions from the colonel. It was evident now that the wood could only be held at great sacrifice, and by determined hand-to-hand fighting. The Boche outnumbered us by at least four to one, and French help had not yet arrived in sufficient strength. I walked behind two rows of French and British infantry, lying ready in shallow newly-dug trenches. They looked grave and thoughtful; some of them had removed their tunics. I remember noting that of four hundred men I passed not one was talking to his neighbour. I remember noticing a few horses waiting behind, and motor-cyclist messengers hurriedly arriving and hurriedly departing. I remember most of all the mournful, desolate howling of a dog, tied up to one of the now deserted huts - the poor friendly French pointer who the day before had snuggled his nose into my hand. Near the hedge leading to the hut where I should find the colonel stood a group of infantry officers. One of them, a tall lieutenant-colonel, I recognised as Colonel —— who had dined with us in our mess in the quarry a few nights before the offensive started. His head was heavily bandaged. I learned some days afterwards that he had been wounded while leading a company of his battalion in a counter-attack; and that not long after I passed him that morning in the wood he reorganised and exhorted his men, facing terrific rifle and machine-gun fire - and indeed showed such glorious and inspiring courage that he gained the Victoria Cross.

1 P.M.: The mounted orderlies had delivered orders to the batteries to retire, and D Battery was already trekking along the road the other

side of Villequier Aumont. Machine-gun fire in the wood we had left was hotter than ever. And the German guns were moving up, as could be told when long-range efforts began to be made on the villages behind Villequier Aumont. Half a dozen high-velocity shells struck the road we had traversed, one of them knocking out a Horse Artillery waggon and three horses. Two other horses had to be shot, and the sixth bolted. From the markings on a good horse that I found tied to our own lines later in the day, I concluded that the runaway had strayed in our direction; and in the matter of strayed horses - good horses, that is - the sergeant-major always worked on the principle, "It's all in the same firm." At any rate, we had a valuable spare horse for the trying march that followed.

2.30 P.M.: The colonel had selected the new positions for the batteries, and two of them were already in. While we waited the arrival of the others, we flung ourselves down in a hay-field and watched the now continuous stream of men, batteries, transport lorries, and ambulance cars coming up the hill leading from Villequier Aumont, and toiling past us towards Ugny. There was no doubting it now: it was a retreat on a big scale.

All round us were rolling fields, rich of soil, and tilled and tended with that French care and thoroughness that the war has intensified. Even small irregular patches at road-crossings have been cultivated for the precious grain these last two years. "The Boche will get all this, curse him!" muttered the colonel.

Major Bullivant of B Battery came over the hill on the pet grey mare that, in spite of three changes from one Division to another, he had managed to keep with him all the time he had been in France. He didn't dismount in drill-book fashion; he just fell off. It was spirit, not physique, that was keeping him going. Unshaven, wild-eyed, dirty, he probably didn't know it. His mind centred on nothing but the business in hand. "My battery is coming through Villequier Aumont now, sir," he informed the colonel. "For a few minutes I was afraid we weren't going to get out. My damn fool of a sergeant-major, for some reason or other, took the gun-teams back to the waggon lines this morning. Said he was going to change them and bring fresh teams up after breakfast or something. When Beadle came up with the teams we were under machine-gun fire. Got one man killed and three wounded, and we have a few scratches on the shields…. If I don't get up, sir, I shall fall fast asleep," he exclaimed suddenly. "Where are our new positions, sir?"

The colonel handed him his flask, and he smiled. "As a matter of fact, sir, I've kept going on ration rum."

When the colonel and Major Bullivant went off, up rode Beadle in an extraordinary get-up: British warm, gum-boots, and pyjamas. He had been able to get no change since the Boche 8-inch had wiped out B Battery's mess at the opening of the Hun bombardment on the 21st. It was an amazing thing, but neither of us had remembered to eat anything since breakfast until that moment. The day's excitements had caused us to ignore time altogether, and to forget hunger. But Beadle's tired grin brought me back to such worldly matters, and we fell to on a tin of bully and a hunk of cheese that the signalling-sergeant discovered for us.

"They say we've done jolly well up north," said Beadle, his mouth full. "Got as far as Cambrai, and 25,000 prisoners taken at Ypres."

"Who told you that?" I asked, at the same time ready to believe. Did not this entirely support my belief of the early morning? Certainly we must be doing something up north!

"I heard it at the waggon lines," went on Beadle. "They say it's in Corps orders."

The line of retreating traffic and of loaded ambulance cars in front of us maintained its monotonous length. But the retirement continued to be orderly and under full control, although now and again a block in the next village kept the main road lined with immobile horses and men, while high-velocity shells, directed at the road, whizzed viciously to right and left of them. One kilted Scot passed us leading a young cow. He paid no heed to the jests and the noisy whistling of "To be a Farmer's Boy" that greeted him. "The milk 'ull be a' richt the morn's morn, ye ken," was his comfortable retort. And once a red-headed Yorkshireman broke the strain of the wait under shell-fire by calling out, "It's a good job we're winnin'!"

The colonel came back after showing Major Bullivant his new battery position, and told me to ride off at once to Ugny, where Divisional Artillery Headquarters had stationed themselves, and inform the staff captain that the ammunition dump on the roadside contained no ammunition. "Find out something definite," he ordered.

D.A. had settled themselves in two rooms in a deserted house, and the staff captain quickly sketched out the arrangements he had made for ammunition supply. "A Divisional ammunition column is too cumbersome for this moving warfare," he said, "and your Brigade will be supplied by No. 1 section acting as B.A.C. There's an ammunition park at ——, and if you will supply guides here (pointing to the map) at 6.30 to-night, your B.A.C. will supply direct to your waggon lines. And that arrangement will continue so long as we are conducting this sort of warfare. Is that clear?… Right!"

As I was about to depart, in came the brigade-major, who had been in consultation with the brigadier-general. "Ah, ——," he said, calling me by name, "you can give me some information. Is the colonel far away?"

"He's with the batteries, sir, giving them targets from their new positions."

"Right! Can you tell me how many guns you have in action now?"

I was able to do this, and also told him where our batteries were going to establish waggon lines for the night.

"That won't do," he interrupted; "you'll be too far north. The Boche is coming down that main road. You'd better tell the colonel that any further retirement must be south-west, because the Boche is pinching us on our left. I'll show you the line as it runs at present. I've just got it."

We bent over his large-scale map, and I copied the curved line on to my own map. "The French are properly in now," added the brigade-major, "and we are going to fight for that line. There's to be no more retiring."

"Is it true, sir, that we've done well up north? Most encouraging rumours flying round."

"I don't know," he replied with a tired smile. "I hope so."

A smile and a cheering word from the General, who said, "I've just seen the colonel, and I've put two of your batteries farther forward. They'll help to hold Villequier Aumont a bit longer." Then outside I met Beadle, and gave him the time and place where battery guides had to meet the B.A.C. ammunition waggons, and sent off my groom to convey this information officially to all the battery waggon lines. After which I cantered back, and discovered the colonel inspecting the two batteries that the General had moved to more forward positions.

It was 6 P.M., and the enemy advance machine-gun parties were now certainly closing in on Villequier Aumont, which lay in the hollow beneath us. But I shall always remember the handling of our composite A and C batteries on that occasion. It so exactly fulfilled drill-book requirements, it might all have been done on parade. The noses of the four 18-pdrs. peeped out from under a clump of beeches, close to a pond under the brow of a hill. Dumble had climbed to the top of a tower three-quarters of a mile from the battery, and directed the shooting from the end of a roughly laid telephone wire. He reported only fleeting glimpses of Huns, but could guess pretty well the spots at which they were congregating, and issued his orders accordingly. Young Eames, the officer passing the orders to the gunners, stood very upright, close to the battery telephonist, and let his voice ring out in crisp staccato tones that would have won him full marks at Larkhill or Shoeburyness: "Aiming point top of tower. All guns... Four 0 degrees Right... Concentrate Two 0 minutes on Number One... Corrector 152... Why didn't you shout out your Fuze Number 3?... Three Two-fifty - Two Nine-fifty... Will you acknowledge orders, Sergeant Kyle?..."

The colonel, who was standing well behind Eames, smiled and said to me, "Good young officer that. If he keeps as cool all the time, the battery ought to shoot well."

Hun aeroplanes were beginning to come over. Trench war customs had made it almost axiomatic that firing should cease when enemy aircraft appeared. Three times the battery stopped firing at the cry, "Aeroplane up!"

The colonel intervened. "Don't stop because of aeroplanes now," he said sharply. "We're fighting moving warfare, and the enemy haven't time to concentrate all their attention on this battery."

7 P.M.: The colonel and I walked slowly back to the roadway. "I've sent back to Bushman, and told him to bring Headquarters waggon lines up here," he said. "They are too far back the other side of Ugny, and we're only a small unit: we can move more quickly than a battery. We'll unhook on the side of that hill there, away from the road. It will be quite warm to-night, and we can lie down under those trees."… A dozen or so 5·9's rushed through the air, and burst with terrifying ear-racking crashes along the road in front of us. A charred, jagged rent showed in the wall of a farm building. Three hundred yards farther along we saw the Headquarter vehicles drawn up on the roadside. The drivers and the signallers were drinking tea, and seemed to be preparing to settle for the night in a barn whose lofty doors opened on to the road. "Look at those fellows," ejaculated the colonel testily. "They're never happy unless they can stuff themselves under a roof. Fetch 'em out, and tell 'em to pull up to the top of that hill there. As long as you keep away from villages and marked roads you can escape most of the shelling."

7.30 P.M.: We had tied up the horses, and parked the G.S. waggon and the telephone and mess carts. Twilight had almost merged into night now, but the moon was rising, and it was to be another amazingly lustrous moon. The cook had started a small log-fire to make tea for the colonel, Bushman, and myself, and after that we intended to lie down and get some sleep. "Swiffy" and the doctor seemed to have disappeared. Must be at one of the battery waggon lines, we concluded.

"While tea is getting ready, I'll walk down to D Battery again. They're pretty close up to the infantry, and I want to make sure they can get out easily if they have to make a rapid move," remarked the colonel, and he disappeared over the hill, taking his servant with him.

The kettle had not had time to boil. The colonel had only been away ten minutes. The tired drivers were unrolling their blankets and preparing for slumber. Suddenly my ear caught a voice calling up the hillside - the colonel's - followed twice by the stentorian tones of his servant.

The cry was, "Saddle-up!"

CHAPTER VII

STILL IN RETREAT

8.15 P.M.: "I found that D Battery had moved off - gone towards the other side of Ugny, and A and C were also on the march," explained the colonel, when Headquarter carts and waggons - parked out for the night only half an hour before - had again got under way (taking the road between Villequier Aumont and Ugny) for the third time during twenty-two hours. "Division got news that the Boche was putting in two fresh divisions, and intended to attack by moonlight," he added, "and they thought our guns were too close up to be safe; so the brigade-major hurried down and told the batteries to move back at once. We turn south-west from Ugny and make for Commenchon, and come into action there as soon as we get further news from Division. I have sent out orders to all the batteries, and they are marching to Commenchon independently."

It was a radiant night. The moon rode high in a star-spangled sky; there was a glow and a sense of beauty in the air - a beauty that exalted soul and mind, and turned one's thoughts to music and loveliness and home. The dry hard roads glistened white and clean; and in the silvery light the silhouettes of men marching steadily, purposefully, took on a certain dignity that the garish sun had not allowed to be revealed.

Whether we spoke of it or not, each one of us listened expectantly for the swift-rushing scream of a high-velocity shell, or the long-drawn sough of an approaching 5·9. This main road, along which our retreating columns were winding their slow even way, was bound to be strafed.

We rode through Ugny, two days ago a Corps H.Q., deserted now save for the military police, and for odd parties of engineers, signallers, and stretcher-bearers. Then our way took us down a wide sunken road, through an undulating countryside that stretched up to remote pine-tipped hills to right and left of us. A battalion of French infantry had halted by the roadside; their voices, softer, more tuneful than those of our men, seemed in keeping with the moonlit scene; and in their long field-blue coats they somehow seemed bigger, more matured, than our foot-soldiers.

We had marched five miles when a horseman on a broad-backed black came towards us. He looked intently at every one he passed as he rode the length of our column. "Is that the adjutant, sir?" he asked when he came level with me; and then, sure of my identity, went on, "I've got our supply waggon with me, sir - halted it at the next cross-roads. I heard the Brigade was moving, sir, and came to find the best spot to pick you up. The battery supply waggons will be passing this way in about half an hour, sir."

Keeping daily touch with your supply column is one of the fine arts of moving warfare, and the resourceful M'Donald had again proved his worth. "Refilling point, to-morrow, will be at Baboeuf, sir," he added, "and after to-morrow it will be only iron rations. Good forage to-day, sir."

11 P.M.: Brigade Headquarters had pulled into the right of the road behind B Battery, just outside a village that up to the 21st had been a sort of rest-village, well behind the lines. Army Ordnance, Army Service Corps, and battalions out of the line were the only units represented there, and a fair proportion of the civil population had re-established itself after the German retreat in the spring of 1917. Now all was abandoned again, furniture and cattle bundled out, and houses locked up in the hope that shortly the Boche would be thrust back and the village re-occupied by its rightful owners.

The colonel had ridden forward with young Bushman to meet the brigade-major and to settle where the Brigade would camp. More French infantry passed, going up to the Front by the way we had come back. Twice, big lasting flares illuminated the sky over there where the fighting was - stores being burnt to prevent them falling into German hands, we concluded. Presently, Bushman returned and pointed out a particular area where Brigade Headquarters could settle down.

The small village green would do for horse lines and for parking our vehicles. I sent off the sergeant-major to scout for water supply, and took possession of a newly-roofed barn in which the men might sleep. There was a roomy shed for the officers' horses and a stone outhouse for the men's kitchen. Now about a billet for the colonel!

"There's a big house at the back, sir, with an artillery mess in it," said the sergeant-major, who had finished watering and feeding the horses. "Perhaps there's a spare room there for the colonel."

I went round and came upon the officers of a 6-inch how. battery, who had reached the village two hours before, and were finishing their evening meal. They offered me dinner, which I refused, and then a whisky, which I accepted; but there were no spare rooms. They had got away from the neighbourhood of the canal with the loss of two hows., but told me of a 9.2 battery at ——, that it had been absolutely impossible to get out. "I believe it is true that we've done very well up north," replied their Irish captain cheerfully. "Lots of prisoners at Ypres, they say…. Have another whisky!"

"We have one tent, haven't we?" I asked the sergeant-major when I got outside.

"Yes, sir, but there's a cottage where Meddings has put the officers' cook-house. It looks all right, and there might be something there for the colonel."

The cottage certainly looked clean and neat from the outside, but the door was locked, and it is the rule that British troops only enter French houses with the consent of the owners. However, I climbed through the window and found two empty rooms each with bed and mattress. Times were not for picking and choosing. "We'll put the tent up," I decided, "and ask the colonel if he cares to take one of these beds or have the tent. You and I, Bushman, will take what he doesn't want."

When I took a turn round to see if the men were comfortably settled for the night, I learnt that the skurried departure of the A.S.C. had provided them with unexampled opportunity of legitimate loot. There was one outbuilding crammed with blankets, shirts, socks, and underwear - and our men certainly rose to the occasion. Even the old wheeler chuckled when he discovered a brand-new saw and a drill. The sergeant-major fastened on to a gramophone; and that caused me for the first time to remember my Columbia graphophone that I had loaned to C Battery before I went home wounded from Zillebeke. Hang it, it must have been left behind at Villequier Aumont. The Germans had probably got it by now.

It was half-past twelve before the colonel returned. "I'll have my camp-bed put up there," he said promptly, indicating an airy cart-shed, and he refused altogether to look at the empty cottage. So Bushman and I had beds made up in the tent, and then the three of us sat down to a welcome and memorable *al fresco* supper opposite our horse lines. Our table was a door balanced on a tree stump, and Meddings provided a wonderful Lincolnshire pork-pie. He also managed hot potatoes as an extra surprise, and as it was our first set meal since 5.30 A.M. breakfast, there was a period of steady, quiet, happy munching. One cigarette, then the colonel tucked himself up in his valise, and in three minutes was deep in his first sleep for three successive nights.

"I'll tell you what I'm going to do," I said to Bushman when we got in our tent. "I'm going to take my clothes off and put on pyjamas. You never know these days when you'll get another chance."

I had pulled off my jacket, when I heard a jingling sound outside and French voices. Looking out, I saw a couple of troops of French cavalry picketing their tall leggy horses on the village green. I just had time to rush out and prevent two troopers stabling their officers' chargers in the cart-shed where the colonel was resting. They seemed startled when I whispered that it was "mon colonel" who lay there, but they apologised with the politeness of their race, and I pointed out a much better stable higher up the street.

About 3 A.M. the piquet woke me to introduce an artillery officer with a Caledonian accent, who asked if I could tell him where a brigade I knew nothing at all about were quartered in the village. The next thing I remember was the colonel's servant telling me the colonel was up and wanted me immediately.

CHAPTER VIII

A LAST FIFTY ROUNDS

5.30 A.M.: "No orders have reached me from Division yet," said the colonel, shaving as he talked, his pocket mirror precariously poised on a six-inch nail stuck in one of the props that held up the roof of his cart-shed boudoir. "And I'm still waiting for reports from A and D that they've arrived at the positions I gave them on the orders sent out last night. I want you to go off and find the batteries. I will wait here for orders from Division. Have your breakfast first. You'll find the batteries somewhere along that contour," pointing with the little finger of the hand that held the safety razor to a 1/100,000th map on his bed.

Again I realised as I set out, followed by my groom, that the Boche had moved forward during the night. The village we had occupied at 11 P.M. was now within range of his guns. Two 5·9's dropped even at that moment within 200 yards of our horses. Moreover, I hadn't ridden far along the main street before I met some of our divisional infantry. A company commander told me that the French had come through and relieved them. His brigadier had arrived at Commenchon at 4 A.M., and was lying down - in the white house at the corner. "The Boche gave us no rest at all last night," he went on. "He'd got two fresh divisions opposite us, and shoved up thousands of men after ten o'clock. We killed hundreds of 'em, but there was no stopping them. And aren't they hot with the machine-gun? They must have been specially trained for this sort of warfare. They snipe you at 700 yards as if the machine-gun were a rifle, and their infantry hasn't needed a barrage to prepare the way. There's so many of 'em."

I trotted on, and at the top of the street leading out of the village recognised a mounted orderly of the battery I had belonged to before coming to Brigade Headquarters. He was riding hard, but pulled up when he saw me and handed me a note, saying, "Major Bartlett sent me with this to Brigade Headquarters, sir."

I recognised the brigade-major's handwriting on an ordinary Army message form. It was a note stating that we were to remain in support of the French after our own divisional infantry had fallen back, but that the French Divisional General hoped to relieve our artillery by 9 A.M. We were to fire on certain points until that hour, and then withdraw to a village still farther south-west, and again co-operate with our own infantry.

"Do you know if Major Bartlett read this?" I asked.

"Yes, sir; I saw him read it."

"Is the battery in action?"

"Yes, sir; they were firing when I came away."

Good! I knew then that Major Bartlett, on his own initiative, was acting on the instructions contained in the brigade-major's note, and that the other batteries would not be delayed in getting into action if I sent the note direct to the colonel.

I took the orderly another quarter of a mile along the road, so that he could point out the nearest way to Major Bartlett's battery; and then told my groom to take him direct to the colonel, after which the pair of them would rejoin me.

I found the major in good fettle, and, as I had guessed, blazing off at the targets given by the B.M. As also he had passed on the orders to B Battery, who were three hundred yards away, we at any rate had two batteries in action. He explained to me that the Division despatch-rider had somehow failed to find Brigade Headquarters, but had come across him. He had got his battery into position at about two o'clock, and they had dossed down beside the guns.

The major didn't know the whereabouts of D and A Batteries, so I got on my horse again and searched a village that was farther south, but on the same map-contour. Judge of my relief when I encountered Fentiman, who told me that D and A would be along in ten minutes. I emphasised the need for despatch, and he told me that the previous night his battery's waggon lines had been taken back farther than they should have been; the horses being thoroughly done, they had had a proper halt at midnight. "We'll be firing in twenty minutes," he added optimistically. "I'll dash along and work out the targets with Major Bartlett."

A couple of Horse Artillery batteries had come into action a quarter of a mile behind ours, and shells began to fly in the direction of the enemy in business-like fashion. From the ridge we looked into a village that sloped up again to a thick belt of trees three thousand yards in front of us and to blue distances away on the right. Down the slopes tiny blue figures could be seen feverishly throwing up earth; parties of twenty and thirty men, khaki-clad, every now and then emerged from the wood, and in single file dipped down to the valley and came towards the village I had just left. The problem would undoubtedly be how far the retirement would proceed before French reinforcements made the line massive enough for a proper stand. The colonel was now with the batteries, checking their lines of fire, and encouraging battery commanders to do their damnedest until the French artillery came along. My groom told me that the colonel had had a very narrow escape as he passed through Commenchon. A shell dropped thirty yards from him, and a splinter had wounded his mare.

8.30 A.M.: The eternal machine-guns were spluttering devilishly in the wood opposite. Our infantry were coming back in larger numbers now, and I thought glumly of what the brigade-major had said the previous evening, "We are going to fight for this line." The colonel had conferred with the colonel of the Horse Artillery, who said that his orders were to pull out at 9.15, come what may. "The Corps are particularly anxious that no more guns should be lost." The veterinary sergeant of a Horse Artillery battery had dressed the colonel's mare, although she was too excited for him to get the splinter out. "I think she deserves to have a wound stripe up," smiled the colonel, who was exceedingly fond of her.

9 A.M.: No signs yet of the French artillery. There seemed to be a curious lull in the fighting. Only the Boche long-range guns were firing, and their shells were going well over our heads. And no more French infantry were coming up.

9.20 A.M.: The two Horse Artillery batteries were away. Our teams and limbers had come up, all except one team of C Battery. We waited for the colonel to give the word.

Suddenly the "chug-chug-chug" of a motor-cycle: a despatch-rider from Division! The colonel tore open the envelope. "A Battery... Limber-up and retire," he ordered; "B and D will follow."

"The French artillery has been stopped," he explained shortly. "We are going to make the stand at Béthancourt, three miles farther back."

An officer of C Battery ran across to say that through the binoculars grey forms could be seen in the belt of trees opposite.

The colonel's eyes gleamed. "Got any ammunition left after filling up the limbers?" he asked quickly.

"Yes, sir - about fifty rounds."

"Right; give it 'em, and then pull out at once."

The officer saluted and hurried off. The colonel lighted a cigarette and stood under a tree. "One of the most difficult things to decide upon in war," he soliloquised, "is to know the exact moment at which to retire."

The sharp crack of C's 18-pdrs. firing fifty rounds as fast as the guns could be loaded. Then silence. Still no sign of the missing team of horses. A corporal went by at the gallop to find out what had happened.

The colonel was now on the ridge searching the trees opposite with his glasses. Three guns had been limbered up. Every other battery had gone. The battery commander looked puzzled and annoyed. "The guns that are ready can move off," said the colonel calmly. "An officer is to wait here until the team arrives to take away the other gun."

Even as the three guns took the road the missing team and limber came out of the village.

"The off-leader had cast a shoe, and they had to send back for the farrier, sir," reported the corporal.

"Good," observed the colonel, "but some of you fellows will have to remember that there's a war on, and put more 'nip' into your work."

CHAPTER IX

FASTER AND FASTER

1 A.M.: It needed cool counsels and a high and steadfast faith during the next twenty-four hours. The sunken track along which our own and other British Artillery brigades were retreating was full of ruts and choked with dust, and we thanked our stars that the weather had held. That road churned into the mud-slime to which a few hours' rain could change it, would have become impassable for wheeled traffic. But the chief trouble was that the French "75's" coming up to relieve us had had to turn and go back the same way as ourselves. For the best part of a mile both sides of the narrow roads were occupied, and only patience, forbearance, and steady command eased the block. The Boche could not be far behind, and there was just a possibility that we might be trapped with little chance of putting up a fight. It was a lovely day again, baking hot, and the birds were singing their gayest; but most of us felt savagely doleful. "I hope it *is* a strategic retreat," said Fentiman viciously, "but we've had no letters and no papers for days, and we know Blink All of what's going on. A strategic retreat is all right, but if the fellow behind follows you close enough to keep on kicking your tail hard all the time, you may retreat farther than you intend. When the Boche retreated last year we never got close enough to kick his tail - damn him."

Two welcome diversions! The road at the point we had now reached rose to the level of the stubble-fields, and three batteries of "75's," with much "*Hue*-ing" of the horses, pulled off the track and made across the fields to another roadway. At the same time the "heavies" woke up, and the sound of the big shells grunting through the air above our heads and on towards the enemy who pursued us was *très agréable*.

When we reached the village of Béthancourt we found two brigades of our divisional infantry already there. Trenches were being dug, and our B Battery had pulled their six guns behind the mile-long ridge that ran southward from the village. The colonel joined our brigadier, who was conferring with the two Infantry brigadiers and the G.S.O. I., and as a result of this war council, D Battery was ordered to continue the march and take up a reserve position on the next ridge, two miles farther back, south of the village of Caillouel. A and C, the composite battery, would come into action alongside B.

Telephone lines were run out from the two batteries to look-out posts on the top of the ridge 700 yards away, and the colonel ordered firing at the rate of one round a minute. Half a dozen "75" batteries were being loosed off with what always looks like gay abandon on the part of the French gunners. Young Bushman was whisked off to inform the staff captain, now at Caillouel, of the batteries' new positions, so that ammunition supply should be kept up. We then awaited developments.

The view westwards from the Béthancourt ridge that day provided one of the most picturesque panoramas of the retreat. The centre of Béthancourt, ridded the night before of its civilian inhabitants, was chock-a-block with troops and military traffic; and the straight road that led down into the valley, across the stream, and up again to Caillouel, was a two-mile ribbon of blue and khaki, and waggons and lorries, and camp kitchens - sometimes moving, oh, so slowly! once at a standstill for over an hour. A long way to the right high rocks and thick masses of dark trees rose, aloof; below them, thousands of horses and hundreds of supply and ammunition waggons, some halted in lines, some making slowly across the valley towards Caillouel. Directly in front of us more horses, more waggons. A road at the foot of the valley wound away to the left and then round behind the Caillouel ridge. The valley would have served admirably for a field-day in home training.

The colonel called Major Bullivant and pointed out that the stream at the bottom was crossed by only one bridge, that over which the main road ran. "If you are relying on that bridge for a withdrawal you will certainly be cut off. You'd better cut down some trees and make a bridge directly behind your battery. Of course, there's the road round by the left, but it will be best to have another way."

1 P.M.: A cavalry officer, hot and dusty, came up and said he had hurried back because some of our artillery fire was dropping dangerously near the French infantry. The colonel and he made a joint inspection of maps, and the cavalry officer pointed out certain spots which we still held.

"That's all right," replied the colonel. "My batteries are not firing on that part, but I will pass word round." And he sent me to some neighbouring batteries to explain and to warn.

An infantry runner came to ask the colonel if he would go across to see the Infantry brigadier. "More moving," said the colonel when he returned. "We are to fall back on Caillouel now. Will you get back and see that telephone wire is brought up? You know where D Battery have gone; the other batteries will come into line with them. You can keep H.Q. waggon line just behind Caillouel."

I rode off, accompanied by Beadle of A Battery, still dressed in overcoat and pyjamas. The stream of retreating traffic on the road between Béthancourt and Caillouel was thicker than ever; the centre of Caillouel was as packed as a Fen village during a hiring fair; the divisional horse-master, the C.R.E., and the D.A.Q.M.G. were among the officers trying to sort out the muddle; and in front of the Mairie, like a policeman on point duty, stood a perspiring staff captain. "That'll mean the Military Cross at least," grinned Beadle. "Life's very hard sometimes, isn't it?"

3 P.M.: The batteries were now in position on Caillouel ridge, and one brigade of the Divisional Infantry had arrived and commenced to dig. "I must have turned up half France since we started this retreat," growled one swarthy private, resting on his pick. "And I was a navvy before the war, and joined up for a change."

I stood by the composite battery and saw four of the waggons come up with ammunition. They had had to climb a long punishing slope over meadow-lands and orchards, and the last five hundred yards was across ploughed fields. The horses were blowing hard. "They've kept their condition well, considering the work they have had to do this last four days," remarked Dumble. "I hope the Supply Column won't fail us, though. The horses want as much corn as they can get now."

"Well, the A.S.C. have had plenty of practice getting up supplies this last three years. They ought to be able to keep touch with us, however irregular our movements - and M'Klown is a pretty smart fellow," I answered.

"Rather amusing just now to recall that 'Truth' a short while ago was saying there were too many horses in the Field Artillery, isn't it?" went on Dumble. "They said one team a battery to pull the guns into position from off the road would be enough, and that motor-traction could do the rest. Never mind; the old horse has earned his keep these last few days, hasn't he?"

"Look here," he added, "come along with me and I'll show you a find. You're thirsty, aren't you?"

"I shall say a grand Amen if you offer me a drink," said I, taking a deep breath.

"Well, come along - there's a cellar full of cider in this house here. I've left a man in charge to see there's no hanky-panky. I'm giving my men some, but under surveillance. No one allowed more than a pint."

It was the coolest, best-tasting cider I have ever drunk, not too sweet, not too tart. A gunner tipped up the barrel and poured it into a dilapidated-looking enamelled mug. How good it was! I quaffed half a pint at a gulp, and said "Rather!" when asked if I would have more.

"Glad you liked it," said Dumble. "I must confess that that was my third."

The General, suave, keen-eyed, and pleasant-spoken, came up with the colonel and the brigade-major as we got back to the battery. The General spoke encouragingly to most of us, and told the subalterns that gunnery rules were as important in this sort of warfare as on the drill-ground. "But don't forget that a cool head and common-sense are as good assets as any," he added.

We were looking now from the Caillouel ridge towards the Béthancourt ridge, which we had occupied in the forenoon, - another fine landscape with a vast plain to the right which was being keenly watched for enemy movement. My signalling-sergeant had run out a telephone line about 600 yards in front of the composite battery, and the

General, the colonel, and the brigade-major went along to the O.P. to see Major Bartlett register his guns on certain points where the General thought it likely the enemy would collect.

The report that our Brigade was to be relieved and our guns taken over by our companion brigade, who had lost practically all their guns on the 21st, became more than a report when Colonel —— and his battery commanders assembled to meet the General. One of the battery commanders, a new-comer to the Brigade, was a well-known golfer whom I had last seen fighting a most exciting match in the 1914 amateur championship at Sandwich. He laughed when he recognised me. "A bit of leave and a bit of golf would be a nice change now, eh? I'm afraid we shan't know what leave is for a long time, though. But do you know what I did the last time I was on leave and had a few rounds over my home course ——?"

But the return of the General prevented my knowing the golf exploit he was going to tell me. The colonel called me for further instructions.

"The ——rd Brigade are taking over our guns to-morrow morning at 6.30," he said. "I shall stay here until then with General —— (the Infantry brigadier). I'll keep young Bushman with me, and my groom with our horses. You had better remain at the waggon line and keep in touch with the battery waggon lines. Will you send up my British warm when you get back, some sandwiches for Bushman and myself, and my Thermos flask?"

The almost paralysing block of traffic between Béthancourt and Caillouel had thinned out now. It was easy enough also to move along the road from Caillouel to Grandru, whither three hours ago I had despatched H.Q. waggons to get them out of the way. For two hours, also, there had been a marked cessation of hostile fire. And as I rode towards Grandru I thought of those reports of big British successes at Ypres and at Cambrai. They seemed feasible enough. What if they were true, and what if the offensive on this front had been checked because of the happenings North? It was a pleasant thought, and I rather hugged it.

Later there was grim proof that the lull merely meant that the Hun was bringing up his guns and putting in fresh divisions to buffet and press our tired worn men.

5 P.M.: When I reached Grandru and sat down in a hay-field while my servant brought me a cup of tea and some bread and cheese, I gave my mind to a five minutes' reconstruction of the incidents and aspects of the last four days. It had all been so hurried, and each particular emergency had demanded such complete concentration, that it was more than difficult to realise that so short a time had elapsed since the German hordes began their rush. I longed to see a newspaper, to read a lucid and measured account of the mighty conflict in which our brigade, the centre of my present workaday world, could only have played such a tiny part. I longed for a chance to let my friends in England know that all was well with me. However ——

The regimental sergeant-major had established the H.Q. horse lines in a roadside field just outside the village. I wouldn't let him unload the waggons, but the brigade clerk, devout adherent of orderliness and routine, had already opened the brigade office in the first cottage on the right of the village street, while the cook was in possession next door. It was the first village we had come to during the retreat, whence all the civilian inhabitants had not fled, and the cook talked of fresh eggs for breakfast. I shaved and had a scrub down, put on a clean collar, and gained a healthier outlook on life generally. I sent out the four cycle orderlies to scout around and find the battery waggon lines, which I knew were coming to this vicinity, and the A.S.C. supply officer rode up and discussed the best place for unloading the morrow's food and forage for the brigade. That settled, I wrote out the formal information for the batteries, and then decided to stroll round the village before dinner. "I've got a rabbit for your dinner to-night, sir," called the cook from his kitchen door, "a fresh rabbit." So I promised to be back by 8 o'clock.

When I came back there was an awkward surprise. All our waggons had been shifted and a French heavy battery were hauling their howitzers up the incline that led from the road to the field. The senior French officer was polite but firm. He was sorry to disturb us, but this was the most suitable spot for his howitzers to fire from.

The sergeant-major asked me whether I would like to shift the horses to such-and-such a spot in the field, but I said "No" to that. "These guns will be firing all night, and the horses will be only thirty yards away from them. They'll have no rest whatever, and they want every minute they can get. No, the Brigade are coming out of action to-morrow morning. We'll shift our waggon line right away to the other side of the village. Saddle-up at once, and get away before it is dark. Move well away from the village while you are about it, and camp by the roadside."

The cook looked glum and said my rabbit was cooked to a turn. "Keep it for me until we get settled down again," I said. I posted a cycle orderly to wait at the spot we were leaving, so as to re-direct messengers arriving from Division or from the colonel; the brigade clerk asked to be allowed to stay behind until the three other orderlies returned from the batteries - he wouldn't feel justified in leaving before then, he assured me. It was 8.15 P.M. when our little procession headed by the sergeant-major passed through the village.

I had sent my horses on, and it was on the point of darkness when I strode through the village, some way behind the column. A few officers of the Pioneer battalion that was moving out any moment stood at open doorways, and a group of drivers waited near the bridge ready to harness up their mules. Three aged women dressed in faded black, one of them carrying a bird-cage, had come out of a cottage and walked with feeble ungainly step towards the bridge. A couple of ancient men, pushing wheel-barrows piled high with household goods, followed.

Out of the distance came the brooding whine of an approaching howitzer shell. A mighty rush of air, a blinding flash, and an appalling crash. An 8-inch had fallen in the middle of the street.

A running to and fro; a heartrending, whimpering cry from one of the women; and groans and curses farther up the street. None of the poor terror-stricken old people were hurt, thank God! but three of the drivers had been hit and two mules killed outright. The men were quickly lifted into the shelter of the nearest house, and the civilian refugees took cover in a doorway just before the second shell tore a great rent in the village green on the other side of the bridge. Five shells fell in all, and an officer afterwards tried to persuade the old women to take a lift in a G.S. waggon that was about to start. But they refused to leave their men, who would not abandon the wheel-barrows. When I walked away the five were again beginning their slow hazardous pilgrimage to the next village.

11 P.M.: That night I lay rolled up in a blanket at the foot of a tree. The H.Q. waggon line was duly settled for the night when I arrived - horses "hayed-up" and most of the men asleep on the ground. The cook insisted on producing the boiled rabbit, and I ate it, sitting on the shaft of the mess cart. I arranged with the N.C.O. of the piquet to change every two hours the orderly posted at the spot we had left so hurriedly - it was only ten minutes' ride on a cycle - and kept another sentry on the watch for messengers who might come searching for us. It was again a beautiful clear night, with a resplendent moon; a few long-range shells whizzed over, but none near enough to worry us; a pioneer party worked right through the night, putting up a stout line of barbed wire that went within thirty yards of where I lay; retreating baggage-waggons, French and British, passed along the road; restless flashes along the eastern skyline showed our guns in active defence.

I cannot say that I slept. The ground was hard, and it got very cold about 2 A.M. I could hear the sergeant-major snoring comfortably on the straw palliasse he had managed to "commandeer" for himself. At about 3 A.M. my ear caught the "chug-chug" of a motor-cycle. It came nearer and then stopped, and I heard the rider and our sentry talking. I got up and found it was the Divisional Artillery signalling-officer.

"Rather important," he said, without preamble. "The General says it is essential to get all transport vehicles over the canal to-night. There's bound to be a hell of a crush in the morning. Headquarters R.A. will be at Varesnes by to-morrow morning, so I should move as far that way as you can. I've just come over the canal, and there are two ways of crossing from here. I think you'll find the Appilly route the least crowded. The great thing is to hurry. I'm going to look for the colonel now. I'll tell him you are moving."

We bade each other "Good-night." While the horses were being hooked in, I scribbled an order explaining the situation, and instructing all battery waggon lines to move towards Varesnes at once. I knew that in view of the 6.30 A.M. relief by the ———rd Brigade, horses would be sent up for the officers and men at the guns, and it was possible that the guns would now be brought back from the Caillouel ridge before that time. The Boche was clearly coming on once more.

Cycle orderlies sped away with the notes, and I was sending a signaller on a cycle to tell the sentry posted at Grandru to rejoin us, when I discovered that the brigade clerk had not yet turned up. I told the signaller to send him along as well.

Two of the orderlies returned and reported that B and D Batteries had received my instructions and had started. With the return of the next orderly I explained where we were to go to the sergeant-major, and told him to move off. I would come along behind with the others.

To my astonishment the signaller and the sentry came back without the brigade clerk. "Can't find him anywhere, sir," said the signaller. "Didn't you see him while you were there?" I asked the orderly who had been doing sentry. "No, sir. I saw no lights in that house where the office was, and there's no one there now."

This was something unexpected, not to say perturbing. I turned to one of the cycle orderlies who stood by. "Go back and make a thorough search for Briercliffe. Don't come back until you are satisfied he's not in the village. I'll wait here. You others, except one cyclist, go on and catch up the column."

A quarter of an hour, twenty minutes, half an hour! The orderly returned alone. "I can't find Briercliffe, sir. I've been into every house in Grandru. He's not there."

I couldn't understand it. The amazingly conscientious, thoroughly correct, highly efficient Briercliffe to be missing. "I can't wait any longer," I said, mounting my horse. "He's quite wide awake and should be all right. We'll get on."

CHAPTER X

THE SCRAMBLE AT VARESNES

4 A.M.: For the best part of a mile my groom and I had the moonlit road to ourselves. We passed at the walk through the stone-flagged streets of Baboeuf, our horses' hoofs making clattering echoes in what might have been a dead city. Along the whole length of the tortuous main street were only two indications that there was life behind the closed doors and fastened shutters. Two French soldiers, leaning against a wall and talking, moved away as we rode up; then a door banged, and all was quiet. Once, too, a cat ran stealthily across and startled my horse: I remember that distinctly, because it was the first cat I had seen since coming back to the fighting area.

At the junction, where the way from Baboeuf joined the main road that ran parallel with the canal, stood a single British lorry. A grey-headed lieutenant, who was lighting a cigarette, came up when I hailed him, and told me our waggons had passed. He had pointed out the way, and they had gone to the left. "The first turning on the right after that will bring you to the bridge," he ended.

Our column was now moving along one of France's wonderful main roads - perfectly straight, tree-bordered, half its width laid with pavé. On either side good-sized villas, well-kept front gardens, "highly desirable residences" - comfortable happy homes a week before, now shattered, silent, deserted. The road as we followed it led direct to the battle-front.

We had gone a mile past the railway station, and were in open country, and had still to reach the first turning to the right. I asked the sergeant-major to trot ahead and let me know how much farther we had to go. "Over a mile yet, sir," was his report.

At last, however, a sign-post loomed up, and we struck right along a track that led over dreary waste lands. Before long we were forging through a damp clinging mist, that obviously came from the canal. Somewhere near the point towards which we were making, shells from a Boche big gun were exploding with dull heavy boomings. I sent the sergeant-major forward again, and he came back with the bewildering report, "We're on the wrong road, sir!"

"Wrong road!" I repeated. "What do you mean?"

"There are some French lorries in front, sir, and the sentry won't open the bridge gates to let them cross."

I felt puzzled and angered, and rode forward to question the French sentry. Half a dozen protesting lorry-drivers stood round him.

The bridge did lead to Varesnes, he admitted, but it was only a light bridge, and he had orders to allow no military traffic over it. I became almost eloquent in describing the extreme lightness of my vehicles; but a *sous-officier* stepped out of a little hut and said he was sorry, the orders were very strict, and he could not open the gates. The bridge we wanted was approached by the next turning to the right, off the main road. He assured me that it was a much better way, and, in any case, he couldn't open the gates.

There was nothing else for it: we made the long tedious journey back, out of the fog and into it again, and so got on the right track.

Weariness through lack of sleep and the dampness of the air made one feel chilly, and I got off my horse and walked. The horses stepped out mechanically; the men had lost their chirpiness. There was a half-hour or so when I felt melancholy and depressed: the feeling of helplessness against the triumphant efficiency of the Boche got on one's nerves. Wasn't this talk of luring him on a myth? Why was he allowed to sweep forward at this overpowering pace, day after day, when each of our big advances had been limited to one hard, costly attack - and then stop? I quickened my step, and walked forward to where A Battery moved along the same road.

"Hullo, Dumble," I said. "You and C are running as separate batteries again, aren't you? How did you leave the cider-cellar?"

"We came back from there at about 5 P.M." There was a big discussion as to whether we should come farther back. The colonel wanted to stay, and the ———rd's B Battery were in action there until four this morning. It was a Divisional decision that there should be a retirement to the next ridge. The poor old infantry were fed to the teeth. They'd sweated blood digging trenches all day on the Caillouel ridge, and then in the evening had to fall back and start digging again.

"Have you seen the colonel?" I asked.

"He was still there with General —— when we came away. The ———rd relieved us last night, instead of first thing this morning; and we got down to Grandru, and had three hours' sleep before your note arrived."

"Battery's pretty done, I suppose?"

"Well, it was just about time we came out of action. Men and horses would have been all-in in another day."

We crossed the fine broad canal, watched by the French soldiers guarding the bridge. Dumble was silent for some seconds, and then muttered, "You know, I hate to be coming back like this with the French looking on."

"Yes, I know," I replied,———" but they are good soldiers, and they understand."

"Yes - when I think of poor old Harville, and the fight he put up ———" he broke off; and we trudged along.

"Do you know Harville always kept that speech of Beatty's in his pocket-book, that speech where he said England would have to be chastened and turn to a new way of life before we finished the war?" said Dumble later.

"Yes, he was like that - old Harville," I said quietly.

Over another bridge; and I still walked with Dumble at the head of his battery. There was a long wait while a line of French waggons moved out of our way. Some of the men were yawning with the sleepiness that comes from being cold as well as tired. We were now on the outskirts of a village that lay four miles from Varesnes.

"What do you say if we stop at this place and go on after a rest?" said Dumble. I agreed.

I put Headquarter waggons and horses into an orchard, and found a straw-loft where the men could lie down.

It was six in the morning, and I told the sergeant-major to have breakfast up at 7.30. There was a cottage opposite the orchard; some French soldiers were inside breakfasting. As I looked through the window I felt I would give anything for a sleep. The old housewife, a woman with a rosy Punch-like face, waited on the men. I asked her if she would let me have a room. She demurred a while, said everything was dirty and in disorder: the French *sous-officier* was not gone yet. Then I think she noticed how fagged I was. In two minutes my servant had brought my valise in. "I'm going to take my clothes off," I said, "but don't let me sleep after 7.30."

7.30 A.M.: I woke to find the sun streaming through the window. The booming of guns sounded nearer than before. I got off the bed and looked out. The fifty Headquarter men were breakfasting or smoking. Something prompted me: I had the feeling that we ought to leave the village at once. I shouted through the window for the sergeant-major. The column could be ready to move in a quarter of an hour, he answered. My servant brought me a change of boots and leggings, and I shaved. "Won't you wait and have breakfast, sir?" asked the sergeant-major. "No. Pack up everything; we'll get to Varesnes as soon as you are ready."

I went round to see Dumble before we started, but he said he wasn't going to hurry. "I'll let the men have a proper clean-up and march off about eleven," he decided.

The Headquarter column wound away from the village, and set out on a long smooth road that ran through a wood and edged away from the canal. Two miles from Varesnes we met the brigade-major. His tired eyes lighted up when he saw me. "What batteries have actually got over the canal?" he questioned. I told him that A were in the village I had just left. "C and B are coming round by the Noyon bridge," he informed me. "I expect we shall send Headquarters and B on to Thiescourt to get you out of the way - and give you some rest." And he nodded and rode on.

It looked as if the German rush was not expected to go much farther, for Varesnes was the first little town fully occupied by civilians that we had come to. Most of them were preparing to leave, and roomy French farm carts, piled high with curious medleys of mattresses, chairs and tables, clothing, carpets, kitchen utensils, clocks and pictures, kept moving off. But children played about the streets; girls stood and talked to French and British soldiers; and M. le Maire continued to function.

The colonel, neat and unruffled, but pale with fatigue, stood waiting in the main thoroughfare as we came in. I informed him at once where I had left A Battery and what the brigade-major had mentioned. He told me he had remained with the Infantry brigadier until 6.30 A.M., the hour at which Colonel —— of the ——rd had formally to relieve him; and he had only just crossed the canal. The infantry were still falling back. "I've lost Laneridge and my two horses," he added, shaking his head. "Laneridge missed me in the fog when I sent for him, and I'm half afraid he went towards the Hun lines. It was very puzzling to get your bearings up there this morning. I walked part of the way here and got a lift in a lorry."

9.30 A.M.: The colonel had seen the C.R.A. and received instructions about continuing the march. We were going on another ten miles to the place which a week ago was to have become the rest area for Divisional Headquarters. I had come across a section of the D.A.C. who had arrived the night before and secured a billet, and they gave the colonel and myself breakfast. I had discovered B Battery's mess in another cottage, every officer deep in a regular Rip Van Winkle slumber that told of long arrears of sleep. And I had been greatly cheered by the sudden appearance, mounted on a horse, of Briercliffe, the missing brigade clerk. He explained his absence. When one of the orderlies returned to Grandru, saying he couldn't find B Battery's waggon lines, the admirable Briercliffe had retorted that they must be found, and he went in quest of them himself. Then when he heard the sudden order to cross the canal he had the common-sense to come along with B Battery.

Neither C Battery nor A Battery had yet arrived. The colonel, having shaved, felt ready for the fray again, dictated the route-march orders, and told me to fix 11.30 A.M. as the time of starting. Fortunately his horses and his groom had turned up. The traffic down the main street, with its old-fashioned plaster houses, its squat green doors, and the Mairie with its railed double-stone steps, was getting more congested. Infantry transport and French heavy guns were quickening their pace as they came through. The inhabitants were moving out in earnest now, not hurriedly, but losing no time. A group of hatless women stood haranguing on the Mairie steps; a good-looking girl, wearing high heels and bangles, unloaded a barrow-load of household goods into a van the Maire had provided, and hastened home with the barrow to fill it again; a sweet-faced old dame, sightless, bent with rheumatism, pathetic in her helpless resignation, sat on a wicker-chair outside her doorway, waiting for a farm cart to take her away: by her side, a wide-eyed solemn-faced little girl, dressed in her Sunday best, and trying bravely not to cry.

10.15 A.M.: The colonel met me in the street; he had just come from seeing the C.R.A. again. "Better tell B and D Batteries to move off at once, B leading. Headquarters can start as well. It will be best to get out of this place as quickly as possible. The enemy is coming on fast, and there will be an awkward crush shortly."

11 A.M.: The Boche machine-guns could be heard now as plainly as if they were fighting along the canal banks. B Battery had marched out with their waggons, Headquarters behind them. I stood with the colonel in the square to watch the whole brigade go through. Young Bushman had ridden off towards the canal to seek news of C Battery.

And now the first enemy shell: a swishing rush of air and a vicious crack - a 4·2 H.V. It fell two streets from us. Another and another followed. Shouts from behind! The drivers spurred their horses to a trot. Clouds of dust rose. Odd civilians alternately cowered against the wall and ran panting for the open country, making frightened cries as each shell came over. A butcher's cart and a loaded market cart got swept into the hurrying military traffic.

"I don't like this," muttered the colonel, frowning. "It would be stupid to have a panic."

On the Mairie steps I could see M. le Maire ringing a hand-bell and shouting some sort of proclamation. With a certain dignity, and certainly with little apparent recognition that shells were falling close, he descended the steps and strode along the street and through the square, all the time determinedly shaking his bell. As he passed, I asked him gravely why he rang the bell. He stared over his glasses with astonishment, responded simply "Pour partir, m'sieur," and walked on, still ringing. A bizarre incident, but an instance of duty, highly conceived and carried out to the end.

A colonel of one of our Pioneer battalions rode by and hailed the colonel. "We seem to be driving it pretty close," he said. "There's a lot more artillery to cross yet, and they are shelling the bridge hard. Which way do you go from here?"

"I've got two batteries to come, and I'm afraid one of 'em's still over the bridge," responded the colonel. "We go to Thiescourt from here."

11.30 A.M.: D Battery was passing now, with A not far behind. The stream of traffic making for beyond the town was continuous as ever, but the shelling had quietened, and the horses were kept at the walk. The colonel stood and accepted the salutes of his batteries, and criticised points of turn-out and horse-mastership as though he were making an ordinary route-march inspection. And this compelling them to think of something other than the physical dangers around and behind them, had its moral effect upon the men. They held themselves more erect, showed something of pride of regiment and race, and looked men fit and worthy to fight again.

Civilians were still hurrying out of the town. A family passed us, the husband in his best suit of dull black, top-hat, and white tie and all, pushing a perambulator loaded with clothes, household ornaments, and cooking requisites, his three children dragging at their mother's skirts and weeping piteously. A fine-looking *vieillard*, with clean-cut waxen features and white flowing moustaches, who wore his brown velvet jacket and sombrero with an air, walked by erect and slow, taking what he could of his belongings on a wheel-barrow. Even the conjunction of the wheel-barrow could not prevent him looking dignified and resolute.

And a terrier and a young retriever, oblivious of the tragedy around them, gambolled up and down the Mairie steps and chased each other across the street.

12 noon: Bigger shells had begun to fall, and still C Battery had not come. The colonel glanced at his watch. One shell came near enough to send a chimney-pot and some slates clattering to the ground, making a pair of water-cart horses plunge wildly; a French soldier was killed farther down the street. An officer cantered by and directed a Horse Artillery battery that had passed a few minutes before, and had a clear half-mile of road in front of it, to break into a trot. Voices in rear could be heard shouting to those in front to go faster. Two riderless, runaway wheelers, dragging a smashed limber-pole, raced after the Horse Artillery battery. "I'm afraid we shall have to say Good-bye to C Battery," said the colonel seriously.

I walked to the end of the square and looked down the road towards the canal. Dust rose in clouds, and straining horses still came on. Out of the welter I saw young Bushman's horse on the pathway coming towards me. "C Battery's all right," he shouted to me, and a minute later I heard him explaining to the colonel.

"C Battery's over now, sir. It has been touch-and-go. Some Horse Artillery in front had a waggon hit, and that caused a stoppage; and there were a lot of other waggons in front as well. They are putting shells all round the bridge now, sir. C Battery have had two gunners wounded, but they are over now, sir."

C Battery came through at a trot, but the colonel regarded their general appearance as soldierly. We remained in the square and saw the tail-end of their mess cart.

"And now," observed the colonel, lighting a cigarette and noting the time, "we may as well gather our horses and get along ourselves."

"I feel very relieved about C Battery," he said five minutes later as we rode along; and he smiled for the first time for quite three hours.

CHAPTER XI

THE G IN GAP

1 P.M.: For some miles after leaving Varesnes it was retreat - rapid, undisguised, and yet with a plan. Thousands of men, scores of guns and transport vehicles, hundreds of civilians caught in the last rush, all struggling to evade the mighty pincers' clutch of the German masses who, day after day, were crushing our attempts to rally against their weight and fury. Unless collectedly, in order, and with intercommunications unbroken, we could pass behind the strong divisions hurrying to preserve the precious contact between French and British, we should be trapped. And when I say we, I mean the very large force of which our Brigade formed one tiny part. Not even the colonel knew much at this moment of the wider strategy that was being worked out. The plain and immediate task was to free the Brigade, with its seven hundred odd men and its horses and waggons, from the welter of general traffic pouring on to the main roads, and bring it intact to the village that Division had fixed as our destination. And as we had now become a non-fighting body, a brigade of Field Artillery without guns, it was more than ever our business to get out of the way.

Our men found room for some of the aged civilians in motor-lorries and G.S. waggons; but I shall always remember one silver-haired dame who refused to be separated from the wheel-barrow heaped up with her belongings, which she was pushing to a place seven miles away. For some reason she would not allow a gunner to wheel the barrow for her. Poor obstinate old soul! I hope she got away; if she didn't, I trust the Boche was merciful.

The colonel and I rode through a forest in order to catch up the batteries. As we emerged from the wood we came upon five brigades of cavalry - three French and two British - fresh as paint, magnificently mounted, ready and waiting. "The most cheering sight we've seen this morning," remarked the colonel.

We came up with C Battery, and rode at their head. Despite the spurt to cross the canal, their turn-out was smart and soldierly, and there was satisfaction in the colonel's quick, comprehensive glance. Through Pontoise, another village from which the inhabitants had fled the day before, and past the outskirts of Noyon, with its grey cathedral and quaint tower. The evacuation here had been frantic, and we heard stories of pillage and looting and of drunken men - not, one is glad to say it, British soldiers. In all that galling, muddling week I did not see a single drunken soldier. As we were near a considerable town, I gave my groom twenty francs, and told him to buy what food he could: we might be very short by nightfall. He returned with some sardines, some tinned tunny fish, and a few biscuits, the sardines costing five francs a small tin. At one cross-road a dozen American Red Cross cars were drawn up, and I recall the alacrity of a middle-aged American doctor, wearing gold pince-nez, in hopping off his ambulance and snapshotting the colonel at the head of the battery. I wondered bitterly whether that photograph would subsequently be published under the heading, "British Artillery in Retreat."

2.30 P.M.: The four batteries were now ranged alongside a railway siding at a point where the road by which we had journeyed joined the main road to Compiègne. For several hours this great traffic artery had been packed with troops and transport moving to and from the battle-front. It was hot and dusty, and our men and horses were glad of the half-hour's halt, although the respite had only lasted so long because the traffic on the main route had been too continuous for us to turn on to it and reach the road fifty yards farther down along which we had to continue. Remembering a lesson of the Mons retreat emphasised by a Horse Artillery major lecturing at Larkhill - that his horses kept their condition because every time there was a forced halt near a village he despatched his gunners with the water-buckets - I had told my groom to search around until he found water for my two horses. Then I stood under the trees lining the main road and watched three battalions of

French infantry march past, moving north of the part of the front our brigade had just left. They were older, smaller, more town-bred French soldiers than those we had seen during the two previous days, more spectacles among them, and a more abstracted expression. The thought came to me that here must be last-line reserves. Up on the steep hills that overlooked the railway siding bearded French troops were deepening trenches and strengthening barbed wire.

3 P.M.: We were anxious to get on now, and longed for a couple of City of London traffic policemen to stand in majestic and impartial control of these road junctions. The colonel and Major Bullivant, after expostulating five minutes with a French major, had got our leading battery across. Then the long line of traffic on the main route resumed its apparently endless flow. An R.A.M.C. captain came out and stood by as I stationed myself opposite the road we wanted our three remaining batteries to turn down, watching to take quick advantage of the G in the first possible GAP. "Pretty lively here last night," volunteered the R.A.M.C. captain. "General scramble to get out, and some unusual sights. There was a big ordnance store, and they hadn't enough lorries to get the stuff away, so they handed out all manner of goods to prevent them being wasted. The men got pretty well *carte blanche* in blankets, boots, and puttees, and you should have seen them carting off officers' shirts and underclothing. There was a lot of champagne going begging too, and hundreds of bottles were smashed to make sure the men had no chance of getting blind. And there was an old sapper colonel who made it his business to get hold of the stragglers. He kept at it about six hours, and bunged scores of wanderers into a prisoners-of-war cage; then he had 'em marched off to a collecting station. He was hot stuff, I can tell you."

A gap came at last on the main route, but something also that would dam the opening we had awaited for over an hour.

A tremendous line of French lorries was moving towards me on the road opposite. The French officer in charge had come forward to reconnoitre the crossing. Three British lorries, loading up, also stood on the road along which we wanted to go. If the French lorries reached that spot first, our batteries might be held up another hour. It was a moment for unscrupulous action. I told my groom to dash off and tell Major Bartlett to come along at the trot; then I slipped across and engaged the French captain in conversation. If I could prevent him signalling back for his lorries to quicken speed, all would be well. If Major Bartlett failed, there would be a most unholy mix up near the three stationary lorries. Major Bartlett responded nobly. His leading team reached the three lorries while the first French motor-waggon was still thirty yards away. The gap between the stationary lorry and the moving one narrowed to eight yards; but the waggon and six horses were through, and the battery now commanded the position with a line of horsed waggons and baggage-carts stretching back along the fifty yards of the main road, with A and B Batteries following in column of route past the railway siding. The line of French lorries extended back far as the eye could see. The French officer turned sharply, cursed impatiently, and asserted volubly that his lorries must come through. I explained soothingly what a long time we had waited, and asked his forbearance. Meanwhile C Battery continued to trot through the gap, and I called Heaven to witness that the whole of our Brigade would be through and away before ten minutes passed. I ran back to urge A and B Batteries to keep up the pace. When our very last water-cart, mess-cart, and G.S. waggon had passed, I thanked the French officer with great sincerity, and felt I had done a proper job of work.

4.30 P.M.: We sat by the roadside eating bread-and-cheese - the colonel, young Bushman, and I. The batteries were well on the way to their destination; and we three, jogging along in rear, had encountered Bombardier M'Donald, triumphant at having filled his forage and rations waggon for yet another day. So we and our grooms helped ourselves to bread-and-cheese and satisfied hefty appetites, and drank the cider with which Bushman had filled his flask at Caillouel the day before.

Another of the mournful side-spectacles of the retreat was being enacted under our eyes. Opposite a small cottage a cart packed to a great height, but marvellously balanced on its two huge wheels, stood ready to move off. A wrinkled sad-eyed woman, perched on top, held beside her her grandchild - a silent, wondering little girl. A darkly handsome, strongly-built daughter had tied a cow to the back of the cart. A bent old man began to lead the wide-backed Percheron mare that was yoked to the shafts with the mixture of straps and bits of rope that French farm folk find does well enough for harness. But the cow, bellowing in an abandonment of grief, tugged backwards, and the cart did not move. The daughter, proud-eyed, self-reliant, explained that the cow was calling for her calf. The calf would never be able to make the journey, and they had been compelled to sell it, and it would be killed for food. It was hard, but it was war.

They tried again; but the cow refused to be comforted, and tugged until the rope threatened to strangle her. They brought the calf out again and tied him alongside his now pacified mother; but this time, when the cart moved forward, he protested in fear and bewilderment, and tried to drag himself free. The cart was still there when we rode off.

Our way ran through a noble stretch of hilly country, well wooded, with sparkling streams plashing down the hillsides - a landscape of uninhabited quiet. Two aeroplanes droned overhead - the first Allied planes we had seen since the retreat began. "The old French line," observed the colonel, pointing out a wide system of well-planned trenches, deep dug-outs, and broad belts of rusted barbed wire. "The Boche ought not to get through here."

Up and over a hill, and down into a tiny hamlet which more stricken civilians were preparing to leave. As our little cavalcade drew near, a shrinking old woman, standing in a doorway, drew a frightened little girl towards her, and held a hand over the child's eyes. "I believe they took us to be Germans at first," said the colonel when we had passed.

In another village a woman was trying to make a cow pull a heavily-laden waggon up the hill. With streaming eyes and piteous gestures she besought us to assist with our horses. She would pay us money. Twice before she had lost everything through the Boche, she pleaded. The colonel looked grieved, but shook his head. "We'll send back a pair of draught-horses if we can," was all he said to me. And we did.

6 P.M.: We had reached Thiescourt, a hillside village that had thought never to be threatened by the Germans again. Dwellings damaged during their last visit had been repaired. New houses made of fine white stone, quarried in the district, had been built, and were building. The bitterness of it, if the foul devastating Boche were to come again! There were many evidences of the hurried flight of the last two days, - torn letters and papers, unswept fire-grates, unconsumed food and drinks, beds with sheets in them, drawers hurriedly searched for articles that could be taken away, disconsolate wandering dogs. A few days before it had been arranged that the major-general, his Divisional Staff, Ordnance, the Divisional brass band, and all the usual appurtenances of a Divisional Headquarters, should come and make this village a Divisional rest area. Few even of the first preparations for visitation were left now. D.A.D.O.S., blue-tabbed and business-like, was in the main street, bewailing the scarcity of lorries for removing his wares to an area still farther back. He had several rifles he would be pleased to hand out to our batteries. There was a large quantity of clothing which would have to be left in the store he had established. Any we didn't want would we burn, or drop in the stream before we left? No lorry to remove the Divisional canteen. Would we distribute the supplies free to our men? Biscuits, chocolate, potted meats, tooth-paste, and cigarettes went like wildfire.

Brigade H.Q. mess was installed in a new house that had chalked messages scrawled on doors, walls, and mirrors, telling searching relations and friends the address in a distant town to which the occupants of the house had fled. In another dwelling that Boche aeroplanes had already bombed, we discovered sleeping quarters. At 7 P.M. a lieutenant on a motor-cycle arrived with Corps orders for the morrow. We were to leave for Elincourt immediately the tactical situation demanded it.

We dined early, and sought our beds early too. I had been asleep two minutes, as I thought - really about an hour and a half - when Dumble woke me up. "Cavalry are coming through," he said, shining his electric torch right in my eyes, "and they say the enemy is at Lagny. Hadn't you better let the colonel know?"

"No," I retorted with some asperity.

"But listen; can you hear all that traffic? It's our infantry coming back."

"Can you hear machine-gun fire?" I asked resentfully.

"No."

"Well, I'm damned if I disturb the colonel until you can tell me that, at least," I said finally, turning on my right side.

CHAPTER XII

OUT OF THE WAY

THE USUAL MONOTONOUS spectacle when we woke next morning: the narrow streets of what a few days before had been a tranquil, out-of-the-war village choked with worn-out troops marching to go into rest. Now that we had become a brigade of artillery without guns, a British non-fighting unit struggling to get out of the way of a manoeuvring French army, our one great hope was that Corps would send us right back to a depot where we could refit ourselves with fresh guns and reinforcements, to some spot where we need not be wondering every five minutes whether the enemy was at our heels. Men who have fought four days and nights on end feel like that when the strain of actual battle ceases.

The Boche guns sounded nearer, and the colonel had ordered a mounted officer to go back and seek definite information upon the situation. By 10 A.M. a retiring French battalion marched through, and reported that the line was again being withdrawn. By 11 A.M. two batteries of "75's" came back. Which decided the colonel that the tactical situation demanded our departure, and the Brigade began the march to Elincourt. On past more evacuated villages. Abandoned farm carts - some of which our batteries eagerly adopted for transporting stores and kit - and the carcases of dogs, shot or poisoned, lying by the roadside, told their own story of the rush from the Hun. By 1 P.M. we reached Elincourt, a medieval town whose gable-ends and belfry towers, and straight rows of hoary lime-trees, breathed the grace and charm of the real France. I made immediately for the Mairie, bent upon securing billets for officers and men; but standing at the gateway was a Corps despatch-rider who handed over instructions for the Brigade to continue the march to Estree St Denis, a town twenty kilometres distant.

5 P.M.: Estree St Denis, to which I rode in advance with a billeting officer from each battery, proved to be a drab smoky town of mean-looking, jerry-built houses. One thought instinctively of the grimiest parts of Lancashire and the Five Towns. The wide and interminably long main street was filled with dust-laden big guns and heavy hows., four rows of them. Every retreating Division in France seemed to be arriving and to be bringing more dust. Hundreds of refugees from villages now in Boche possession had come, too. What a place to be sent to! It was useless looking for billets, so I fixed upon a vast field on the outskirts of the town where we could establish our horse lines and pitch tents and bivouacs. This was satisfactory enough, but the watering problem was bound to be difficult. Four small pumps in the main street and one tiny brackish pond totalled the facilities. It would take each battery an hour and a half to water its horses. "Corps moves in most mysterious ways," crooned Stone. "Why did they send us here?" We rode and walked until we were tired, but found nothing that would improve matters. Then Fentiman, Stone, and I found the Café de la Place, and entered the "Officers only" room, where we sat down to a bottle of wine and devoured the Continental 'Daily Mail' of March 23, the first paper we had seen since starting the retreat. Madame informed us that some officers of Divisional Headquarters had turned up the day before and were dining there. As we went out to go and meet the batteries and lead them to the waggon lines, there was a shout of recognition, and "Swiffy" and the little American doctor ran up, grinning and rather shamefaced. "We thought of posting you as deserters," I said with pretended seriousness, "not having seen you since the afternoon of the 23rd." It was now the 26th. They narrated a long and somewhat sheepish story that, boiled down, told of a barn that promised a sound afternoon's nap, an awakening to find every one vanished; then a worried and wearied tramp in search of us, with nothing to eat except what they could beg or buy at ruinous prices; one perturbing two hours when they found themselves walking into the arms of the oncoming Hun; and finally, a confirmed resolve never to stray far from the Brigade mess-cart again.

7 P.M.: When the batteries were settled in their waggon lines, I led the colonel and "Swiffy" and the doctor through the crowded dusty streets into the Café de la Place. The restaurant was filled with French and British officers. "Swiffy" insisted on cracking a bottle of champagne to celebrate the return of the doctor and himself to the fold; then I spotted Ronny Hertford, the Divisional salvage officer, who was full of talk and good cheer, and said he had got his news from the new G.S.O. II., who had just come from England, travelling with a certain politician. "It's all right, old boy," bubbled Ronny. "The War Office is quite calm about it now; we've got 'em stone-cold. Foch is in supreme command, and there are any number of Divisions in reserve which haven't been called on. We're only waiting to know if this is the real push, or only a feint, and then we strike. We've got 'em trapped, old top, no doubt about that."

"Right-o, strategist!" I retorted in the same vein.

"Do you want to buy a calf, old boy?" he switched off. "Look here - there's one under the table. About 110 lbs. of meat at 3 francs a pound. Dirt cheap these times. A Frenchman has left it with Madame to sell. We'd buy it for our mess, but we've got a goose for dinner to-night. Stay and dine with us, old boy."

Through the glass door that showed into the café one saw a little group of civilians, dressed in their Sunday black, waiting for carts to take them from the town. A mother was suckling a wailing child. An old cripple nodded his head helplessly over hands propped up by his stick. A smart young French soldier came in at the door, and Madame's fair-haired daughter rushed to his arms and held him while she wept. They talked fast, and the civilians listened with strained faces. "Her fiancé," quietly explained an interpreter who came through the café to join us in the "Officers only" room. "He's just come from Montdidier with a motor-transport. He says he was fired at by machine-guns, which shows that the Boche is still coming on."

The camp commandant of the Division, nervously business-like, the baths' officer, D.A.D.O.S., and a couple of padres came in. The Camp Commandant refused to hear of the colonel sleeping in a tent. "We've got a big dormitory at the back here, sir - thirty wire-beds. We can put all your Brigade Headquarter officers up." The colonel protested that we should be quite happy in bivouacs, but he was overruled.

We dined in a tent in the waggon lines. As I made my way there I noticed a blue-painted motor-van, a mobile French wireless station, some distance away in the fields. What really caught my eye when I drew near it was a couple of Camembert cheeses, unopened and unguarded, on the driver's seat. I bethought myself that the operator inside the van might be persuaded to sell one of the cheeses. He wasn't, but he was extremely agreeable, and showed me the evening *communiqué* that had just been "ticked" through. We became friends, which explains why for three days I was able to inform the camp commandant, Ronny Hertford, and all their party, of the latest happenings at the Front, hours before the French newspapers and the Continental 'Daily Mail' arrived.

And what do you think the men of two of our batteries were doing an hour after the camps were pitched and the horses watered? - playing a football match! Marvellous fellows!

We stayed at Estree until the evening of the 28th, days of gossip and of fairly confident expectations, for we knew now that the Boche's first offensive was held - but a time of waiting and of wondering where we were to be sent next. Division was nearly thirty miles away, incorporated with the French Army, and still fighting, while Corps seemed to have forgotten that we needed supplies. Still there was no need to worry about food and forage. Estree was an important railhead, and the supply officer seemed anxious to get his stores distributed as soon as they came in: he was prepared to treat most comers as famine-stricken stragglers. Besides, near the station stood an enormous granary, filled to the brim, simply waiting to be requisitioned.

About noon on the 28th we were very cast down by the news that, to meet the demand for reinforcements, the Brigade might be disbanded, and the gunners hurried off in driblets, to make up losses on various parts of our particular Army's front.

The colonel had instructions to attend a Staff Conference in the afternoon, and each battery was ordered to prepare a list of its available gunners.

There were sore hearts that afternoon. Many of the men had been with the Brigade since it was formed, and to be scattered broadcast after doing well, and coming through a time of stress and danger together, would knock the spirit out of every one. The colonel came back at tea-time, impassive, walking briskly. I knew before he opened his lips that the Brigade was saved. "We move to-night to Pont St Maxence. We are going on to Poix to refit," was all he said.

*   *   *   *   *

Every one was anxious to be off, fearing that the Staff might change its mind. It rained in torrents that night, and owing to the Corps' failure to map out proper accommodation arrangements, we slept anyhow and anywhere, but no one minded much. The Brigade was still in being, and nothing else mattered. I could tell many stories of the next few days - marching and billeting and getting ready for action again; of the village that no English troops had visited before, and the inhabitants that feared us, and afterwards did not want us to leave; of the friendly bearded patron of an estaminet, who flourished an 'Echo de Paris,' and pointed to the words *ténacité anglaise* in an account of the fighting; of the return of the signalling officer, who, while attending a course at an Army School, had been roped in to lead one of Sandeman Carey's infantry platoons; of the magnificently equipped casualty clearing station that a week before the offensive had been twenty-five miles behind the lines, and only got its last patients away two hours before the Boches arrived!

*   *   *   *   *

April 2nd: A few more new guns had come in from the Refitting Depot. We were almost complete to establishment. The horses were out grazing and getting fat again. Most of the men were hard at it, playing their eternal football. The colonel came out of the chateau, which was Brigade Headquarters billet, and settled himself in a deck-chair. He looked sun-tanned and fit.

"If all colonels were as competent and knowledgeable as our colonel, we should have won the war by now," said Dumble as he and I walked away. "What a beautiful day."

"Yes. Oh to be in England, now that April's here," I chimed in.

"Oh to be in England, any bally old time of the year," Dumble corrected me.

THE RETURN PUSH

CHAPTER I

THE DEFENCE OF AMIENS

O N A DAY towards the end of April the colonel and I, riding well ahead of the Brigade, passed through deserted Amiens and stopped when we came upon some fifty horses, nose-bags on, halted under the trees along a boulevard in the eastern outskirts of the city. Officers in groups stood beneath, or leaned against, the high wall of a large civil hospital that flanked the roadway.

Reinforced in guns and personnel, and rested after the excitements and hazards of the March thrust-back, our two brigades of Divisional Field Artillery, and the D.A.C., were bound again for the Front. These waiting officers formed the advance billeting parties.

"We've been obeying Sir Douglas Haig's Order of the Day - getting our backs to the wall," growled the adjutant to me, after he had sprung up and saluted the colonel. "The staff captain met us two hours ago at ——; but they were shelling the place, and he said it wouldn't be safe for waggon lines; so we came on here. He's inside the building now seeing if he can put the whole Divisional Artillery there....

"I'll bet we shan't be ready for the batteries when they come in," he went on gloomily - and then added, like the good soldier that he is, "My groom will show you where the horses can water."

A long-range shell, passing high overhead and exploding among the houses some way behind us, showed that Amiens was no health resort. But horse lines were allotted, and in due course the long corridors of the evacuated building resounded with the clatter-clatter of gunners and drivers marched in to deposit their kits. "You've got a big piece of chalk this morning, haven't you?" grumbled the adjutant to the adjutant of our companion Brigade, complaining that they were portioning off more rooms than they were entitled to. Still he was pleased to find that the room he and I shared contained a wardrobe, and that inside the door was pinned a grotesque, jolly-looking placard of Harry Tate - moustache and all - in "Box o' Tricks." The discovery that a currant cake, about as large as London, sent a few days before from England, had disappeared from our Headquarters' mess-cart during the day's march, led to a tirade on the shortcomings of New Army servants. But he became sympathetic when I explained that the caretakers, two sad-eyed French women, the only civilians we ourselves met that day, were anxious that our men should be warned against prising open locked doors and cupboards. "Tell 'em any man doing that will be shot at dawn," he said, leaving me to reassure the women.

Twenty-four hours later, after another march, our guns were in position. With pick and shovel, and a fresh supply of corrugated iron, the batteries were fortifying their habitations; Brigade Headquarters occupied the only dwelling for miles round, a tiny café that no shell had touched. The colonel had a ground-floor room and a bedstead to himself; the adjutant and myself put down our camp-beds in an attic, with the signalling officer and the American doctor next door, and H.Q. signallers and servants in the adjoining loft that completed the upper storey. It was a rain-proof comfortable shelter, but the C.R.A. didn't altogether approve of it. "You're at a cross-roads, with an ammunition dump alongside of you, and the road outside the front door is mined ready for blowing up should the Boche advance this way," he said grimly, when he visited us. "In any case, he'll shoot by the map on this spot immediately he starts a battle.... I think you ought to have a retiring headquarters in readiness." So I put in two days superintending the erection of a little colony of houses, built of ammunition boxes and corrugated iron, half a mile from the main road. I camouflaged the sloping roofs with loose hay, and, at a distance, our "Garden City" looked like a bunch of small hay-stacks. We got quite proud of our handiwork; and there was a strained moment one midday when the regimental sergeant-major rode hurriedly to the café with a most disturbing report. Riding along the main road he had observed a party of men pulling down our huts, and piling the sheets of corrugated iron into a G.S. waggon. When he cantered across, the driver whipped up his horses, and the G.S. waggon bounded over the open fields for half a mile before the sergeant-major got sufficiently near to order it to halt. "They belong to the ———st Brigade, sir," the sergeant-major informed the adjutant, "and I've told the sergeant in charge of the party to consider himself under arrest until you have seen him."

The adjutant, eye flashing, nostrils dilated, was already out of the café walking hard, and breathing dire threats against the servant who had been posted to guard our new home. Apparently he had gone away to complain that the cook was late in sending his dinner.

The sergeant and his assistant "pirates" were restoring the dismantled huts by the time the adjutant and myself drew near. The sergeant was plainly a disciple of the "It's all in the same firm" school. He submitted, with great respect, that he was innocent of criminal intent. There was nothing to show that the huts were in use... and his battery wanted iron for their gun-pits.

"None of your old soldier talk with me," blustered the adjutant, shaking a ponderous forefinger. "You knew you were doing wrong.... Why did you send the waggon off when you saw the sergeant-major?"

"I went after it and stopped it when he told me to, sir," returned the sergeant.

The sergeant-major admitted that, strictly speaking, this was a correct statement. There was a ten seconds' pause, and I wondered what the adjutant's next thrust would be.

"The waggon was trotting away, was it?" he demanded slowly.

"Yes, sir," replied the sergeant.

"And you made no attempt to prevent it trotting until the sergeant-major told you to stop it?"

"No, sir."

"And you know it's forbidden for waggons to be trotted except in very exceptional circumstances?"

"Ye-s, sir."

"Very well, I put you under arrest for contravening G.R.O. by trotting draught-horses."

"Artful beggar - I know him of old," chuckled the adjutant, as he and I returned to the café. "He was a gunner in my battery when I was sergeant-major of —— Battery, R.H.A."

The Boche was expected to attack on St George's Day. Our Brigade was defending a reserve line, and would not fire unless the enemy swept over our first-line system. Fresh trenches were being dug, and new and stout rows of wire entanglement put down. Corps orders were distinct and unmistakable. The fight here would be a fight *à outrance*. On March 21 our retirement had been a strategic one. But this Front had to be held at all costs, and we should throw in every reserve we had. Only once during our stay in the café did the adjutant and myself sleep in pyjamas. "These walls are so thin one 5·9 would knock the whole place out; if we have to clear we may as well be ready," he said meaningly. The ridge, three-quarters of a mile in front of us, was shelled regularly, and every night enemy bombing planes came over, but, strangely enough, the Boche gunners neglected our cross-roads; we even kicked a football about until one afternoon a trench-mortar officer misdirected it on to the main road, and an expressive "pop!" told of its finish under the wheel of a motor-lorry. St George's Day, and still no Boche attack! We began to talk of the peaceful backwater in which we were moored. Manning, our mess waiter, decorated the stained, peeling walls of the mess with some New Art picture post-cards. I found a quiet corner, and wrote out a 'Punch' idea that a demand for our water-troughs to be camouflaged had put into my head. Major Bullivant, who had succeeded poor Harville in the command of A Battery, and Major Bartlett of C Battery, dined with us that night, and the best story told concerned an extremely non-military subaltern, newly attached to the D.A.C. When instructed to deliver an important message to "Div. Arty." - the Army condensation for "Divisional Artillery" - he pored long and hopelessly over a map. Finally he appealed to a brother officer. "I can't find the village of 'DIVARTY' on the map," he said, and, of course, sprang into immediate fame throughout the Division.

April 24: About 4 A.M. a shell burst that shook the café. Then the steady whistling scream of high-velocity shells going overhead. I lighted a candle and looked at the adjutant as he poked his red face and tousled grey hair from under his blankets. "They've started," he muttered solemnly. "The old Hun always shells the back areas when he attacks."

We got up slowly, and fastened boots and leggings. "I suppose we ought to put on revolvers," he went on dubiously, and then added with sudden warmth, "I hope he gets it in the neck to-day."

Our telephone pit in the cellar below the café was alive with industry. Our batteries were not firing, but the colonel had already asked the battery commanders whether any shells, particularly gas shells, had come their way. A couple of 4·2's had landed close to C Battery, but they seemed to be stray shots; it did not seem likely that the enemy knew where the batteries were sited. The Boche bombardment continued.

After breakfast, a 5·9 exploding 200 yards from our café, blew out the largest pane in the unshuttered window. Shells had dropped by now in most spots around us; but the cross-roads remained untouched. A cyclist orderly from our waggon line, two miles back, brought news that a direct hit had blown the telephone cart to bits; fortunately, neither man nor horse had been touched. The adjutant was outside exhorting four infantry stragglers to try and find their units by returning to the battle line. A Royal Fusilier, wounded in the head, had fainted while waiting at the cross-roads for an ambulance; our cook had lifted him on to a bench inside the café and was giving him tea. The colonel, who remained in the mess, in telephone touch with the brigadier-general, C.R.A., and the brigade-major, had never seemed so preoccupied. Days afterwards, he confided to me that when the Hun bombardment started he feared a repetition of the overpowering assault of March 21.

"They had tanks out to-day," a boy captain of infantry, his arm in a sling, told me, as he climbed into a motor ambulance. "By Gad, I saw a topping sight near Villers Bretonneux. The Boche attacked in force there and pushed us back, and one of his old tanks came sailing merrily on. But just over the crest, near a sunken road, was a single 18-pdr.; it didn't fire until the Boche tank climbed into view on top of the crest.

Then they let him have it at about 100 yards' range. Best series of upper-cuts I've ever seen. The old tank sheered off and must have got it hot." I learnt afterwards that this was a single gun detachment belonging to our companion brigade, who had been pushed forward as soon as news came that the enemy was being held.

By tea-time we ourselves had been ordered forward to relieve a brigade that had suffered considerably in the opening stages of the assault. And, after all, we didn't occupy the "Garden City" headquarters I had been at such pains to build. We handed it over to the brigade we were relieving, and their colonel congratulated our colonel on his forethought.

The colonel decided that only the doctor, the signalling officer, and myself should go forward. The adjutant could settle at the waggon lines and occupy himself with reinforcements, clothing, and salvage returns, Army Form B 213, watering and forage arrangements, and suchlike administrative duties. My task would be the "Forward" or "G" branch - *i.e.*, assisting the colonel with the details of his fighting programmes.

The colonel and I lay down that night in a hole scooped out of a chalk bank. The corrugated iron above our heads admitted a draught at only one corner; as our sleeping-bags were spread out on a couple of spring mattresses, moved by some one at some time from some neighbouring homestead, we could not complain of lack of comfort.

April 24 was the last day on which our Brigade awaited and prepared to meet a Boche attack of the first magnitude. But it was not until the month of July that any of us conceived, or dared to believe in, the possibility of his mighty armies being forced upon the defensive again.

During May and June we accepted it that our rôle would be to stick it out until the Americans came along *en masse* in 1919. The swift and glorious reversal of things from August onwards surprised no one more than the actual fighting units of the British armies.

CHAPTER II

THE RED-ROOFED HOUSE

"WE'RE DOING AN attack to-morrow morning," said the colonel, returning about tea-time from a visit to the C.R.A. "We are under the ——th Divisional Artillery while we're up here, and we shall get the orders from them. You'd better let the batteries know. Don't say anything over the wire, of course.... Any papers for me to see?" he added, pulling out his leather cigarette case.

I handed him the gun and personnel returns, showing how many men and guns the Brigade had in action; and the daily ammunition reports that in collated form find their way from Divisional Artillery to Corps, and from Corps to Army, and play their part in informing the strategic minds at the back of the Front of the ebb and flow of fighting activity all along the vast battle line, enabling them to shape their plans accordingly. "D Battery are a bit low in smoke shells," remarked the colonel. "You'd better warn Major Veasey that he'll want some for to-morrow morning."

"B Battery... two casualties... how was that?" he continued, before signing another paper.

"About an hour ago, sir. Their mess cart was coming up, and got shelled half a mile from the battery position. Two of the servants were wounded."

"I've never seen an order worded quite like that," he smiled, when I showed him a typed communication just arrived from the Divisional Artillery, under whose orders we were now acting. It gave the map co-ordinates of the stretch of front our guns were to fire upon in response to S.O.S. calls. The passage the colonel referred to began -

"By kind consent of the colonel of the ———th French Artillery, the S.O.S. barrage on our front will be strengthened as follows:…"

"Sounds as if the French colonel were lending his batteries like a regimental band at a Bank Holiday sports meeting, sir," I ventured.

"Yes, we are learning to conduct war in the grand manner," smiled the colonel, opening his copy of 'The Times.'

Our mess, under a couple of curved iron "elephants" stuck against the bank, had looked a miserable affair when we came to it; but judicious planting of sandbags and bits of "scrounged" boarding and a vigorous clean-up had made it more habitable. Manning, the mess servant, had unearthed from a disused dug-out a heavy handsome table with a lacquered top, and a truly regal chair for the colonel - green plush seating and a back of plush and scrolled oak - the kind of chair that provincial photographers bring out for their most dignified sitters. By the light of our acetylene lamp we had dined, and there had been two rubbers of bridge, the colonel and the little American doctor bringing about the downfall of Wilde, the signalling officer, and myself, in spite of the doctor's tendency to finesse against his own partner. The doctor had never played bridge before joining us, and his mind still ran to poker. The Reconnaissance Officer of the ———th Divisional Artillery had rung up at 10 o'clock to tell us that an officer was on his way with a watch synchronised to Corps time, and that we should receive orders for the next morning's operation *viâ* a certain Field Artillery Brigade who were somewhere in our vicinity. I had told the brigade clerk that he could go to bed in his 3 feet by 6 feet cubby-hole, and that the orderlies waiting to convey the battle orders to the batteries ought to snatch some rest also. It was 11 P.M. now. Wilde and the doctor had gone off to their own dug-out. It was very dark when I looked outside the mess. We were in a lonely stretch of moorland; the nearest habitation was the shell-mauled cottage at the railway crossing, two miles away. Every ten minutes or so enemy shells screamed and flopped into the valley between us and the road alongside which D Battery lay.

"We'll try and hurry these people up," said the colonel, picking up the telephone. Even as he told the signaller on duty to get him Divisional

Artillery, a call came through. It was the Artillery Brigade from whom we expected a messenger with the orders.

"No!" I heard the colonel say sharply. "We've had nothing.... No! no one has been here with a watch.... You want an officer to come over to you?... But I haven't any one who knows where you are."

A pause. Then the colonel continued. "Yes, but you know where we are, don't you?... Umph.... Well, where are you to be found?... You can't give a co-ordinate over the telephone?... That's not very helpful."

He rang off, but I knew by his expression that the matter was not yet settled. He got through to the ———th Divisional Artillery and told the brigade-major that it was now 11.20 P.M., that no officer with a synchronised watch had arrived, and that the other brigade were now asking us to send an officer to them for orders for the coming battle. "I have no one who knows where they are," he went on. "They must know our location - we relieved one of their brigades. Why can't they send to us as arranged? I may have some one wandering about half the night trying to find them."

In a little while the telephone bell tinkled again. "I'll answer them," said the colonel abruptly.

"All right, I'll send to them," he replied stonily. "Where are we to find them, since they won't give us co-ordinates over the telephone?... A house with a red roof!... You can't tell us anything more definite?... Very well.... Good-bye."

He put down the telephone with a little "Tchat!" that meant all forms of protest, annoyance, and sense of grievance. But now that no possible concession was to be gained, and certain precise work had to be done by us, he became the inexorable matter-of-fact executive leader again. "There's nothing for it," he said, looking at me. "You will have to go."

Buildings with red roofs are not marked as such on military maps, and I bent glumly over the map board. However, houses were exceedingly few in this neighbourhood, and the chateau on the other side of the railway could be ruled out immediately. It was known as "The White Chateau," and I had noticed it in daytime. Besides, it had been so heavily shelled that our companion brigade had evacuated it two days before. "It's pretty certain to be somewhere in this area," observed the colonel, bending over me, and indicating a particular three thousand square yards on the map. "I expect that's the place - on the other side of the railway," and he pointed to a tiny oblong patch. I estimated that the house was three miles from where we were. It wanted but five minutes to midnight.

I went outside, and flickering my electric torch stumbled across ruts and past occasional shell-holes to the copse, three hundred yards away, that sheltered the officers' chargers. I crackled a way among twigs and undergrowth until the piquet called out, "Who goes there?"

"I think your groom's here, sir," he said, and the trees were so close set that my shoulder brushed the hindquarters of a row of mules as he piloted me along. "Are you there, Morgan?" he shouted, pulling open a waterproof ground-sheet that was fastened over a hole in the ground. "No - go away," called a voice angrily. "Where's Morgan sleep? Mr. ——— wants him," persevered the piquet.

We found my groom in another hole in the ground about thirty yards away. He listened sleepily while I told him to get my horses ready immediately. "Do you want feeds on, sir?" he asked, with visions apparently of an all-night ride.

There was no moon, and I gazed gratefully at the only constellation that showed in a damp unfriendly sky - the Great Bear. I let my horse find his own way the first few hundred yards, until we struck a track, then we broke into a trot. The swish and plop of gas shells in the valley towards which we were descending made me pause. I calculated that they were falling short of the railway crossing I wanted to reach, and decided that a wide sweep to the right would be the safest course. We cantered alongside some ploughed land, and the motion of the horse, and the thought that with luck I might finish my task quickly, and earn a word of commendation from the colonel, brought a certain sense of exhilaration. The shelling of the valley increased; my horse stumbled going down a bank, and for the next five minutes we walked over broken ground. "Getting a bit too much to the right," I said to myself, and turned my horse's head. Further thoughts were cut short by the discovery that his forelegs were up against a belt of barbed wire.

For ten minutes I walked in front of the wire, searching for an opening, and getting nearer to where the shells were falling. All the time I looked earnestly for the railway line. I began to feel bitter and resentful. "If our own Divisional Artillery had been doing to-morrow's show I shouldn't have had to turn out on a job of this kind," I reflected. "Damn the ——th Division. Why can't they do their work properly?"

But little gusts of anger sometimes bring with them the extra bit of energy that carries a job through. We had reached a ruined wall now, and there was still no opening in the wire. I could see telegraph posts, and knew that the railway was just ahead. I got off my horse, told the groom to wait behind the broken wall, and, climbing through the barbed wire, picked my way along smashed sleepers and twisted rails until I came to the crossing.

I followed the deserted shell-torn road that led from the level-crossing, searching for a track on the left that would lead to the house I sought. A motor-cyclist, with the blue-and-white band of the Signal Service round his arm, came through the hedge.

"Is there a house on top of that hill?" I asked him, after a preliminary flicker of my torch.

"Yes, sir."

"Is it a red-roofed house?"

"Well,… I don't know, sir."

"Who's up there?"

"Smith's group, sir."

"Oh, hang! that tells me nothing. What are they - artillery?"

"Yes, sir - heavies, I think, sir."

I felt myself at a standstill. Orders for us were not likely to be with a group of heavy artillery. "Whom are you from?" I asked finally, preparing to move on.

"From the ——th Div. Artillery, sir."

"Oh!" - with a rush of hopefulness - "you have no orders, I suppose, for the ——nd Brigade?" - mentioning our Brigade.

"No, sir."

I broke off and strode up the hillside, determined at any rate to gather some sort of information from the house the motor-cyclist had just left. I came upon a bare-looking, two-storied brick building with plain doors and windows. Through the keyhole of the front door I could see a light coming from an inside room. I opened the door and walked down the passage, calling, "Is this the ———rd Field Artillery Brigade?"

"No! This is the ———nd Field Company," replied a fair-moustached sapper captain, who was lying on a mattress in the room from which the light came, reading a book of O. Henry stories.

"Sorry to trouble you," I said, "but I'm trying to find the ———rd Brigade. Do you know if they are round here?"

"I don't, I'm afraid. We only came in this afternoon."

"It's a house with a red roof," I went on, rather hopelessly.

"I think I know the place," chimed in a voice from an inner room. "It's a shooting-box, isn't it? Your best way is to get on the road again and take the next track on the left. I noticed a red-roofed house up there when we came by."

I trudged back and got on to the new track, feeling very martyred but very resigned. I suppose I ought to have kept my eyes open more, I thought. Next time I go to a new part of the country I won't miss a single distinguishing feature.

It was now 1.15 A.M. I came to a lonely house fronted by a neatly railed garden. I hammered noisily on the door and found that it opened into a darkened passage. A torch flashed into my face. "Is this the ———rd Brigade?" I began.

"Yes," a voice shouted, and suddenly a door opened and a spurt of light revealed a youthful pink-cheeked staff lieutenant. "Are you from the ———nd Brigade?" he asked. "Oh, bon! bon! - I've been waiting for you."

"Waiting for me!" I retorted, nettled by his airy manner. "Hard luck on me having to traipse at this time of night to a place I don't know to get orders you ought to have sent out."

"Yes, I know," he replied cheerfully. "We're awfully sorry, but it's the French Division, you know. We've only just got the orders out of them. It's really their show.... And I'm afraid the first part of your orders have been sent off to the wrong place." Saying which, he led me into a large sombre room in which four or five officers sat immersed in papers and message forms. An elderly colonel looked up and nodded over his glasses. The young staff officer handed me some barrage maps and a quantity of type-written operation orders.

"Zero hour is 5.10 A.M.," he began, "and here is the part of your orders that has gone astray. I can't give you this copy. Will you take the orders down from this?"

I commenced writing out the operation order, and was struck to find that the barrage "lifts" were in hundreds of metres instead of hundreds of yards. "Yes, the French insisted on that," explained the staff lieutenant briskly.

"But we haven't metres on our range-drums," I said with an air of abandonment.

"Yes, I know, but the French insisted on it, because of their infantry.... Oh! there's a para. there about smoke-shells - that's important."

"The para. about smoke-shells is deleted... there will be no smoke-shells," put in the elderly colonel, looking up.

"Oh, is it, sir?" said the staff lieutenant, turning round.

"Yes; the correction has just come through."

"Right, sir."

I synchronised my watch, thrust the bundle of papers into my hip-pocket, and hurried away to find my horses. It was half-past one, and the attack was timed to start at 5.10. The colonel would require to deal with the orders, and the battery commanders would have but the barest time to work out their individual "lifts." I started back at the gallop, skirting the side of the valley. I remember wishing to heaven that the clumps and hillocks of this part of France did not look so consistently alike. If only it were light enough for me to pick out the mustard field that lay, a bright yellow landmark, behind our chalk bank!

The colonel was in bed when I got back, but I held a candle while he read through the orders, and got out his ivory ruler, and apportioned a barrage lane to each battery. "Metres will have to become yards," was one of his remarks.

By twenty-to-three the orderlies had set out with the battle orders to the batteries, while I spoke on the telephone to an officer of each battery, and synchronised watches.

When I turned in, after a whisky-and-soda and a couple of biscuits, the colonel was fast asleep. I felt satisfied, however, that I had done my share that night towards beating the Hun.

By 7 A.M. we were up again, and until 7 P.M. the telephone buzzed continuously. It was a day of hard infantry fighting, of attacks that were held up and had to be renewed, of German counter-efforts to shift us from points won at the opening of our attack. All day long F.O.O.'s and liaison officers telephoned reports of changes in our front line, and five times I turned on our batteries to respond to S.O.S. calls. By the end of the day we held three parts of the ground that our Higher Command had planned to seize.

CHAPTER III

AN AUSTRALIAN "HAND-OVER"

THERE FOLLOWED THREE months of varied kinds of soldiering: short spells holding the line, odd days in rest areas, quick shifts to other parts of the Front, occasional participation in carefully prepared raids on Hun trenches, one whole fortnight in a riverside village where even the Boche night-bombers did not come, and where we held a joyous race-meeting - seventy riders in one race - and a spit-and-polish horse show. There was the fresh burst by the Hun armies that seemed to spell the doom of Reims. We began to notice larger and larger bodies of arriving Americans, but did not expect them to be in the war on an impressive scale until 1918 was out. Leave to England remained at a standstill. The universal phrase of 1916 and 1917, "Roll on Duration," had almost entirely disappeared from the men's letters that came before me for censoring. Yet no one seemed depressed. Every one appeared possessed of a sane and calm belief that things would work out right in the long-run. We should just have to hold the Hun off this year, and by honest endeavour during training opportunities fit ourselves to fight with added effectiveness in 1919, when America would be properly in the field and the Allies' turn would come.

The second week in May the Brigade, after a fourteen-mile march, came again into the land of rolling heights and sunken roads in which for three and a half years most of our fighting had been done. A "sausage" balloon anchored to the ground, a pumping-station and four square-shaped water-troughs, and a dozen or so shanties built of sandbags and rusted iron, dotted the green-and-brown landscape.

Waggon tracks had cut ugly brown ways through clover-fields and grasslands. A new system of trenches stretched to north and to south from the main road along which the Brigade were moving. Men of the Labour Corps were stolidly filling shell-holes in the road surface with broken stones, and digging sump-holes for draining away the rain-and-mud torrents that were sure to come. A long dark wood crowned the ridge three miles in front of us. In the centre a slender spire tipped the tree-tops.

"That's Baisieux Church," said Major Bullivant, with whom I was riding along the horse track at the side of the road. "Do you know the latest motto for the Labour Corps?" he added inconsequentially, looking down at a bespectacled man in khaki who eased up as we passed. *"Infra dig.,"* he went on, with a humorous side-glance, and without pausing for my answer.

Away to the east muffled boomings as if giants were shaking blankets. My mind turned to July 1916, when first I arrived in France and came along this very road at 3.30 one morning as the sun's rim began to peep above the long dark wood. How easy to recall that morning! I had brought fifty-three men from the Base, reinforcements for the Divisional Artillery, and half-believed that the war could not proceed unless I delivered them to their destination in the shortest possible time; and my indignant keenness when I reached the village behind the long dark wood and learned that no one there knew anything about the two lorries that were to transport my party the remainder of the journey to the Front! Did I not rouse a frowning town major and two amazed sergeant-majors before 5 A.M. and demand that they should do something in the matter? And did not my fifty-three men eventually complete a triumphant pilgrimage in no fewer than thirteen ammunition lorries - to find that they and myself had arrived a day earlier than we were expected? And here was I again in the same stretch of country, and the British line not so far forward as it had been two years before.

We pitched tents and tethered our horses in the wood, and before nightfall I walked into the village to look at the spot beneath the church tower where I had halted my fifty-three men, and to view again the barn in which I had roused the most helpful of the two sergeant-majors. Alas for the sentiment! All French villages seem much alike, with their mud-wall barns and tiled cottages, when you have passed through scores of them, as I have done since July 1916. I could not be certain of the building.

Coming back to our camp through the heart of the wood, I chanced upon a place of worship that only a being of fancy and imagination and devoutness could have fashioned. Inside a high oval hedge, close-woven with much patient labour, stood an altar made of banked-up turf, surmounted by a plain wooden cross. Turf benches to seat a hundred and fifty worshippers faced the altar. Above, the wind rustled softly through the branches of tall birches and larch trees, bent over until they touched, and made one think of Gothic arches. There was wonderful peace and rest in the place. Some one told me afterwards that the chaplain of a London Division had built it. It was a happy thought.

*   *   *   *   *

In the morning I went with the colonel through the village, and a mile and a half along a road leading east that for half a mile was lined with camouflage screens. "The Boche holds the ridge over there," remarked the colonel, stretching an arm towards high ground swathed in a blue haze five miles away. A painted notice-board told all and sundry that horse traffic was not permitted on the road until after dusk. We struck off to the left, dropped into a trench where we saw a red triangular flag flying, and said "Good-day" to the brigade-major of the Infantry brigade who had made their headquarters at this spot. Then we got out of the trench again, and walked along the top until we came to what was to be our future home - the headquarters of the Australian Field Artillery Brigade that we were to relieve by 10 P.M. We received a cheery welcome from a plump, youngish Australian colonel, and a fair-haired adjutant with blue sparkling eyes.

When a brigade of artillery relieves another brigade of artillery, there is a ceremony, known as "handing-over," to be gone through.

The outgoing brigade presents to the in-coming brigade maps and documents showing the positions of the batteries, the O.P.'s, the liaison duties with the infantry, the amount of ammunition to be kept at the gun positions, the zones covered, the S.O.S. arrangements, and similar information detailing daily work and responsibilities. I can recall no "hand-over" so perfect in its way as this one. The Australian Brigade's defence file was a beautifully arranged, typed document, and a child could have understood the indexing. True, the extent and number of their headquarters staff was astonishing. Against our two clerks they had three clerks, and a skilled draughtsman for map-making; also an N.C.O. whose sole *magnum opus* was the weekly compiling of Army Form B. 213. But there could be no doubt that they carried on war in a most business-like way.

The colonel went off with the Australian colonel to inspect the battery positions and view the front line from the O.P.'s, and sent me back to bring up our mess cart and to arrange for the fetching of our kit. By tea-time we were properly installed; and indeed the Australian colonel and his adjutant remained as our guests at dinner.

The mess, cut out of the side of the trench and lined with corrugated iron, possessed an ingeniously manufactured door - part of a drum-tight wing of a French aeroplane. The officers' sleeping quarters were thirty feet below ground, in an old French dug-out, with steps so unequal in height that it was the prudent course to descend backwards with your hands grasping the steps nearest your chin.

The Australian colonel dipped his hand for the fifth time into the box of canteen chocolates that Manning had placed on the table with the port. "That's a nice Sam Browne of yours," he observed, noticing the gloss on our adjutant's belt.

"I hope you don't take a fancy to it, sir," replied our adjutant quickly. "We're all afraid of you, you know. I've put a double piquet on our waggon lines for fear some of your fellows take a liking to our horses."

The Australian colonel and his adjutant laughed good-naturedly, and the colonel told us a story of a captain and a sergeant-major in another Australian brigade who were accomplished "looters."

One night the pair were hauling down a tent which they thought was empty, when a yell made them aware that an officer was sleeping in it. The captain took to his heels, but the sergeant-major was captured.

"The next day," concluded the Australian colonel, "the captain had to go and make all sorts of apologies to get his sergeant-major off. The other people agreed, provided the officer ransomed him with half a dozen pit-props and ten sheets of corrugated iron. For a long time afterwards we used to chaff the captain, and tell him that he valued his sergeant-major at six pit-props and ten sheets of iron."

Hot sweltering days followed. Most mornings I spent at the O.P. watching our batteries' efforts to knock out suspected enemy trench mortars, or staring through my binoculars trying to pick out Boche transport, or fresh digging operations. The tramp back at midday along the communication trenches was boiling-hot going. I used to think "People working in London will be pining just now for green fields and country air. For myself, I'd give anything for a cool ride on a London bus." In the afternoons there were reserve battery positions - in case of a swift Hun advance - to be reconnoitred, gaps in the barbed-wire systems to be located, and bits of trenches that would have to be filled in to allow our waggons to cross. Divisional Artillery were insistent upon timed reports of hostile shelling, particularly gas shelling, and this formed another portion of my special work. One day intimation came from Division that Fentiman and Robson had been accepted for the Air Service. "It's the only way to get leave to England," said Robson jocularly. Fentiman's chief regret was that he would have to leave behind a mare that he had got from the Tank Corps. "She pulls so," he told me one afternoon when I met him jogging along the road, "that if I turned on to the grass at this moment and put spurs into her, she wouldn't stop till she got to Amiens…. No one in the Tank Corps has been able to pull her up under four miles, and only then when she came to a seven-foot hedge…. But I was beginning to understand her."

When I accompanied the colonel on his visits to the Infantry brigades all the talk was of the training of the youngsters, who now formed so considerable a portion of the battalion strengths. "They are good stuff,"

I heard one of the brigadiers say, "and I keep drumming into them that they are fighting for England, and that the Boche mustn't gain another yard of ground." He was a fighter, this brigadier - although I have never yet met another officer who took it as a matter of course that his camp-bed should be equipped with linen sheets when he was living in the firing line.

About three-quarters of a mile from our headquarters was a tiny cemetery, set in a grove of trees on a bare hillside, sequestered, beautiful in its peacefulness and quiet. One morning, very early, I walked out to view it more closely. It had escaped severe shelling, although chipped tombstones and broken railings and scattered pieces of painted wire wreaths showed that the hell-blast of destruction had not altogether passed it by. I went softly into the little chapel. On the floor, muddy, noisy-sleeping soldiers lay sprawled in ungainly attitudes. Rifles were piled against the wall; mess-tins and water-bottles lay even upon the altar. And somehow there seemed nothing incongruous about the spectacle, nothing that would hurt a profoundly religious mind. It was all part of the war.

And one night when I was restless, and even the heavy drugging warmth of the dug-out did not dull me to sleep, I climbed up into the open air. It was a lovely night. The long dark wood stood out black and distinct in the clear moonlight; the stars twinkled in their calm abode. Suddenly a near-by battery of long-range guns cracked out an ear-splitting salvo. And before the desolating rush of the shells had faded from the ear a nightingale hidden among the trees burst into song. That also was part of the war.

CHAPTER IV

HAPPY DAYS!

URING THE MONTH of June Brigade Headquarters
retired from the trench dug-out and settled in the end house
of the village, a white-walled, vine-clad building, with a courtyard and
stables and a neat garden that only one Boche shell had smitten. On the
door of the large room that we chose for the mess there still remained
a request in French, written in a clear painstaking hand, that billeted
officers should keep to the linoleum strips laid across the carpet when
proceeding to the two inner rooms. But there was no linoleum now,
and no carpet. On the otherwise bare wall was hung a massively-framed
portrait of the proprietor - a clean-shaven middle-aged Frenchman of
obviously high intelligence. A family press-cutting album contained
an underlined report from a local newspaper of a concert given in the
village on June 6, 1914:-

> *Très remarque le duo de mandoline avec accompagnement de*
> *violon exécuté par trois gracieuses jeunes filles qui font à chacune de*
> *nos soirées admirer par les amateurs du beau, leur talent d'artiste!*

I gathered that the three young girls were daughters of the house; I
also noted that *trois gracieuses jeunes filles* was doubly underlined.

One of our servants used to be a professional gardener, and in a couple
of days he had weeded the paths and brought skill and knowledge to
bear on the neglected vegetable beds. We had excellent salad from that
garden and fresh strawberries, while there were roses to spare for the
tall vases on the mantelpiece in the mess; and before we came away our
gardener had looked to the future and planted lettuce and turnips and
leeks, and even English pansies. The Boche gunners never got a line on

to that house, and though aeroplanes cruised above us every night not a single bomb dropped near.

The town major, a learned and discursive subaltern, relieved on account of rheumatic troubles from more strenuous duties with an Infantry regiment, joined our mess and proved a valuable addition. He was a talented mathematician whose researches had carried him to where mathematics soar into the realms of imagination; he had a horror of misplaced relatives, and possessed a reliable palate in the matter of red wines. One dinner-time he talked himself out on the possibilities of the metric system, and pictured the effects of a right angle with a hundred instead of ninety degrees. Another night he walked me up and down the garden until 2 A.M., expatiating on astronomy. He tried to make me realise the beyond comprehension remoteness of the new star by explaining that astronomers did not calculate its distance from the earth in thousands of miles. "Light travels at 186,000 miles a second; to astronomers the new star is 2000 years away," he concluded.

As I have said, he was a valuable addition to our mess. One day he took me to a neighbouring village and introduced me to a fat comfortable-looking Maire, who spread his hands on his capacious knees and invited us to try a cooling nip of absinthe. After which he produced from a small choice store a bottle of fifty-year-old brandy, and made the town major take it away in token of a friendship that began in the way-back days of 1915.

All this may not sound like war, but I am trying to write down some of the average daily happenings in a field-artillery brigade that has seen as much service as any brigade in the new armies.

For several days Wilde, the signalling officer, and the doctor conducted an acrid argument that arose from the doctor's astounding assertion that he had seen a Philadelphia base-ball player smite a base-ball so clean and hard that it travelled 400 yards before it pitched. Wilde, with supreme scorn, pointed out that no such claim had been made even for a golf ball. The doctor made play with the names of Speaker, Cobb, and other transatlantic celebrities. Then one day Wilde rushed into the mess flourishing a London Sunday paper that referred in glowing terms to a mighty base-ball hit of 136 yards, made on the Royal Arsenal football ground; after which the doctor retired to cope with the plague of boils that had descended upon the Brigade. This and a severe outbreak of Spanish 'flue provided him with a regular hundred patients a day. He himself had bitter personal experience of the boils. We never saw him without one for ten weeks. His own method of dealing with their excruciating tenderness was to swathe his face in cotton-wool and sticking-plaster. "Damn me, doctor, if you don't look like a loose imitation of Von Tirpitz," burst out the adjutant one day, when the doctor, with a large boil on either side of his chin, appeared plastered accordingly.

By July we had side-stepped north and were housed in a chateau that really deserved the appellation, though it was far from being as massively built as an average English country seat of like importance. It belonged to one of the oldest families in France. Wide noble staircases led to vast rooms made untenable by shell fire. Fragments of rare stained glass littered the vacant private chapel. The most valuable paintings, the best of the Louis XV. furniture, and the choicest tapestry had been removed to safety. In one room I entered some bucolic wag had clothed a bust of Venus in a lance-corporal's cap and field-service jacket, and affixed a box-respirator in the alert position. We made the mess in what had been the nursery, and the adjutant and myself slept in bunks off an elaborately mined passage, in making which British tunnellers had worked so hard that cracks showed in the wall above, and the whole wing appeared undecided whether or not to sink. We learned that there were two schools of opinion regarding the safety of the passage. The Engineers of one Division thought the wing would not subside; some equally competent Engineers shook their heads and said no civil authority would dream of passing the passage as safe. The adjutant and myself relied upon the optimists; at any rate, we should be safe from the Hun gunners, who treated the chateau as one of their datum points.

We were relieving an Army Field Artillery brigade commanded by a well-known scientific gunner, and on the afternoon that we arrived he took the colonel and myself on an explanatory tour of the battery positions and the "O.P.'s." They were leaving their guns in position for us to use. There was a Corps standing order that steel helmets should be worn and box-respirators kept in the alert position in this part of the line. So first we girded up ourselves in compliance with orders. Then our guide made us walk in single file and keep close to the houses as we walked along the main street. "He has a beautiful view of the chateau gates and can see movement in the centre of the road," he informed us.

It was a terribly battered village. The church tower had been knocked out of shape. Roofs that had escaped being smashed in were threadbare, or seemed to be slipping off skeleton houses. Mutilated telegraph-poles and broken straggly wires, evil-smelling pools of water, scattered bricks, torn roadways, and walls blackened and scarred by bomb and shell, completed a scene of mournfulness and desolation. We passed one corner house on the shutters of which some "infanteers" had chalked the inviting saucy sign, "Ben Jonson's Café." Then we struck across a fast-ripening wheat-field and put up a mother partridge who was agonised with fear lest we should discover her young ones. "It will be a pity if these crops can't be gathered in," remarked our colonel. To right and left of us, and beyond the ruined village that lay immediately in front, were yellow fields ready for the harvesters. "Does he shell much?" continued the colonel.

"Not consistently," replied the other colonel. "I don't think he does much observed shooting. He's copying our method of sudden bursts of fire, though."

We inspected two O.P.'s on one side of the wide valley that led towards the front line, picked up, through binoculars, the chief reference points in Bocheland, and had a look at two heavily-camouflaged anti-tank guns that were a feature of the defence in this part of the front. Myriads of fat overfed flies buzzed in the trenches through which we passed. Hot and dusty, we came back about 6 P.M., and entered the chateau kitchen-garden through a hole that had been knocked in the high, ancient, russet-red brick wall. The sudden scent of box and of sweet-smelling herbs roused a tingling sense of pleasure and of recollection. I never failed afterwards to return to the chateau by that way.

The other colonel came out with us again next morning, although our batteries were now in possession, and his own officers and men had gone a long way back. He wanted to show our colonel some observation points from the O.P. on the other side of the valley.

A certain incident resulted. As we passed A Battery's position we saw Dumble, the battery captain, looking through the dial-sight of his No. 1 gun, apparently trying to discover whether a black-and-white signalling-pole, planted fifty yards in front of the gun, was in line with a piece of hop-pole fifty yards farther on. Both colonels stared fixedly at the spectacle. "What's become of the aiming-posts?" said the other colonel, puzzled and stern.

When a gun has fired satisfactorily on a certain target, which is also a well-defined point on the map, and it is desired to make this particular line of fire the standard line, or, as it is commonly called, the zero line, the normal method is to align two aiming-posts with such accuracy that, no matter what other targets are fired upon, the gun can always be brought back to its zero line by means of the aiming-posts. Absolute accuracy being essential, the aiming-posts are specially designed and are of a settled pattern. Judge of the two colonels' astonishment then when they perceived Dumble's impromptu contrivance.

"Have you no aiming-posts?" our colonel asked Dumble sharply.

"No, sir, the other battery would not leave theirs behind. I had understood it was arranged that we should hand over ours at the waggon line, and that they should leave theirs here to give us the lines of fire."

"Of course," interrupted the other colonel; "but what are you doing now? You can't get your line with those things."

"I'm trying to do the best I can, sir, until my own aiming-posts arrive."

"Yes, but it's hopeless trying to fix those ridiculous things in the same positions as the aiming-posts. Who was it gave the order to remove the aiming-posts?"

"The subaltern who was waiting for us to relieve your battery, sir."

"The battery commander wasn't here then?"

"No, sir. I believe he'd gone on ahead to the waggon lines."

"I'm exceedingly sorry this has happened," said the other colonel, turning to our colonel. "I'll have the battery commander and the other officer up here at once, and they can go forward with your officer when he registers the guns again. It's disgraceful. I'll stop their next leave for this." He disappeared into the battery telephone pit to send through orders for the recalling of the delinquent officers.

"Not a bad idea to make an inspection round the day after you have handed over," remarked our colonel to me drily. "This is rather an instructive example."

These were our last days of waiting and wondering whether the Boche would attack; of the artillery duels and the minor raids by which each side sought to feel and test the other's strength. I recall two or three further incidents of our stay in that part of the line. The G.O.C., R.A., of Corps decided that a rare opportunity presented itself for training junior officers in quick picking up of targets, shooting over open sights, and voice-command of batteries from near sighting-places where telephone wires could be dispensed with and orders shouted through a megaphone. "It will quite likely come to that," he observed. "The next fighting will be of the real open warfare type, and the value of almost mechanical acquaintance with drill is that the officer possessing such knowledge can use all his spare brains to deal with the changing phases of the actual battle." So a single 18-pdr. used to be pulled out for practice purposes, and Generals and infantry officers came to see gunner subalterns schooled and tested. It was better practice than Shoeburyness or Larkhill, because though the shoots were carried out on the gunnery school model the shells were directed at real targets. During one series a distinguished red-tabbed party was dispersed because the Hun did an area strafe in front, behind, and around the single gun. Another time the descent of an 8-inch saved the *amour-propre* of a worried second lieutenant, who, after jockeying with his angle of sight, had got into abject difficulties with his range and corrector.

One morning I was up forward carrying out instructions to keep in daily touch with the infantry battalions, finding out their requirements, and discovering what new artillery targets they could suggest. As it was also my business to know what the Heavies were doing, I stopped at an O.P. in a trench to ask a very young R.G.A. officer observing for a 6-inch how. such questions as what he had fired upon that morning, and whether he had noted any fresh Boche movement. I had passed along the winding trench and descended the dug-out headquarters of one of our infantry battalions, and was inquiring if the commanding officer had any suggestions or complaints to make, when the boyish R.G.A. officer came down the steps and, not noticing me in the dim candle-light, asked in hurried tones: "Excuse me, sir, but could you identify an artillery officer who said he was coming here? He stopped and asked me some extraordinary questions… and" - hesitatingly - "you have to be careful talking to people in the front line."

The adjutant and the intelligence officer of the infantry battalion were smiling broadly. Finally the colonel had to laugh. "Yes," he said, "I can identify the artillery officer. Here he is. You haven't discovered a spy this time."

The young officer looked abashed, and when later I passed his "O.P.," apologised with much sincerity. I replied by asking him to have a good look at me, so that he wouldn't mistake me next time we met. After which we both laughed. We did meet again, not long afterwards, and in much more exciting circumstances.

When the Brigade left that part of the line, Marshal Foch had begun his momentous counter-effort between Soissons and Château-Thierry. In a very short time we also were to be engaged in a swift and eventful movement that changed the whole tenor of the war: a time of hard ceaseless fighting, countless episodes of heroism and sacrifice, and vivid conquering achievement.

CHAPTER V

BEFORE THE
GREAT ATTACK

O N THE EVENING of August 3, an evening with a sinister lowering sky, we settled in our newest headquarters: wooden huts, perched on the long steep slope of a quarry just outside the crumbling ruins of Heilly, celebrated in the war annals of 1916 for an officers' tearooms, where three pretty daughters of the house acted as waitresses.

Excitement was in the air. Marshal Foch's bold strategy at Soissons had had dramatic effect. The initiative was passing again to the Allies. A faint rumour had developed into an official fact. There was to be a big attack on our immediate front. Yet few of us dared to conceive the mark in history that August 8 was to make. All we really hoped for was a series of stout resolute operations that would bring Germany's great offensive to a deadlock.

Along the road that wound past the quarry - offshoot of a main route that will for ever be associated with the War - there flowed a ceaseless stream of ammunition waggons. "This goes on for three nights.... My Gad, they're getting something ready for him," remarked our new adjutant to me. Gallant, red-faced, roaring old Castle had been transferred to command the Small Arms Ammunition section of the D.A.C., where his love of horses was given full play, and had already gained his section many prizes at our Horse Show a week before.

Rain descended in stinging torrents, and the Australian colonel and his adjutant, who would leave as soon as they heard that our batteries had relieved theirs, looked out disgustedly. I called for a bottle of whisky, and when the Australian adjutant toasted me with "Here's to the skin of your nose," I gathered that his gloom was lessening. The soup came in and we started dinner.

Talk ran upon the extraordinary precautions taken to surprise the enemy. Field-guns were not to be moved up to their battle positions until the night before the attack. There was to be no digging in of guns, no earth was to be upturned. Reconnaissance likely to come under enemy observation had to be carried out with a minimum of movement. As few officers and men as was possible were to be made aware of the date and the scope of the operation. On a still night the creaking rattle of ammunition waggons on the move may be heard a very long way off. To prevent this noise of movement wheel tyres were lapped with rope; the play of the wheels was muffled by the use of leather washers. Straw had even to be laid on some of the roads - as straw is laid in front of houses where the seriously sick are lying.

"I think," said the Australian signalling officer, "that the funniest thing is the suggestion in orders that telephone conversations should be camouflaged. I suppose that if some indiscreet individual asks over the 'phone whether, for instance, a new telephone line has been laid to a certain map point it is advisable to reply, 'No, he's dining out to-night.'"

"Why not try a whistling code?" put in our adjutant. "Suppose you whistled the first line of 'Where my Caravan has rested,' that could mean 'At the waggon line.'"

"And 'Tell me the old, old Story' would be 'Send in your ammunition returns at once,'" laughed Wilde, our signalling officer, who had been angered many times because his line to Divisional Artillery had been held up for that purpose.

"And 'It's a long way to Tipperary' could be taken as 'Lengthen your Range,'" said one of the Australian officers in his soft drawl; while the exuberance reached its climax when some one suggested that "Waiting for the Robert E. Lee" might be whistled to indicate that the Divisional Commander was expected at any moment.

"You've had some of the Americans with you, haven't you?" asked our colonel of the Australian colonel. "How do you find them? We heard a humorous report that some of the Australian infantry were rather startled by their bloodthirstiness and the vigour of their language."

The Australian colonel - one of those big, ugly, good-tempered men who attract friendship - laughed and replied, "I did hear one good story. A slightly wounded Boche was being carried on a stretcher to the dressing station by an American and one of our men. The Boche spoke a bit of English, and was talkative. 'English no good,' he said. 'French no good, Americans no good.' The stretcher-bearers walked on without answering. The Boche began again. 'The English think they're going to win the war, - they're wrong. You Americans think you've come to win, - you're wrong.'

"Then the American spoke for the first and last time. 'You think you're going to be carried to hospital, - you're wrong. Put him down, Digger!' And that ended that.

"Speaking seriously, though," he went on, "the Americans who have been attached to us are good stuff - keen to learn, and the right age and stamp. When they pick up more old-soldier cunning, they'll be mighty good."

"From all we hear, you fellows will teach them that," answered our colonel. "I'm told that your infantry do practically what they like with the Boche on their sector over the river. What was that story a Corps officer told me the other day? Oh, I know! They say your infantry send out patrols each day to find out how the Boche is getting on with his new trenches. When he has dug well down and is making himself comfortable, one of the patrol party reports, 'I think it's deep enough now, sir'; and there is a raid, and the Australians make themselves at home in the trench the Boche has sweated to make."

The Australian colonel nodded with pleasure. "Yes, our lot are pretty good at the cuckoo game," he agreed.

Next morning our shaving operations were enlivened by the swift rush of three high-velocity shells that seemed to singe the roof of the hut I was in. They scattered mud, and made holes in the road below. "The nasty fellow!" ejaculated our new American doctor, hastening outside, with the active curiosity of the new arrival who has been little under shell fire, to see where the shells had burst. Our little Philadelphia medico had gone, a week before, to join the American forces. His successor was broad-built, choleric, but kind of heart, and came from

Ohio. I suspected the new doctor of a sense of humour, as well as of an understanding of current smart-set satire. "They kept me at your base two months," he told me, "but I wanted to see the war. I also heard an English doctor say he would be glad of a move, as the base was full of P.U.O. and O.B.E.'s."

After breakfast the colonel and myself passed through the battered relics of Heilly on our way to the batteries. The rain and the tremendous traffic of the previous night had churned the streets into slush, but the feeling that we were on the eve of great events made me look more towards things of cheer. The sign-board, "———th Division Rest House," on a tumble-down dwelling ringed round with shell-holes, seemed over-optimistic, but the intention was good. At the little railway station a couple of straw-stuffed dummies, side by side on a platform seat as if waiting for a train, showed that a waggish spirit was abroad. One figure was made up with a black swallow-tailed coat, blue trousers, and a bowler hat set at a jaunty angle; the other with a woman's summer skirt and blouse and an open parasol. B Battery, who had discovered excellent dug-outs in the railway cutting, reported that their only trouble was the flies, which were illimitable. A and C had their own particular note of satisfaction. They were sharing a row of dug-outs equipped with German wire beds, tables, mirrors, and other home comforts. "We adopted the Solomon method of division," explained Major Bullivant. "I picked out two lots of quarters, and then gave C first choice."

"We've got to select positions still farther forward for the batteries to move to if the attack proves a success," said the colonel next day; and on that morning's outing we walked a long way up to the infantry outposts. We struck a hard main road that led due east across a wide unwooded stretch of country. A drizzling rain had set in; a few big shells grunted and wheezed high over our heads; at intervals we passed litters of dead horses, rotting and stinking, and blown up like balloons. At a cross-road we came to a quarry where a number of sappers were working. The captain in charge smiled when the colonel asked what was the task in hand. "General ——— hopes it will become his headquarters three hours after zero hour, sir."

"That ammunition's well hidden," remarked the colonel as we followed a lane to the right, and noted some neat heaps of 18-pdr. shells tucked under a hedge. We found other small dumps of ammunition hidden among the corn, and stowed in roadside recesses. Studying his map, the colonel led the way across some disused trenches, past a lonely burial-place horribly torn and bespattered by shell fire, and up a wide desolate rise. "This will do very well," said the colonel, marking his map. He looked up at the grey sky and the heavy drifting clouds, and added, "We'll be getting back."

We came back along the main road, meeting occasional small parties of infantry, and turned to the right down a road that led to the nearest village. A Boche 5·9 was firing. The shells fell at minute intervals four hundred yards beyond the road on which we were walking. The colonel was describing to me some of the enjoyments of peace soldiering in India, when there came a violent rushing of air, and a vicious crack, and a shower of earth descended upon us; and dust hung in the air like a giant shroud. A shell had fallen on the road forty yards in front of us.

We had both ducked; the colonel looked up and asked, "Well, do we continue?"

"We might get off the road and go round in a semi-circle, sir," I hazarded. "I think it would be safer moving towards the gun than away from it."

"No, I think that was a round badly 'layed,'" said the colonel. "We'll keep on the road. Besides, we shall have time to get past before the next one comes. But I give you warning," he added with a twinkle, "the next one that comes so near I lie down flat."

"I shall do exactly as you do, sir," I responded in the same spirit.

The colonel was right as usual. The next round went well over the road again, and we walked along comfortably. At the entrance to the village lay two horses, freshly killed. The harness had not been removed. The colonel called to two R.A.M.C. men standing near. "Remove those saddles and the harness," he said, "and place them where they can be salvaged. It will mean cutting the girths when the horses commence to swell."

At 4.30 next morning the batteries were roused to answer an S.O.S. call. The rumble of guns along the whole of our Divisional front lasted for two hours. By lunch-time we learned that strong Hun forces had got into our trenches and penetrated as far as the quarry where the colonel and myself had seen the sappers at work. Twenty sappers and their officer had been caught below ground, in what had been destined to become General ——'s headquarters. Our counter-attack had won back only part of the lost ground.

"I'm afraid they'll spot all that ammunition. They are almost certain now to know that something's afoot," said the colonel thoughtfully.

"Something like this always does happen when we arrange anything," broke in the adjutant gloomily.

There were blank faces that day. We waited to hear whether there would be a change of plan. But after dark the ammunition waggons again poured ceaselessly along the roads that led to the front.

CHAPTER VI

THE BATTLE OF AUGUST 8

O N THE AFTERNOON of August 7 the colonel left us to assume command of the Divisional Artillery, the C.R.A. having fallen ill and the senior colonel being on leave. Major Veasey, a Territorial officer, who was senior to our two regular battery commanders, a sound soldier and a well-liked man, had come over from D Battery to command the Brigade. A determined counter-attack, carried out by one of our Divisional infantry brigades, had won back most of the ground lost to the Boche the day before. Operation orders for the big attack on the morning of the 8th had been circulated to the batteries, and between 9 P.M. and 10 P.M. the guns were to move up to the battle positions. The old wheeler was looking ruefully at the ninety-two steps leading from the quarry up to our mess. Made of wooden pegs and sides of ammunition boxes, the steps had taken him three days to complete. "My gosh! that does seem a waste of labour," commented the American doctor, with a slow smile.

"Doctor, those steps will be a godsend to the next people who come to live here," I explained. "That's one of the ways in which life is made possible out here."

We dined at eight, and it was arranged that Major Veasey, the adjutant, and the signalling officer should go on ahead, leaving me to keep in telephone touch with batteries and Divisional Artillery until communications were complete at the new headquarters.

Down below the regimental sergeant-major was loading up the G.S. waggon and the Maltese cart. An ejaculation from Wilde, the signalling officer, caused every one to stare through the mess door. "Why, they're putting a bed on,... and look at the size of it.... Hi! you can't take that," he called out to the party below.

The doctor rose from his seat and looked down. "Why, that's *my* bed," he said.

"But, doctor, you can't take a thing like that," interposed the adjutant.

The doctor's face flushed. This being his baptismal experience of the Front, he regarded the broad wire bed he had found in his hut as a prize; he seemed unaware that in this part of the world similar beds could be counted in hundreds.

"But I like that bed. I can sleep on it. I want it, and mean to have it," he went on warmly.

"Sorry, doctor," answered the adjutant firmly. "Our carts have as much as they can carry already."

The doctor seemed disposed to have the matter out; but Major Veasey, who had been regarding him fixedly, and looked amused, stopped further argument by saying, "Don't worry, doctor. There are plenty of beds at the new position."

The doctor sat down silent but troubled, and when the others went he said he would stay behind with me. I think he wanted my sympathy, but the telephone kept me so busy - messages that certain batteries had started to move, demands from the staff captain for a final return showing the shortage of gas-shell gauntlets, and for lists of area stores that we expected to hand over, and a request from the adjutant to bring the barometer that he had overlooked - that there was little time for talk.

It was half-past ten when word having come that full communication had been established at the new position, I told the two signallers who had remained with me to disconnect the wires; and the doctor and I set off. It was a murky night, and the air was warmly moist. The familiar rumble of guns doing night-firing sounded all along the Front; enemy shells were falling in the village towards which we were walking. There was a short cut across the river and the railway and then on through corn-fields. To strike it we ought to pass through a particular skeleton house in the village we were leaving, out by the back garden, and thence along a narrow track that led across a swamp. In the dark I failed to find the house; so we plodded on, past the church, and took to a main road. After walking two kilometres we switched south along a by-road that led to the position A Battery had occupied. Not a soul had passed since we took to the main road; the Boche shells, now arriving in greater numbers, seemed, as is always the case at night, nearer than they actually were.

Sounds of horses and of orders sharply given! It was the last section of A Battery pulling out; in command young Stenson, a round-faced, newly-joined officer, alert and eager, and not ill-pleased with the responsibility placed upon him. "Have the other sections got up all right?" I asked him. "Yes," he answered, "although they were shelled just before getting in and Bannister was wounded - hit in the face, not seriously, I think." Bannister, poor fellow, died three days later.

The doctor and I passed on, following a shell-plastered road that wound towards a rough wooden bridge, put up a week before; thence across soggy ground and over the railway crossing. There was a slight smell of gas, and without a word to each other we placed our box-respirators in the alert position. To avoid the passage of a column of ammunition waggons crunching along one of the narrow streets we stepped inside a crumbling house. No sign of furniture, no stove, but in one corner - quaint relic of less eventful days - a sewing-machine, not even rusted.

A grove of poplars embowered the quarry that we were seeking; and soon our steps were guided by the neighing of horses, and by the raised voice of the R.S.M. hectoring his drivers. The doctor and I were to share a smelly dug-out, in which all the flies in the world seemed to have congregated. The doctor examined at length the Boche wire bed allotted to him, and refused to admit that it was as comfortable as the one left behind. However, he expressed satisfaction with the mahogany side-board that some previous occupant had loaned from a neighbouring house; our servants had bespread it with newspapers and made a washing-table of it.

The doctor quickly settled himself to sleep, but there were tasks

German troops advance in the sector near Villers-Bretonneux during the opening phases of the Kaiserschlacht, Germany's last major effort to secure victory on the Western Front.

A German shell bursts on the ground near a group of artillery horse lines close to La Bassée Canal.

Forward with the guns: A battery of the Royal Horse Artillery galloping into action.

Crowded ways of war: British troops and transport on the way to meet the German offensive.

Ready at the bridge: British field gunners guarding a canal crossing in France.

Captured British soldiers are allowed by their German guards to salvage the personal effects of comrades killed in action during the German advance.

Gunners of 101ˢᵗ Siege Battery, Royal Garrison Artillery, prepare 6-inch Howitzer shells for firing near Merville, 12ᵗʰ April 1918.

The crew of a Royal Field Artillery 18-pounder battery prepare to open fire near Meteren during the fighting for Hazebrouck, 13ᵗʰ April 1918.

A British Lewis Gun post awaits the advancing Germans on the bank of the Lys Canal near Marquois, 13th April 1918.

Three British Lewis gunners manning a barricade at a bridge crossing the Lys Canal at Marquois, 13th April 1918.

Men of the 1st Battalion, Middlesex Regiment, manning a street barricade in the town of Bailleul, 15th April 1918. The barricade is built up of all sorts of things from wheelbarrows to wastepaper baskets, chairs and shutters.

Outpost of the 1st Battalion, Middlesex Regiment, on the Meteren-Moulehouck line, 16th April 1918.

Men of 31ˢᵗ Division man a Lewis gun post beside a railway line near Merris during the Battle of Hazebrouck.

A rest interval for the retreating British forces during a time of great trial.

Gunners of the Royal Field Artillery manhandle an 18-pounder field gun into a firing position beside a ruined house in the village of Saint Floris, 2nd May 1918.

Gunners struggle to pull a huge piece of artillery through mud. A makeshift caterpillar tread has been fitted to the wheels of the gun.

for me. "This is where I'm the nasty man," exclaimed Major Veasey, descending the dug-out with a signalling watch in his hand. "I'm afraid I shall have to ask you to take the time round to the batteries and to the ——th Brigade, who aren't in communication yet with Divisional Artillery. Sorry to fire you out in the dark - but secrecy, you know."

Zero hour was timed for 4.20 A.M.; it was now 11.30 P.M.; so I donned steel helmet and box-respirator, and was moving off when a loud clear voice called from the road, "Is this ——nd Brigade Headquarters?" It was Major Simpson of B Battery, buoyant and debonair. "Hallo!" he burst forth, noticing me. "Where are you bound for?… Um - yes!… I think I can save you part of the journey…. I'm here, and Lamswell is coming along…. We're both going to the new positions."

Captain Lamswell of C Battery suddenly appearing, accompanied by young Beale of A Battery, we made our way to the mess, where Major Veasey and the adjutant were sorting out alterations in the operation orders just brought by a D.A. despatch-rider. Beale and Major Simpson slaughtered a few dozen flies, and accepted whiskies-and-sodas. Then I synchronised watches with representatives of the three batteries present, and young Beale said that he would check the time with D Battery, who were only two minutes' walk from A. That left me to call upon the ——th Brigade, who lay on the far side of the village three parts of a mile out.

We set out, talking and jesting. There was a high expectancy in the air that affected all of us. Major Simpson broke off humming "We are the Robbers of the Wood" to say, "Well, if this show comes off to-morrow, leave ought to start again." "I should shay sho," put in Lamswell in his best Robey-cum-Billy Merson manner. "Doesn't interest me much," said I. "I'm such a long way down the list that it will be Christmas before I can hope to go. The colonel told me to put in for a few days in Paris while we were out at rest last month, but I've heard nothing more about it."

When Major Simpson, Lamswell, and Beale, with cheery "Good-night," made for the sunken road that led past the dressing station, and then over the crest to their new positions, I kept on my way, leaving a red-brick, barn-like factory on my left, and farther along a tiny cemetery. Now that I was in open country and alone, I became more keenly sensitive to the damp mournfulness of the night. What if to-morrow should result in failure? It was only four months since the Hun was swamping us with his tempestuous might! Brooding menace seemed in the air. A sudden burst of fire from four 5·9's on to the cross-roads I had just passed whipped my nerves into still greater tension.

I strode on, bending my mind to the task in hand.

*   *   *   *   *

At 4.40 A.M. I lifted my head to listen to the sound of the opening barrage - a ceaseless crackle and rumble up in front. I had not taken off my clothes, and quickly I ascended the dug-out steps. Five hundred yards away a 60-pdr. battery belched forth noise and flame; two 8-inch hows. on the far side of the road numbed the hearing and made the earth tremble. A pleasant enough morning: the sun just climbing above the shell-shattered, leaf-bare woods in front; the moon dying palely on the other horizon; even a school of fast-wheeling birds in the middle distance. Ten minutes, a quarter of an hour, half an hour. Still no enemy shells in this support area. Could it be that the attack had really surprised the Boche?

I turned into the adjutant's dug-out and found him lying down, telephone to ear. "Enemy reply barrage only slight," he was repeating.

"Any news?" I asked.

"Some of the tanks missed their way," he answered. "A Battery have had a gun knocked out and four men hit. No communication with any of the other batteries."

By seven o'clock we were breakfasting, and Major Veasey announced his intention of going forward to seek information. A grey clinging mist had enveloped the countryside. "Something like March 21st," said the major as he and I set out. "We said it helped the Boche then. I hope we don't have to use it as an excuse for any failure to-day. Difficult for observers," he added thoughtfully.

At the dressing station in the sunken road we learned that one battery of our companion Field Artillery Brigade had suffered severely from gas. All the officers had been sent down, and a large proportion of the gunners. The sickly-sweet smell hung faintly over most of the ground in the neighbourhood of our batteries as well. A and C were now firing fifty rounds an hour. "The major's asleep in that dug-out," volunteered Beale of A, pointing to a hole in a bank that allowed at least two feet of air space above Major Bullivant's recumbent form. The major was unshaven; his fair hair was tousled. He had turned up the collar of his British warm. Beale also looked unkempt, but he said he had had three hours' sleep before the barrage started and felt quite fresh. "Our casualties came just after we got the guns in," he told me. "They dropped two whizz-bangs between No. 1 gun and No. 2."

Major Simpson was up and eating hot sizzling bacon in a trench, with a cable drum for a seat and an ammunition-box as table. Two of his subalterns - Overbury, who won the M.C. on March 21st, and Bob Pottinger, all smiles and appetite, at any rate this morning - had also fallen to, and wanted Major Veasey and myself to drink tea. "We're taking a short rest," remarked Major Simpson cheerfully. "I'm glad I moved the battery away from the track over there. No shell has come within three hundred yards of us…. We have had a difficulty about the wires. Wilde said he laid wires from Brigade to all the new positions before we came in last night, but my signallers haven't found their wire yet; so we laid a line to A and got through that way."

Infantry Brigade Headquarters was in a ravine four hundred yards away. A batch of prisoners had just arrived and were being questioned by an Intelligence officer: youngish men most of them, sallow-skinned, with any arrogance they may have possessed knocked out of them by now. They were the first Huns I remember seeing with steel helmets daubed with staring colours by way of camouflage. "They say we were not expected to attack to-day," I heard the Intelligence officer mention to the G.S.O. II. of the Division, who had just come up.

"Is that one of your batteries?" asked the Infantry Brigade signalling officer, an old friend of mine, pointing to our D Battery, a hundred yards from Brigade Headquarters. "What a noise they made. We haven't had a wink of sleep. How many thousand rounds have they fired?"

"Oh, it'll be about 1500 by midday, I expect," I answered. "Any news?"

"It's going all right now, I believe. Bit sticky at the start - my communications have gone perfectly, so far - touch wood."

More prisoners kept coming in; limping, bandaged men passed on their way down; infantry runners in khaki shorts, and motor-cycle despatch-riders hurried up and buzzed around the Brigade Headquarters; inside when the telephone bell wasn't ringing the brigade-major could be heard demanding reports from battalions, or issuing fresh instructions. There was so little fuss that numbers of quiet self-contained men seemed to be standing about doing nothing. Occasional high-velocity shells whizzed over our heads.

Major Veasey suddenly emerged from the brigade-major's quarters, looking at his map. "Some of the Tanks and two companies of the ——s lost their way at the start," he told me, "but things have been pulled straight now. The ——rd Brigade have gone right ahead. A hundred and twenty prisoners up to date. Down south the Australians are on their final objective. Yoicks! - this is the stuff to give 'em! Now we'll go and have a look at my battery."

Captain Drysdale, who was commanding during Major Veasey's absence from the 4·5 battery, said that the programme had been carried through without a hitch, although it had been difficult in the night to get the hows. on to their aiming-posts without lights. "Kelly has gone forward, and has got a message through. He says he saw some of our firing, and the line was extraordinarily good."

"Good old Kelly!" said Major Veasey, puffing at his pipe. "I don't know whether we shall be ordered to move forward to-day; we shan't until the situation is thoroughly clear. But I shall go forward now with Simpson and Bullivant to spy out the land. You'd better cut back to Headquarters with what news we've got" - this was said to me - "Division will be wanting something definite."

When about 3 P.M. Major Veasey returned, footsore and wearied, he brought news that the Infantry Brigade that had reached its final objective had had to come back, owing to the stoutness of the machine-gun opposition. The attack would be renewed in the morning, and the batteries would not move forward that evening.

The adjutant was opening the latest batch of official envelopes from Divisional Artillery. With a laugh he flourished a yellow paper. "Here's your leave to Paris," he called out.

"Certainly, I should take it," was Major Veasey's comment. "Why, I knew one C.R.A. who never stopped officers' leave when they were in action. It was only when the Division was at rest that he wouldn't let them go. Said he wanted them for training then. You pop off."

And as this is a true tale, I hereby record that I did go to Paris, and returned in full time to participate in the brave days that witnessed Britain's greatest triumphs of the war.

CHAPTER VII

SHORT LEAVE
TO PARIS

S HORT LEAVE TO Paris ought to bequeath a main impression of swift transition from the dirt, danger, and comfortlessness of the trenches to broad pavements, shop windows, well-dressed women, smooth courtliness, and restaurant luxuries; to fresh incisive talks on politics and the Arts, to meetings with old friends and visits to well-remembered haunts of the Paris one knew before August 1914. Instead, the wearing discomforts of the journey are likely to retain chief hold upon the memory. Can I ever forget how we waited seven hours for a train due at 9.25 P.M. at a station that possessed no forms to sit upon, so that some of the men lay at full length and slept on the asphalt platform? And is there not a corner of my memory for the crawling fusty leave-train that had bare planks nailed across the door spaces of some of the "officers'" compartments; a train so packed that we three officers took turns on the one spare seat in an "other ranks" carriage? And then about 8 A.M. we landed at a well-known "all-change" siding, a spot of such vivid recollections that some one had pencilled in the ablution-house, "If the Huns ever take —— Camp and have to hold it they'll give up the war in disgust."

But in the queue of officers waiting at the Y.M.C.A. hut for tea and boiled eggs was the brigade-major of a celebrated Divisional Artillery. He stood in front of me looking bored and dejected. I happened to pass him a cup of tea. As he thanked me he asked, "Aren't you fed up with this journey? Let's see the R.T.O. and inquire about a civilian train!" "If you'll take me under your wing, sir," I responded quickly. So we entered Paris by a fast train, - as did my two companions of the night before, who had followed my tip of doing what I did without letting outsiders see that there was collusion.

The brigade-major's wife was awaiting him in Paris, and I dined with them at the Ritz and took them to lunch next day at Henry's, where the frogs' legs were delicious and the chicken a recompense for that nightmare of a train journey. Viel's was another restaurant which retained a proper touch of the Paris before the war - perfect cooking, courtly waiting, and prices not too high. I have pleasant recollections also of Fouquet's in the Champs Elysées, and of an almost divine meal at the Tour d'Argent, on the other side of the river, where Frederic of the Ibsen whiskers used once to reign: the delicacy of the *soufflée* of turbot! the succulent tenderness of the *caneton à la presse!* the seductive flavour of the raspberries and whipped cream!

The French Government apparently realise that the famous restaurants of Paris are a national asset. There was no shortage of waiters; and, though the choice of dishes was much more limited than it used to be, the real curtailment extended only to cheese, sugar, and butter. Our bread-tickets brought us as much bread as we could reasonably expect.

One day, in the Rue de la Paix, I met a well-known English producer of plays, and he piloted me to the Café de Paris, which seemed to have lost nothing of its special atmosphere of smartness and costliness. Louis the Rotund, who in the early days of the war went off to guard bridges and gasometers, was playing his more accustomed rôle of *maître d'hôtel*, explaining with suave gravity the unpreventable altitude of prices. And for at least the tenth time he told me how in his young-man soldiering days he came upon the spring whose waters have since become world-famous.

Another night I ascended Montmartre, and dined under the volatile guidance of Paul, who used to be a pillar of the Abbaye Thélème. Paul came once to London, in the halcyon days of the Four Hundred Club, when nothing disturbed him more than open windows and doors. "Keep the guests dancing and the windows tight-closed, and you sell your champagne," was his business motto. However, he was pleased to see me again, and insisted on showing me his own particular way of serving Cantelupe melon. Before scooping out each mouthful you inserted the prongs of your fork into a lemon, and this lent the slightest of lemon flavouring to the luscious sweetness of the melon.

America seemed to be in full possession of the restaurant and boulevard life of Paris during those August days. Young American officers, with plenty of money to spend, were everywhere. "You see," a Parisienne explained, "before the war the Americans we had seen had been mostly rich, middle-aged, business men. But when the American officers came, Paris found that they were many, that many of them were young as well as well-off, and that many of them were well-off, young, and good-looking. It is quite *chic* to lunch or dine with an American officer."

The Americans carried out their propaganda in their usual thorough, enthusiastic fashion. I was taken to the Elysée Palace Hotel, where I found experienced publicists and numbers of charming well-bred women busy preparing information for the newspapers, and arranging public entertainments and sight-seeing tours for American troops in Paris, all with the idea of emphasising that Americans were now pouring into France in thousands. One night a smiling grey-haired lady stopped before a table where four of us, all British officers, were dining, and said, "You're English, aren't you? Well, have you been with any of 'our boys'?... Have you seen them in action?... They're fine, aren't they?" We were surprised, a little taken aback at first, but we showed sympathetic understanding of the American lady's enthusiasm, and responded in a manner that left her pleased as ever.

Before returning to the Front I got in a day's golf at La Boulie, and also made a train journey to a village the other side of Fontainebleau, where an old friend, invalided from the French army, had settled on a considerable estate, and thought of nothing but the fruits and vegetables and dairy produce he was striving to improve and increase. I did not visit many theatres; it struck me that the Paris stage, like that of London, was undergoing a war phase - unsophisticated, ready-to-be-pleased audiences bringing prosperity to very mediocre plays.

*   *   *   *   *

My journey back to the line included a stay at a depot where officers were speedily reminded that they had left the smooth luxuriousness of Paris behind them. The mess regulations opened with "Try to treat the mess as a mess and not as a public-house," and contained such additional instructions as, "Do not place glasses on the floor," and "Officers will always see that they are in possession of sufficient cash to pay mess bills."

I found the brigade three and a half miles in advance of where I had left them. There had been a lot of stiff fighting, and on our front the British forces had not gone so far forward as the corps immediately south of us had done. Big things were afoot, however, and that very night batteries and Brigade Headquarters moved up another three thousand yards. A snack of bully beef and bread and cheese at 7 P.M., and the colonel and a monocled Irish major, who was working under the colonel as "learner" for command of a brigade, went off to see the batteries. The adjutant and myself, bound for the new Headquarters, followed ten minutes later.

"You know that poor old Lamswell has gone," he said, as we crossed a grassy stretch, taking a ruined aerodrome as our guiding mark. "Poor chap, he was wounded at the battery position the day after you left. Only a slight wound in the leg from a gas-shell, and every one thought he had got a comfortable 'Blighty.' But gangrene set in, and he was dead in three days. Beastly things those gas-shells!... Kent, too, got one through the shoulder from a sniper, and he's gone to England. The colonel was with him at the O.P., and tried to get the sniper afterwards with a rifle."

"How is the colonel?" I asked.

"Oh, he's going very strong; active as ever. Colonel —— is back from leave and doing C.R.A. now. We're under the ——th Division at the moment."

"You remember Colonel —— who got the V.C. in the Retreat," he went on; "he was killed on August 8th - went out to clear up a machine-gun pocket.... Damned nice fellow, wasn't he?"

We reached a narrow road, crowded with battery ammunition waggons going up to the new positions. Darkness had descended, and when you got off the road to avoid returning vehicles it was necessary to walk warily to escape tumbling into shell-holes. "The blighters have got a new way of worrying us now," went on the adjutant. "They've planted land-mines all over the place, particularly near tracks. Lead-horses are always liable to put a foot against the wire that connects with the mine, and when the thing goes off some one is nearly always hurt. D Battery had a nasty experience this afternoon. Kelly tried to take a section forward, and the Boche spotted them and shelled them to blazes. As they came back to get away from observation one of the teams disturbed a land-mine. The limber was blown up, and one driver and two horses were killed.... Look here, if we move off in this direction we ought to save time; the railway must be over there and the place for our Headquarters is not far from it, in a trench where the O.P. used to be."

We found ourselves on some shell-torn ground that was cut up also by short spans of trenches. One part of it looked exactly like another, and after ten minutes or so we decided that we were wandering to no purpose. "There are some old German gun-pits close by," panted the adjutant in further explanation of the place we were seeking. All at once I saw a thin shaft of light, and blundered my way towards it. It proved to be a battery mess, made in a recess of a trench, with a stout tarpaulin drawn tight over the entrance. I hailed the occupants through the tarpaulin, and on their invitation scrambled a passage inside. A young captain and two subalterns listened to what I had to say, and gave me map co-ordinates of the spot on which we now were. When I mentioned German gun-pits the captain responded with more helpful suggestions. "It's difficult finding your way across country, because the trenches wind about so, but follow this trench as it curves to the right, and when you come to an old British dug-out blown right in, go due north across country; then you'll come to the railway," he said.

We thanked him, plodded on, reached a point on the railway quite half a mile beyond the spot we wanted, and then out of the darkness heard the voice of Henry of C Battery. We drew near, and found him in the mood of a man ready to fight the whole world. "Dam fools," he grumbled: "there's a sergeant of A Battery who's taken a wrong turning and gone into the blue, and half a dozen of my waggons have followed him…. And B Battery have a waggon tipped over on the railway line, just where we all cross, and that's holding everything else up."

As we could be of no assistance to the distressful Henry we continued our own search, and, by hailing all within call, eventually reached our trench, where we found the colonel, always in good mood when something practical wanted doing, superintending Headquarters' occupation of the place. "Major Mallaby-Kelby, the doctor, the adjutant, and myself can fix up under here," he said, pointing to a large tarpaulin fastened across the trench. "The signallers have got the mined dug-out round the corner, and you," he went on, referring to me, "had better start fixing Wilde and yourself up. We'll make that gun-pit with the camouflaged roofing into a mess to-morrow."

With the aid of the servants I gathered six long two-inch planks, and placed them across the part of the trench that seemed best protected from enemy shells. A spare trench cover pulled full stretch on top of these planks lent additional immunity from rain. A little shovelling to level the bottom of the trench, and Wilde's servant and mine laid out our valises. A heap of German wicker ammunition-carriers, sorted out on the ground, served as a rough kind of mattress for the colonel. The doctor had fastened upon a spare stretcher. In half an hour we were all seeking sleep.

Zero hour was at 1 A.M., a most unusual time for the infantry to launch an attack. But this would increase the element of surprise, and the state of the moon favoured the enterprise. When hundreds of guns started their thunder I got up to see, and found the doctor on the top of the trench also. Bursts of flame leapt up all around, and for miles to right and left of us. The noise was deafening. When one has viewed scores of modern artillery barrages one's impressions become routine impressions, so to speak; but the night, and the hundreds and hundreds of vivid jumping flashes, made this 1 A.M. barrage seem the most tremendous, most violently terrible of my experience. The doctor, looking a bit chilled, gazed long and solemnly at the spectacle, and for once his national gift of expressing his feelings failed him.

When news of the results of the operation came to us it was of a surprising character. The infantry had moved forward under cover of the barrage, had reached their first objective, and continued their advance two miles without encountering opposition. The Boche had stolen away before our guns loosed off their fury. I only saw three prisoners brought in, and some one tried to calculate the thousands of pounds worth of ammunition wasted on the "barrage." A message came that we were to hold ourselves in readiness to rejoin our own Divisional Artillery; our companion Field Artillery Brigade, the ———rd, would march also. At 6.30 P.M. the orders arrived. We were to trek northwards, about four thousand yards as the crow flies, and be in touch with our C.R.A. early next morning.

That night rain fell in torrents. When we had dined, and all the kit had been packed up, we sheltered in the gun-pit, awaiting our horses and the baggage-waggons. As the rain found fresh ways of coming through the leaky roof, we shifted the boxes on which we sat; all of us except the colonel, who, allowing his chin to sink upon his breast, slept peacefully for three-quarters of an hour. It was pitch-dark outside, and the trench had become a glissade of slimy mud. It was certain that the drivers would miss their way, and two of the signallers who had gone out to guide them along the greasy track from the railway crossing had come back after an hour's wait. After a time we ceased trying to stem the rivulets that poured into the gun-pit; we ceased talking also, and gave ourselves up to settled gloom, all except the colonel, who had picked upon the one dry spot and still slept.

But things mostly come right in the end. The rain stopped, a misty moon appeared; the vehicles came along, and by 10.30 P.M. the colonel was on his mare, picking a way for our little column around shell-holes, across water-logged country, until we struck a track leading direct to Meaulte, where the Brigade had been billeted during 1915. It was a strangely silent march. There was a rumbling of guns a long way to north of us, and that was all. The Boche had undoubtedly stolen away. For a long time the only sound was the warning shout, passed from front to rear, that told of shell-holes in the roadway.

On the outskirts of the village we saw signs of the Hun evacuation: deserted huts and stables, a couple of abandoned motor-lorries. The village itself was a wreck, a dust-heap, not a wall left whole after our terrific bombardments. Not a soul in the streets, not a single house habitable even for troops. Of the mill that had been Brigade Headquarters three years before, one tiny fragment of a red-brick wall was left. The bridge in front of it had been scattered to the winds; and such deep shell-craters pitted the ground and received the running water, that the very river-bed had dried up. On the other side of the village batteries of our own and of our companion brigade moved slowly along. It was 2 a.m. when we encamped in a wide meadow off the road. When the horses had been tethered and fed and the men had erected their bivouacs, the colonel, Major Mallaby-Kelby, and we five remaining officers turned into one tent, pulled off boots and leggings, and slept the heavy dreamless sleep of healthily tired men.

At 7 a.m. the colonel announced that he and myself would ride up to Bécourt Chateau to visit the C.R.A. We touched the southern edge of Albert, familiar to thousands of British soldiers. The last time I had been there was on my return from leave in January 1917, when I dined and slept at the newly-opened officers' club. Since the Boche swoop last March it had become a target for British gunners, and seemed in as bad a plight as the village we had come through the night before. We had no time to visit it that morning, and trotted on along a road lined with unburied German dead, scattered ammunition, and broken German vehicles. The road dipped into a wood, and the colonel showed me the first battery position he occupied in France, when he commanded a 4·5 how. battery. Bécourt Chateau was so much a chateau now that Divisional Headquarters were living in tents outside. Four motor-cars stood in the courtyard; some thirty chargers were tied to the long high railings; motor despatch-riders kept coming and going. R.A. were on the far side of the chateau, and when our grooms had taken our horses we leapt a couple of trenches and made our way to the brigade-major's tent. The brigade-major was frankly pleased with the situation. "We are going right over the old ground, sir," he told the colonel, "and the Boche has not yet made a proper stand. Our Divisional Infantry are in the line again, and the latest report, timed 6 A.M., comes from Montauban, and says that they are approaching Trones Wood. We shall be supporting them to-morrow morning, and the C.R.A. is anxious for positions to be reconnoitred in X 10 and X 11. The C.R.A. has gone up that way in the car this morning."

I looked into an adjoining tent and found the liaison officer from the heavies busy on the telephone. "A 5·9 battery shooting from the direction of Ginchy. Right! You can't give me a more definite map-spotting? Right-o! We'll attend to it! Give me counter-batteries, will you?"

"Heavies doing good work to-day?" I asked.

"Rather," he returned happily. "Why, we've got a couple of 8-inch hows. as far up as Fricourt. That's more forward than most of the field-guns."

As I stepped out there came the swift screaming rush of three high-velocity shells. They exploded with an echoing crash in the wood below, near where my horse and the colonel's had been taken to water. A team came up the incline toward the chateau at the trot, and I looked rather anxiously for our grooms. They rode up within two minutes, collectedly, but each with a strained look. "Did those come anywhere near you?" I inquired. "We just missed 'em, sir," replied Laneridge. "One of them dropped right among the horses at one trough."

By the colonel's orders I rode back to the waggon lines soon afterwards, bearing instructions to the battery commanders to join the colonel at half-past one. The Brigade might expect to move up that evening.

The battery commanders came back by tea-time with plans for that evening's move-up completed. The waggon lines during the afternoon were full of sleeping gunners; a sensible course, as it proved, for at 6.45 P.M. an orderly brought the adjutant a pencilled message from the colonel who was still with the C.R.A. It ran -

Warn batteries that they must have gun limbers and firing battery waggons within 1000 yards of their positions by 3.30 A.M., as we shall probably move at dawn. Headquarters will be ready to start after an early dinner. I am returning by car.

"Hallo! they're expecting a big advance to-morrow," said the adjutant. The note also decided a discussion in which the adjutant, the signalling officer, and the cook had joined as to whether we should dine early and pack up ready to go, or pack up and have dinner when we got to the new position behind Mametz Wood.

It was a dark night again; other brigades of artillery were taking the same route as ourselves, and, apart from the congestion, our own guns had shelled this part so consistently since August 8 that the going was heavy and hazardous. We passed one team with two horses down; at another point an 18-pdr. had slipped into a shell-hole, and the air rang with staccato shouts of "Heave!" while two lines of men strained on the drag-ropes. We reached a damp valley that lay west of a stretch of tree-stumps and scrubby undergrowth - remnants of what was a thick leafy wood before the hurricane bombardments of July 1916. D Battery had pulled their six hows. into the valley; the three 18-pdr. batteries were taking up positions on top of the eastern slope. Before long it became clear that the Boche 5·9 gunners had marked the place down.

"I'm going farther along to X 30 A.M. as zero hour, and I circulated the news to the batteries. Some time later the telephone bell aroused me, and the adjutant said he wanted to give me the time. Some one had knocked over my stub of candle, and after vainly groping for it on the floor, I kicked Wilde, and succeeded in making him understand that if he would light a candle and check his watch, I would hang on to the telephone. Dazed with sleep, Wilde clambered to his feet, trod once or twice on the doctor, and lighted a candle.

"Are you ready?" asked the voice at the other end of the telephone. "Ready, Wilde?" said I in my turn.

"I'll give it you when it's four minutes to one... thirty seconds to go," went on the adjutant.

Now Wilde always says that the first thing he heard was my calling "thirty seconds to go!" and that I did not give him the "four minutes to one" part of the ceremony. I always tell him he must have been half asleep, and didn't hear me. At any rate, the dialogue continued like this -

Adjutant (over the telephone to me): "Twenty seconds to go."

Me (to Wilde): "Twenty seconds to go."

Wilde: "Twenty seconds."

Adjutant: "Ten seconds to go."

Me: "Ten seconds."

Wilde: "Ten seconds."

Adjutant: "Five seconds."

Me: "Five."

Wilde: "Five."

Adjutant: "Now! Four minutes to one."

Me: "NOW! Four minutes to one."

Wilde (blankly): "But you didn't tell me what time it was going to be."

It was useless arguing, and I had to ring up the adjutant again. As a matter of fact it was the colonel who answered, and supplied me with the "five seconds to go" information; so there was no doubt about the correctness of the time-taking on this occasion, and after I had gone out and roused an officer of each battery, and made him check his watch, I turned in again and sought sleep.

CHAPTER VIII

TRONES WOOD AGAIN

FOR THREE HOURS after zero hour our guns spat fire, fining down from four rounds a gun a minute to the slow rate of one round each minute. The enemy artillery barked back furiously for the first two hours, but got very few shells into our valley; and after a time we paid little heed to the 5·9's and 4·2's that dropped persistently on the top of the western slope. An 8-inch that had landed in the valley about midnight had wrought frightful execution, however. Another brigade lay next to us; in fact one of their batteries had occupied a position intended for our C Battery. The shell fell with a blinding crash among their horses, which they had kept near the guns in readiness for the morning; and for half an hour the darkness was pierced by the cries and groans of wounded men, and the sound of revolvers putting horses out of their pain. Four drivers had been killed and twenty-nine horses knocked out. "A lucky escape for us," was the grim, not unsympathetic comment of C Battery.

All through the morning the messages telephoned to me indicated that the fighting up forward had been hard and relentless. Our infantry had advanced, but twice before eleven o'clock I had to dash out with S.O.S. calls; and at intervals I turned each battery on to enemy points for which special artillery treatment was demanded.

The colonel ordered Wilde and myself to join the forward Headquarters party after lunch. We found them in a small square hut, built at the foot of a range of hills that rose almost sheer 200 feet up, and curled round north-east to Catterpillar Valley in which our batteries had spent a bitter punishing time during the third week of July 1916. The hut contained four wire beds and a five-foot shaft in one corner, where a solitary telephonist crouched uncomfortably at his task. The hut was so cramped for space that one had to shift the table - a map-board laid upon a couple of boxes - in order to move round it.

The winding road outside presented a moving war panorama that afternoon. Two Infantry brigades and their staffs, and some of the battalion commanders, had huts under the hillside, and by four o'clock battalions returned from the battle were digging themselves sheltering holes higher up the hillside. Boche prisoners in slow marching twenties and thirties kept coming along also; some of them used as stretcher-bearers to carry their own and our wounded; others were turned on to the odd jobs that the Army call fatigues. I found one long-haired, red-eyed fellow chopping wood for our cook; my appearance caused a signaller, noted for his Hyde Park Corner method of oratory, to cease abruptly a turgid denunciation of the Hun and all his works.

The talk was all of a counter-attack by which a battalion of Prussian Guards had won back the eastern corner of Trones Wood, one of the day's objectives. One of the Infantry brigadiers, a tall, tireless, fighting soldier, who started the war as a captain, had come round to discuss with the colonel artillery support for the fresh attack his Brigade were to make at 5.45 P.M. This brigadier was rather apt to regard 18-pounders as machine-guns; and it was sometimes instructive to note the cool good-humoured way in which the colonel guided his enthusiasm into other channels. "You're giving me one forward section of 18-pounders there," began the brigadier, marking the map. "Now," - placing a long lean forefinger on a point 150 yards behind our most advanced infantry post, - "couldn't I have another little fellow there? - that would tickle him up."

The colonel smiled through his glasses. "I don't think we should be helping you more, sir, by doing that.... I can shoot on that point with observed fire as well from where the batteries are as from up there; and think of the difficulty of getting ammunition up."

"Right!" responded the General, and turned immediately to the subject of the 4·5 how. targets.

I went outside, and saw Judd at the head of the two guns of B Battery, that were to be the forward section in the attack, going by at the trot. As he passed he gave me an "I'm for it" grin. I knew that he was trotting his teams because the corner of the valley was still under enemy observation, and had been shelled all day. Bob Pottinger was following in rear.

Five minutes after the two guns passed, the Boche began a hellish strafe upon a battery that had perched itself under the crest of the hill. A couple of hundred 5·9's came over, and we had a view of rapid awe-inspiring bursts, and of men rushing for cover. "Good shooting that," remarked the colonel, who had come to the doorway.

The brigadier paid us another visit late that night. He was almost boyish in his glee. "A perfect little show," he told the colonel. "Your forward guns did very fine work indeed. And the 6-inch hows. gave the wood an awful pasting. From the reports that have come in we only took seven Boche prisoners; practically all the rest were killed."

So we took our rest that night, content in the knowledge that things were going well. There being only four beds, one of us would have to doss down on the floor. The colonel insisted on coming into our "odd man out" gamble. The bare boards fell to me; but I slept well. The canvas bag containing my spare socks fitted perfectly into the hollow of my hip - the chief recipe for securing comfort on hard ground.

Réveille was provided by the bursting of an 8-inch shell on the other side of the road. It removed part of the roof of our hut, and smothered the rest with a ponderous shower of earth. We shaved and washed by the roadside, and Major Mallaby-Kelby contrived a rapid and complete change of underclothing, also in the open air.

By 8.30 A.M. the colonel, Major Mallaby-Kelby, and the battery commanders were walking briskly through the valley and on to the rolling country beyond, reconnoitring for positions to which the batteries would move in the afternoon. Wilde and myself accompanied them, and as Judd and Bob Pottinger were also of the party I heard more details of what B Battery's forward section had done the evening before.

"I saw you turn into the valley at the trot," I said to Judd.

"Yes, by Gad," he replied; "and when we got into the valley we made it a canter. Those dead horses will show you what the valley has been like."

We were striding through the valley now - a death-trap passage, two hundred yards across at its widest point, and less than three-quarters of a mile long. I counted twenty-seven dead horses, lying in grotesque attitudes, some of them cruelly mangled. The narrow-gauge railway had become scattered bits of scrap-iron, the ground a churned waste of shell-holes.

"And the worst of it was that the traces of the second team broke," Pottinger chimed in. "Judd had gone on ahead, and we hadn't any spare traces. So I sent that team back out of the way, followed the first gun, and brought the team back to take up the second gun. Damned good team that, E sub-section. You remember the team we were training for the 'Alarm Race' when we were out at St Saveur? That's the one.... And the old Boche was peppering the valley all the time."

"Did the Boche shell much during the attack?" I asked.

"Well," continued Pottinger, "he gave the guns most of the shelling —— I was shooting the battery and Judd was doing F.O.O. with the infantry, - and where Judd was it was mostly machine-guns."

"Yes," said Judd, "I got the wind-up with those machine-guns. I couldn't find the battalion headquarters at first, and it was 150 yards from the wood. The first lot of machine-gun bullets went in front of me; one plopped into a bank just past my foot. It was dam funny. I spun right round.... But the infantry colonel, the colonel of the ——s, was a brave man. We only had a tiny dug-out, and every time you got out the machine-gun started. But he didn't mind; he got out and saw for himself everything that was going on. Didn't seem to worry him at all.... And I shall never forget the way the heavies lammed it into the wood. They had half an hour, six batteries of 6-inch howitzers, before the 18-pounders put in a five minutes' burst of shrapnel.... They say the wood is choked with German dead."

It was this self-same colonel who wrote to his brigadier commending the fine work of Judd and Pottinger on that day. Before October was out each was wearing the M.C. ribbon.

Battery positions being selected, the colonel, Major Mallaby-Kelby, and myself cast round for a headquarters. Some machine-gunners had taken possession of the only possible dug-outs. However, there were numerous huts, abandoned by the Hun, and I was chalking our claim on a neat building with a latched door and glass windows, and a garden-seat outside, when the colonel, who was gazing through his binoculars at the long, dense, hillside wood that marked the eastern edge of the valley, said in his decisive way, "What's that Swiss châlet at the top of the gully in the centre of wood?... Looks a proper sort of place for headquarters!... Let's go and inspect it."

The view through the binoculars was not deceptive; indeed, when we plunged into the wood and made the steep climb up to the châlet, we passed five or six beautifully built huts hidden among the trees. The châlet was equipped with a most attractive verandah; a hundred feet below stood a larger wooden building, covered with black felt and lined with match-boarding. The main room possessed tables obviously made by expert carpenters, and a roomy bench, with a sloping back, that went round two sides of the apartment. An inner bedroom contained a wood-framed bed with a steel spring-mattress and a number of plush-bottomed chairs. The Boche had extended his craftsmanship to the neat slats that covered the joinings of the wall-planks and kept out draughts. All the wood used was new and speckless, and smelt sweet and clean. The other huts were constructed with similar attention to detail. Also, one came across tables and benches in shady nooks, and arbours of the kind found in German beer-gardens.

"Jehoshaphat," gasped Major Mallaby-Kelby, "this is indeed the height of war luxury." The colonel, who was going on leave next day, not having been in England since the early part of January, smiled in his turn, and jested upon the desirability of delaying his departure until we vacated this delightful retreat. Wilde and myself nosed about joyously, chalking the name of our unit on every door within reach. From a Boche artillery map picked up in the châlet we concluded that the place must have been the summer quarters of a Hun artillery group commander.

And then without warning our satisfaction was changed to

disappointment. Major Mallaby-Kelby had just called out that the place was so complete that even a funk-hole had been provided, when a gunner emerged.

"What are you doing here?" inquired the major in surprise.

"I'm left here until our brigade headquarters come in, sir," the gunner replied promptly.

"What brigade?"

"The ——rd, sir," said the gunner, naming our companion Artillery Brigade.

"When did Colonel —— take over?" asked the colonel.

"About an hour ago, sir. He left me to look after the place until Brigade Headquarters came in this afternoon."

We looked solemnly at one another. "We've been forestalled," said the colonel with mock despair. Then with brisk decision, "Well, there are plenty more huts about here. We'll hurry up and get settled before other people come along."

*   *   *   *   *

The colonel left us during the afternoon. The C.R.A.'s car was to come for him at headquarters waggon line early next morning. The doctor, who was now living with the veterinary officer and the French interpreter at the waggon line, had visited our new quarters in the wood, and hoicked off our last but one bottle of whisky. I had despatched a frantic S.O.S., coupled with 100 francs in cash, to the colonel, begging him take the interpreter to Boulogne so as to replenish our mess supplies. Our good friends of the ——rd Brigade had occupied the châlet, and received one sharp reminder that the Boche gunner was still a nasty animal. A high-velocity shell had hit the edge of the gully not ten yards from them, and their adjutant and their intelligence officer had described to me their acrobatic plunge into the funk-hole. Major Mallaby-Kelby was commanding our Brigade in the absence of the colonel, and already our signal-wires buzzed with reports that indicated a very short sojourn in our new home in the wood.

I am making this narrative a plain matter-of-fact record of incidents and episodes in the career of our Brigade - which, let it be noted, was in action from August 1, before the British advance commenced, until November 4, the day of the final decisive thrust - because such an account, however poorly told, offers a picture of real war: the war that is by no means one continuous stretch of heroism and martyrdom *in excelsis*, of guns galloping to death or glory, of bayonets dripping with enemy blood, of "our gallant lads" meeting danger and destruction with "characteristic British humour and cheerfulness," when they are not "seeing red." On that 29th of August, when Major Mallaby-Kelby assumed command, we knew that the campaign had taken a definite turn in our favour, but none of us expected the Boche to be so harried and battered that by November he would be suing for peace. And I am stating bald unimaginative facts if I say that one of the main aspirations among officers and men was to continue the advance in such a way as to make sure of decent quarters o' nights, and to drive the Germans so hard that when winter set in we should be clear of the foul mud tracts and the rat-infested trenches that had formed the battlefields of 1915, '16, and '17. Major Mallaby-Kelby was a keen pushful officer, immensely eager to maintain the well-known efficiency of the Brigade while the colonel was away; but he took me into his confidence on another matter. "Look here!" he began, jocularly and with a sweeping gesture. "I'm going to ask you to make sure that the mess never runs out of white wine. It's most important. Unless I get white wine my efficiency will be impaired." I replied with due solemnity, and said that in this important matter our interpreter should be specially commissioned to scour the countryside.

By 1 P.M. it became so certain that the enemy had inaugurated a retreat that the major issued orders for the Brigade to move forward three miles. We marched steadily down the valley through which Judd and Pottinger had passed on their forward-section adventure, skirted the wood that they had assisted the Divisional Infantry to recapture, and halted for further instructions west of a deserted colony of battered Nissen huts, gaping holes and broken bricks shovelled into piles, still entered on the maps as the village of Guillemont. It would have been a truer description to paint on the sign-boards, "This was Villers Carbonnel," as has been done at one desolate spot between Peronne and Villers Bretonneux. Along the valley we had passed were row after row of solidly-built stables left uncleaned and smelly by the fleeing Hun; rotting horses smothered with flies; abandoned trucks marooned on the few stretches of the narrow-gauge railway left whole by our shell-fire. In the wood stood numerous Boche-built huts, most of them put up since the March onslaught. The Boche, dirty cur that he is, had deliberately fouled them before departing. The undulating waste land east of Trones Wood, hallowed by memories of fierce battles in 1916, had remained untroubled until the last few weeks; and the hundreds of shell-holes, relics of 1916, had become grass-grown. The hummocky greenness reminded one of nothing so much as a seaside golf-course.

CHAPTER IX

DOWN THE ROAD TO COMBLES

A BATTERY HAD been ordered to move about half a mile beyond Guillemont, and to come into action off the road that led towards the extensive, low-lying village of Combles, through which the enemy front line now ran. Major Mallaby-Kelby had gone forward and the three remaining batteries awaited his return.

I clambered my horse over the shell-holes and rubbish heaps of Guillemont, a preliminary to a short reconnaissance of the roads and tracks in the neighbourhood. Old Silvertail, having become a confirmed wind-sucker, had been deported to the Mobile Veterinary Section; Tommy, the shapely bay I was now riding, had been transferred to me by our ex-adjutant, Castle, who had trained him to be well-mannered and adaptable. "A handy little horse," was Castle's stock description, until his increasing weight made Tommy too small for him. I had ridden about six hundred yards past the sunken road in which A Battery's ammunition waggons were waiting, when half a dozen 5·9's crashed round and about them. I turned back and saw more shells descend among the empty Nissen huts in Guillemont. Two drivers of A Battery were being carried away on stretchers and the waggons were coming towards me at a trot. They halted four hundred yards from the spot where they had been shelled, and young Beale said they counted themselves lucky not to have had more casualties.

The Boche by now had got his guns in position and began a two hours' bombardment of Guillemont and its cross-roads. It was not until 7 P.M. that Major Mallaby-Kelby returned. He was tired, but anxious to go forward. "We are the advanced Brigade for to-morrow's show," he said. "The battery positions are only 1600 yards from the Boche, but I think they will be comparatively safe.... I want you all to come along and we'll arrange a headquarters. I've got my eye on a sunken Nissen hut. There's a section commander of another brigade in it, but it ought to be big enough to hold us as well."

So the major, the adjutant, Wilde, and myself walked at a smart pace along the road to Combles. The Boche shells were mostly going over our heads, but whizz-bangs now and again hit the ground to left and right of us; a smashed limber had not been cleared from the road, and fifty yards short of the railway crossing four decomposing horses emitted a sickening stench. "We'll have our headquarters waggon line along there first thing to-morrow," announced the major, stretching a long arm towards a side-road with a four-foot bank.

At the forsaken railway halt we turned off the roadway and followed the line, obeying to the letter the major's warning to bend low and creep along under cover of the low embankment, "Now we'll slip through here," said the major, after a six-hundred-yards' crawl. We hurried through what had been an important German depot. There was one tremendous dump of eight-gallon, basket-covered wine bottles - empty naturally; a street of stables and dwelling-huts; a small mountain of mouldy hay; and several vast barns that had been used for storing clothing and material. Each building was protected from our bombers by rubble revetments, fashioned with the usual German carefulness. "They shell here pretty consistently," added the major encouragingly, and we made for more open land that sloped up towards a well-timbered wood on the wide-stretched ridge, a thousand yards away. The sparse-covered slopes were dotted with living huts, all built since the Boche recovered the ground in his March push. "A Battery have moved to within two hundred yards of Leuze Wood now - you can see the guns," resumed the major. "The other battery positions are on the southern side of the road. The place I have in my eye for headquarters is close to A Battery."

The German artillery had quite evidently understood the likelihood of British batteries occupying the slope, and were acting accordingly. Our party had reached a smashed hut three hundred yards from A

Battery, when the whine of an approaching shell caused us to drop to ground; it fell fifty yards away, and the air became dense with flying pieces of shell and earth showers. As we raised ourselves again we saw Beadle walking at an even pace towards us. "Not a nice spot, sir," he began, saluting the major. "We picked that place for a mess" - pointing to the broken hut - "and five minutes later a shell crashed into it. There's a dead horse round the corner…"

"Have you been shelled much at the battery?" demanded the major.

"We had two sergeants killed a quarter of an hour ago, sir…. Captain Dumble is arranging to shift the guns a bit north of the present position, - do you approve of that, sir?"

"Yes, certainly," responded Major Mallaby-Kelby hastily. "If the direction of the shelling indicates that it would mean more safety for the battery I'm all for shifting." Beadle saluted and went away.

There was not as much spare room in the Nissen hut as the major had thought. He asked me to "organise things" and to "scrounge round" for a trench-cover to separate the subaltern and his gunners from our party; but while I was dodging shells, making the search, he found a small Boche combination hut and dug-out. The opening pointed the wrong way, of course; but there was one tiny chamber twenty feet below ground with a wooden bed in it, and upstairs a table, a cupboard, and a large heap of shavings. It was now eight o'clock, and the major remembered that he had not even had tea.

"Now what are we going to do about a meal?" he broke out. "We can't have many servants up here, there's no room… and it will be difficult to get the mess cart up. Now, who has any suggestions? On these matters I like to hear suggestions."

My own idea was that Meddings the cook, the major's servant, and one other servant should bring up some bully-beef, cheese, and bread, and bacon and tea for the morning. All that we wanted could be carried in a couple of sandbags. We could do without valises and blankets that night. Zero hour for the battle was 5.15 A.M. The mess cart could come along afterwards. The proposition was favourably received, the major's only revision referring to his white wine.

Headquarter waggons had remained the other side of Guillemont, and I volunteered to walk back and bring the servants up. The major thought that Wilde ought to accompany me; it was not too pleasant a pilgrimage with the Boche maintaining his shelling.

But as we climbed the stairs of the dug-out the major made a further decision. "I think you might as well bring the mess cart," he called out. I paused. "Not very easy to bring it round here in the dark, sir," I said, and Wilde raised his eyebrows deprecatingly.

"Yes, I think you had better bring it," continued the major. "There are two officers, and besides, the drivers have to learn the way to come here.... Don't forget my bottle of white wine, old fellow," was his parting reminder as Wilde and I set off.

The nature of the shelling caused us to direct our steps through the Boche depot towards the railway again. "Pity we didn't have something to eat before we came up here," growled Wilde. "What road are we going to bring the cart along when we come back? There's no proper track when we get off the main road."

I looked back towards the hut in which we had left the major and the adjutant. There was little to distinguish it from several other huts. "There's the Red Cross station and that big wooden building at the corner; I think we shall recognise them again," I said.

"Do you see that signalling pole on the roadside? That's a pole crossing, and I know there's a track leading off the road there," added Wilde shrewdly. "That's the way we'd better bring the cart."

It was nearly dark when we reached the Guillemont cross-roads. Small parties of infantrymen were coming along, and ammunition and ration waggons. As we turned up the road leading south-west, a square-shouldered man with a stiff big-peaked cap saluted with the crisp correctness of the regular soldier. I recognised the sergeant-major of A Battery.

"Were you much shelled when you took your waggon lines up there this evening?" I asked him.

"Yes, sir. It got too hot, and Major Bullivant sent us down again half an hour ago. All the batteries have shifted their waggon lines back behind Guillemont, sir."

"All the more exciting for us," muttered Wilde. By the aid of my electric torch we picked our way along a rough track that took us to our waggons. The drivers and spare signallers were waiting orders to settle down for the night. When I told the cook that we only wanted bare necessities in the mess cart, he answered, "That'll mean emptying the cart first. We've got everything aboard now." Such things as the stove, the spare crockery and cutlery, several tins of biscuits, and the officers' kit were quickly dumped upon the ground, and I told off one of the servants to act as guard over it until the morning. "What about this, sir?" inquired the cook, opening a large cardboard box. "The interpreter sent it up this evening." I noted twenty eggs and a cake. "Yes, put that in," I replied quickly.

Wilde detailed a signaller to accompany the driver of the cart, and, with Meddings and two of the servants walking behind, the journey commenced. A ten-minutes' hold-up occurred when Captain Denny of B Battery, a string of waggons behind him, shouted my name through the darkness. He wanted the loan of my torch for a brief study of the shell-holes, as he intended establishing the battery waggon lines in the vicinity.

The Boche had started his night-firing in earnest by the time the mess cart and party passed the cross-roads at Guillemont. A pungent smell of gas led to much coughing and sneezing. The air cleared as the road ascended, but shells continued to fly about us, and no one looked particularly happy. There were nervy, irritating moments when waggons in front halted unaccountably; and, just before the railway crossing, Wilde had to go forward and coax a pair of R.E. mules, who refused to pass the four dead horses lying in the road. The railway crossing passed, we began to look for the black-and-white signalling pole.

"Here it is," called Wilde with relief, as a 5·9 sped over us towards the railway line. "Come along, Miller," he shouted to the mess-cart driver, fifty yards behind us. The cart creaked and wobbled in the bumpy ditch-crossing that led past the pole. "There's the big building," said I, going on ahead, "and here's the Red Cross place. We're getting on fine. We'll tell M'Klown and Tommy Tucker that we'll apply for a job with the 980 company" (the A.S.C. company that supplied the Brigade with forage and rations).

"We want to go half-right from here," I continued, lighting up my torch for four or five seconds. The track led, however, to the left, and we slowed our pace. Another two hundred yards and we came to a junction; one track curved away to the right, the other went back towards the road.

A high-velocity shell screamed over and burst with a weird startling flash of flame a hundred yards away. We followed the right-hand path, and found that it bent to the left again. "This is getting puzzling," I said to Wilde in a low voice. "I think we've come right so far," he replied, "but I shall be glad when we're there."

We went on for another five minutes, the cart following. Then suddenly the situation became really worrying. We were facing a deep impassable trench. "Damn!" said Wilde angrily. "I was afraid this would happen."

"I don't think we can be more than a couple of hundred yards from where we want to get," I answered. "It ought to be in that direction. Let's give 'em a hail."

"They'll be down below - they won't hear us," said Wilde gloomily.

We stood up on the trench and called first the name of the Brigade and then the name of the adjutant. Not a sound in reply. We shouted again, the servants joining in. Another shell, bursting near enough to spray the mess cart with small fragments! At last we heard a cry, and shouted harder than ever. A figure came out of the gloom, and I recognised Stenson, A Battery's round-faced second lieutenant. "Ah! now we're all right," I called out cheerfully. "You see how we're tied up," I said, turning to Stenson. "Our headquarters is close to your battery. Which is the way to it?"

Stenson's face fell. "That's what I was hoping you would tell me," he replied blankly. "I've lost myself."

There was a groan from Wilde.

"I left the battery about half an hour ago because some one was shouting outside in the dark," went on Stenson. "I found a major sitting in a shell-hole; he had lost his way trying to get back to the railway. I managed to put him right - now I can't find the battery."

Another voice came from the far side of the trench, and we peered at the newcomer. It was one of the Brigade orderlies, who also had lost his way trying to find an infantry battalion headquarters. I examined him on his sense of direction, but all I got from him was that if he could reach the road and see the fifth telegraph pole from the wood, he would know that Brigade Headquarters lay on a line due north.

More shells dropped near, and I began to think of Minnie, our patient mess-cart mare. We must get her and the cart out of the way as soon as possible. Close by stood a big Nissen hut, sunk half-way below ground. After consulting with Wilde, I told the servants to unload the cart and carry the stuff into the hut. The cart having gone, we went inside; and, lighting a candle, discovered the usual empty bottles and scattered German illustrated periodicals that indicate a not too hurried Boche evacuation. After a ten minutes' wait, during which the Boche shelling increased in intensity, Stenson, the orderly, and myself went forth with my torch, bent upon trying all the tracks within reach until we found the right one. And though we twice followed ways that disappointed us, and turned and searched with a bitter sense of bafflement, our final path led in the direction to which I had first pointed. We found ourselves close to the shell-stricken hut where I had met Beale of A Battery earlier in the evening. "I know where we are now," I shouted hilariously.

"Who's that?" called some one sharply. I turned my torch on to the owner of the voice. It was Kelly of D Battery, yet another lost soul. "I'm hanged if I know where I am," he explained angrily. "I can't find the battery. I was going to lie down inside here until it got light,... but I have no matches, and I put my hand on a clammy dead Boche."

"Get away with you!" I laughed. "That's a dead horse. I saw it this afternoon."

Sure of my ground now, I walked comfortably towards the dug-out where Major Mallaby-Kelby and the adjutant were waiting. It was 11.15 P.M. now. Tired and hungry and without candles, they had fallen asleep.

"By Gad! you're back," ejaculated the major when I touched him.... "Have you brought my white wine?"

"It is coming, sir, before very long," I responded soothingly.

I stood outside, flashed my torch, and yelled for Wilde. An answering shout was succeeded by Wilde himself. "Why, we were quite close all the time," he said in surprise.

"Now you go back with the orderly and bring Meddings over with something to eat," I went on, "every one's famished." Soon Meddings arrived, striding across shell-holes and treacherous ground with a heavy mess-box balanced on his head.

"Only bully beef to-night, sir," said Meddings to the expectant major as he dumped the box on the floor of the hut.

"My dear fellow, I can eat anything, a crust or a dog-biscuit, I'm so hungry."

Meddings raised the lid and we all crowded round. "By Gad! this is too much," snapped the major.

The box contained nothing but cups and plates and saucers.

When Meddings returned with a second box the major and the adjutant seized some biscuits and munched happily and voraciously. "You devils," said the major, grinning reproachfully at Wilde and myself, "I bet you had whiskies-and-sodas at the waggon line. Why were you so long?"

We didn't go into full explanations then, and I must confess that when the major, in his haste, knocked the bottle of white wine off the table and smashed it, Wilde and myself could scarcely forbear a chuckle. That ought, of course, to be the climax of the story; but it wasn't. I had put two bottles of the major's white wine into the mess cart, so the concluding note was one of content. Also I might add, Stenson called upon us to say that A Battery's mess cart had failed to arrive, and four foodless officers asked us to have pity upon them. So A Battery received a loaf and a big slab of the truly excellent piece of bully, a special kind that Meddings had obtained in some mysterious fashion from a field ambulance that was making a hurried move. "You two fellows have earned your supper," said the now peaceful major to

Wilde and myself. "I didn't think you were going to have so trying a journey." We ate bully sandwiches solidly until 1 A.M. Then the major and the adjutant descended to their little room below ground. I glanced through 'The Times,' and then Wilde and myself found a restful bed upon the shavings. The cook and the servants had gone back to the Nissen hut.

The major's last words as he fell asleep were, "I've to be at the ———th Infantry Brigade Headquarters at 4.45 in the morning. I think I'll take the adjutant with me…. No," - sleepily, - "you'd better come, Wilde."

At 4 A.M., when the major's servant woke us, the major called up the stairs to me, "I think, after all, you'd better come with me." As I had not removed my boots, it didn't take me long to be up and ready.

Before we were fifty yards from the hut the major and I shared in one of the narrowest escapes that have befallen me in France. We heard the shell coming just in time to crouch. According to Meddings, who stood in the doorway of the hut, it fell ten yards from us. Smothered with earth, we moved forward rapidly immediately we regained our feet.

"We shall be right for the rest of the day after that," panted the major. "The ———th Brigade are in the bank along the road from Leuze Wood to Combles," he added, reading from a message form. As we left the dewy grass land and got on to the road that led through the wood, other shells whistled by, but none of them near enough to set our nerves tingling again. Indeed the state of mind of both of us seemed sanguine and rose-coloured. "Fine bit of country this," said the major in his quick jerky way, "and that purple haze is quite beautiful. It ought to be lighter than this. It's not even half morning light yet…. My old uncle in County Clare would be sure to call it dusk. He often used to say when we were arranging a day's fishing, 'Let me see, it will still be dusk at 5 A.M.'"

The major drew an envelope from his pocket and fixed his eyeglass. "Awkward thing sometimes having a double-barrelled name," he continued. "I remember a bright young subaltern in a reserve brigade in England, whose name was Maddock-Smith, or something like that. He complained that the brigade clerk had not noticed the hyphen, and that he was down to do double duty as orderly officer - once as Maddock and once as Smith."

We were now through the wood, and walking down the hill direct to Combles. Everything seemed profoundly quiet; not a soul in the road save ourselves. "Seems strange," observed the major, frowning. "Infantry Brigade Headquarters ought to be about here. They can't be much farther off. The starting line is only a few hundred yards away."

"You'd certainly expect to see plenty of messengers and runners near a brigade headquarters," I put in. "Hullo! here's some one on a bicycle."

It was a New Zealand officer. "Can you tell me where the ——th Brigade Headquarters are?" he asked.

"We are looking for them ourselves," replied the major. "I've to be there by 4.45, and it's past that now."

We went down to where a track crossed the road at right angles. Still no one in sight. "Don't understand it," remarked the New Zealand officer. "I'm going back for more information."

The major and I remained about five minutes longer watching the haze that enveloped the village below commence to lift. Then suddenly we heard the sharp metallic crack of quick-firing guns behind, and dozens of 18-pdr. shells whistled above us. The barrage had started.

Almost immediately red Very lights went up within a stone's-throw as it seemed to me. And now Boche lights leapt up on our left where the haze prevented us seeing the Morval ridge, the highest ground in the neighbourhood, and still in enemy hands. Presently the devilish rattle of machine-guns rapped out, spreading round the half-circle along which the alarm lights were still soaring heavenwards.

"We can't do anything by staying here," decided the major. "My place is with the Infantry Brigade, and I must find them."

"We can report, at any rate, that the Boche lights went up within a few seconds of the start of our barrage, and that the enemy artillery replied within four minutes," I remarked, looking at my wrist-watch, as shells from the direction of the Boche lines poured through the air.

"Yes, we can say that," responded the major, "and —— keep down!" he called out violently.

A number of bullets had swished swiftly past us. We kept close to the bank and walked, bending down, until we came again to the sunken portion of the road.

"We can also report that this road was subjected to machine-gun fire," concluded the major pointedly.

We ducked again with startled celerity just before reaching the wood. This time it was a short-range shell from one of our own guns - there was no mistaking the wheezy, tinny sound of its passage through the air. It fell in front of us on the edge of the road, and delivered its shrapnel as vengefully as if it had fallen in the Boche lines. As we came beyond the wood we met young Stenson with a small party of gunners. His face shone with expectancy. He was on the way to man the forward gun that A Battery had placed overnight under cover of a bank not far from the road the major and I had just walked along.

"Well, old fellow," remarked the major, removing his steel helmet when we got back to headquarters, "a cup of tea, and you'd better go straight down to those trenches the other side of Guillemont and inquire what has become of the Infantry Brigade. And you can deliver our reconnoitring report."

It was a long walk, and I resolved to pick up my horse for the return journey. The Infantry brigadier was taking an early cup of tea when I found his headquarters. His brigade-major told me that there had been a change of plan, and the Brigade did not come forward, as previously arranged. "We couldn't find you to let you know," he explained. "Show me the position of your headquarters on the map.... Oh, we have our advanced headquarters not three hundred yards from you, and you will find the 2nd —— headquarters near there too.... I'm sorry we didn't let you know last night. But none of our despatch-riders could find you."

I rode back the best part of the way, and found the major, the adjutant, and Wilde fortifying themselves with eggs and bacon.

"We'll look round for a better protected headquarters than this after breakfast," said the major briskly.

"When I've had a shave, sir," I answered appealingly. "I can't maintain my efficiency without a shave, you know."

CHAPTER X

A MASTERLY TURNING MOVEMENT

A UGUST 30: Before noon we learned that the battle had gone not altogether our way. Our own Divisional Infantry had fought well and scattered the Boche in the low-lying village of Combles, but the Division on our left had failed to force the enemy from the Morval Heights. Consequently our infantry had been ordered to withdraw their line slightly, while it remained impossible for the Field Artillery to push forward so long as the Boche observers possessed the Morval ridge.

Our batteries, with an S.O.S. range of 1700 yards, were close enough, as it was, to startle strict adherents of siege-war principles. Indeed A Battery's forward section, handled first by Dumble and then by Stenson, had boldly harassed the enemy machine-gunners from under 500 yards' range. Dumble had already been recommended for the Military Cross, and Major Bullivant described Stenson's exploits while visiting Brigade Headquarters during the afternoon.

"Yesterday," he told Major Mallaby-Kelby, "he took a sniping gun on to the crest, and kept it in action for four hours, firing 150 rounds. At one time he was within three hundred yards of the enemy. He wiped out at least two infantry teams and waggons - although the Boche tried hard to knock his gun out with 5·9's and whizz-bangs. This morning he fired 500 rounds over open sights, and the colonel of the ——s tells me he helped our infantry a lot. I understand that more than once, when his gunners got tired, he 'layed' the gun himself - not part of an officer's work, perhaps - but he's a very sound youngster, and I should like to get him something."

"I shall be pleased indeed to put him in," responded Major Mallaby-Kelby. "A word from the infantry would, of course, help."

Our new headquarters, nearer to the Boche depot, consisted simply of a deep stairless shaft with a 40 degrees slope. The props supporting the roof were fusty with mildew and fungus, but the entrance faced away from the German guns. As the colonel of the 2nd ———s was keen to be in liaison with us, he and his adjutant and a couple of signallers shared the shaft. The servants gathered clean straw from the German dump and strewed it down the shaft. Major Mallaby-Kelby and the colonel, a slim soft-voiced young man at least twenty-six years of age, with a proved reputation for bravery and organising powers, had their blankets laid side by side at the top of the shaft; the two adjutants, plus telephones, came next; then a couple of signallers with telephone switch-boards; and, lowest of all, the doctor and myself. Wilde and his signallers, the cook and his servants, had installed themselves in a roomy hut stuck in a big bank thirty yards away. There was a sort of well at the top of the shaft, with steps cut in the earth, leading down from the ground-level. We fastened a tarpaulin across the top of the well and made it our mess. It was not unwise to pick such a well-shielded nook; the Boche gunners flung shells about more in this neighbourhood than along the slope where the batteries were situated.

We slept three nights in the shaft. Each morning on awaking I discovered that I had slipped a couple of yards downhill. I made further full acquaintance, too, with the completeness of the doctor's snoring capabilities. Down in that shaft he must have introduced a new orgy of nasal sounds. It commenced with a gentle snuffling that rather resembled the rustling of the waters against the bows of a racing yacht, and then in smooth even stages crescendoed into one grand triumphant blare.

September 1 proved a day of glory in the history of the Division. Conferences of Generals, and dashing to and fro of despatch-riders, produced ambitious plans for an advance that would more than make up for the set-back of August 30. A brigade of our own Divisional Infantry was again to descend upon the village of Combles, while another brigade, working on the flank, would effect a turning movement northwards towards Fregicourt, a hamlet twelve hundred yards north-east of Combles. Meanwhile the Division on our left intended to make a desperate effort to free the Morval Heights.

My task was to be brigade liaison officer with the ———th Infantry Brigade, who had come up overnight to a quarry a quarter of a mile beyond D Battery's position. It was a crisp invigorating day, with a nip in the air that foretold the approach of autumn, and it would have been a pleasant walk along the valley had not one constantly to get to leeward of the dead horses that littered the way. And I shall always recall a small log-cabin that stood isolated in the centre of the valley - the sort of place that could mean lone settlers or hermit hunters to imaginative boyhood. I felt drawn to the hut. The door hung ajar and I looked in. A young German infantry soldier, dead, his face palely putty-like, his arms hanging loose, sat on a bench before a plain wooden table. There was no disorder in the hut. Many a time have I seen sleeping men in more grotesque attitudes. But the open jacket and the blood-stained shirt told probably of a miserable being who had crept inside to die.

A red triangular flag hanging limply from a lance stuck in the chalk-bank near a roughly-contrived tarpaulin and pit-prop shelter revealed the infantry brigadier's headquarters. The Brigade signalling officer hailed me from a dug-out that flew the blue and white of the signalling company. Outside the brigade-major's hut I found Captain Drysdale of D Battery, and two other gunner officers. "We are kicking our heels, waiting for news like newspaper correspondents during a Cabinet crisis," said Drysdale with a bored smile. "I can't see why they want so many liaison officers.... I went without my dinner to get here from the waggon line last night, and haven't had breakfast yet; and these people haven't told us a scrap of news yet."

"You're doing liaison for Division, aren't you?" I said, "and I'm for Brigade. They can't need us both."

"Except that the General told me he might require me to go forward with him to look for targets," replied Drysdale.

"Well, if you like, you slip along to the battery for breakfast. I'll hold the fort until you come back."

There was, indeed, until well on in the morning, surprisingly little information to be telephoned to the Artillery. What news the Infantry brigade-major did receive, however, was all to the good. The battalions that went into Combles were going strong, and the mopping-up was being done with the old-soldier thoroughness that so many of the young lads who only learnt war during the summer advance seemed to acquire so rapidly. One of the companies engaged in the turning movement had paid the penalty of over-eagerness, and losing touch with a sister company had been badly enfiladed by German machine-gunners; but another company had rushed up to fill their place and the movement was progressing towards its appointed end.

A dozen Boche prisoners were brought in, dirty, hollow-eyed, and furtive. "This one speaks English, sir," said the dapper little private of the East ——s, who had charge of the party, addressing an intelligence officer.

I spoke afterwards to this prisoner, a dark pale-faced infantry man with staring eyes. His English was fair, although he told me he had only visited England once, for a fortnight - in London and Manchester. He had been a telephone manufacturer's employee.

"You were in Combles when you were captured?" I asked.

"Yes."

"How long had you been in the line?"

"Four days; we went down to Combles yesterday morning."

"Did your rations get up last night?" I proceeded, thinking of our all-night burst of fire on enemy cross-roads and approaches.

"We took ours with us, but none came for the others there. They had had nothing for two days."

The marching away of the prisoners prevented further questions. Soon the Divisional Commander with his attendant staff came up, and a conference in the brigadier's headquarters was commenced. After half an hour the G.O.C. came out. His demeanour betokened satisfaction. The manner in which he turned to speak parting words to the brigadier indicated further activities. A captain of the West ——s, who had been in reserve, turned from watching him, and said to me, "I expect we shall be performing this afternoon." Soon the phrase, "exploiting initial success," ran from tongue to tongue.

This was the message that at noon I telephoned to our adjutant:-

7th ——s and East ——s will push forward fighting patrols to exploit success in an easterly and north-easterly direction into St Pierre Vaast Wood, and along the road to S——. Patrols will not penetrate into squares X 120 and Z 130, as ——th Division will continue its advance in Y 140, a and c, under a barrage very shortly.

Artillery have been given tasks of harassing fire east of St Pierre Vaast Wood, and will not fire west of line eastern edge of this wood to A 210, b 05.

Patrols must be pushed out without delay, as it is the intention of the Divisional Commander to exploit initial success with another brigade to-day.

"That's the stuff to give 'em," chortled the Brigade signalling officer, who had been whipping round similar messages to various units.

More prisoners kept coming in; the brigade-major's telephone rang furiously; a heavily-moustached infantry signaller, with a bar to his Military Medal, just back from the eastern side of Combles, was telling his pals how an officer and himself had stalked a Hun sniper. "He was in a hole behind some trees," he said, "and we were walkin' along, when he hit old Alf in the foot ——"

"Is old Alf all right?" asked another signaller quickly.

"Yes" - nodding and grinning - "he's got a nice Blighty - he's all right…. As I was sayin', he hit old Alf in the foot, and Mr. Biles says to me, 'We'll get that blighter.' So we dropped, and Mr. Biles crawled away to the right and I went to the left. He popped off again after about five minutes, and I saw where the shot came from. He had two other goes, and the second time I saw his head. The next time he popped up I loosed off…. We went to have a look afterwards. I'd got him right under the ear."

At three o'clock the brigade-major complained to us that some 18-pdrs. were shooting short. "They mustn't fire in that square," he said excitedly, "we're still mopping up there."

I telephoned to our adjutant, who said he would speak to our batteries. "We are not firing there at all," he informed me five minutes afterwards, and I reported to the brigade-major.

Ten minutes later the brigade-major rushed angrily out of his hut. "Look here!" he said, "that artillery fire has started again. They've killed a subaltern and a sergeant of the East ——s. You must do something!"

I rang up the adjutant again. "It isn't our people," he replied tersely. "It might be the ——th Division on our left," I suggested. "Can you get on to them?"

"I'll get Division to speak to them," he replied.

By five o'clock the number of prisoners roped in by the Division was not far short of a thousand; the Division on the left had gained the Morval ridge, and this, combined with the turning movement from the south, had brought about something like debacle among the enemy forces opposed to us. "That's topping," said the brigade-major when receiving one particular telephone report, and he looked up with a laugh. "The ——s have captured a Boche ambulance waggon, and they have sent it down for receipt on delivery, with horses and driver complete."

Not long afterwards I met Major Veasey, hot and radiant after one of the big adventures of the day. He had gone forward with Kelly, and discovered that the infantry were held up by fierce machine-gun fire. "I was afraid all the time that the major's white breeches would give the show away," Kelly told me, "but we crawled on our bellies to about a hundred yards from the machine-guns - there were two of 'em - and got the exact spot. We went back and told the battery where to fire, and then went forward for another look."

"By Jove, we did pepper 'em. And, hang me, if the major didn't say we must go and make absolutely sure that we had outed 'em. There were nineteen Boches in the trench, and they surrendered to the major.... Look at this pile of revolvers we took from them - fourteen altogether. The major's promised to give this little beauty to the doctor."

And still the day's tale of triumph was not concluded. At seven o'clock the infantry battalion that had been held in reserve made a combined dash with troops of the Division on the left, and drove the tired dispirited Huns out of Sailly-Saillisel, another 2000 yards on.

Our batteries fired harassing crashes all through the night, and were warned to be ready to move first thing in the morning.

CHAPTER XI

ON THE HEELS OF THE BOCHE

SEPTEMBER 2: The side-spectacle that struck me most when I walked by myself through Combles was that of a solitary Royal Engineer playing a grand piano in the open street, with not a soul to listen to him. The house from which the instrument had been dragged was smashed beyond repair; save for some scrapes on the varnish the piano had suffered no harm, and its tone was agreeable to the ear. The pianist possessed technique and played with feeling and earnestness, and it seemed weirdly strange to hear Schumann's "Slumber Song" in such surroundings. But the war has produced more impressive incongruities than that.

The Brigade settled itself in the neighbourhood of Fregicourt. The ——st Infantry Brigade was already established there in a trench; and the first job of work that fell to me was to answer the F.O.O. of another Artillery brigade who had rung up Infantry Brigade Headquarters. "Huns are moving along the road in X 429 b and c," said a voice. "Can you turn one of my batteries on to them?" Our batteries were not yet in position, but I saw, a couple of hundred yards away, two batteries whose trails were lowered; so I hurried across and gave them the target and the map spotting, and before long 18-pdr. shells were on their way to ginger up the aforementioned unlucky Huns. An aeroplane fight within decent observing distance aroused much more interest. No decisive result was obtained, but the enemy airman was finally driven away in full retreat towards his own lines. "Jerry isn't as cheeky as he used to be in Flanders last year, is he?" said Wilde to me. "It must be true that he's running short of 'planes."

The problem of the last few days had been the water supply for the horses. Although the sappers were hard at work in Combles, there was as yet no water within five miles of the batteries. The Boche by smashing all the power-pumps had seen to that; and the waggon lines were too far in rear for moving warfare. "We shall be all right when we get to the canal," had been everybody's consolatory pronouncement. "The horses won't be so hard worked then."

We were still in the area of newly-erected Boche huts, and Headquarters lay that night without considerable hardship. Manning, our mess waiter, a fish-monger by trade, had discovered a large quantity of dried fish left by the departing enemy, and the men enjoyed quite a feast; the sudden appearance in new boots of ninety per cent of them could be similarly explained. The modern soldier is not squeamish in these matters. I overheard one man, who had accepted a pair of leggings from a prisoner, reply to a comrade's mild sneer, "Why not?... I'd take anything from these devils. There was a big brute this morning: I had a good mind to take his false teeth - they had so much gold in 'em." Which rather suggested that he was "telling the tale" to his unsympathetic listener.

Late that night orders informed us that on the morrow we should come under another Divisional Artillery. Our own infantry were being pulled out of the line to bring themselves up to strength. The enemy were still withdrawing, and fresh British troops had to push ahead so as to allow him no respite. A Battery had already advanced their guns another 2000 yards, and through the night fired hotly on the road and approaches east of the canal. Next morning Major Mallaby-Kelby was instructed to reconnoitre positions within easy crossing distance of the canal, but not to move the batteries until further orders came in. Bicycle orderlies chased down to the waggon lines to tell the grooms to bring up our horses. My groom, I remember, had trouble on the road, and did not arrive soon enough for the impatient major; so I borrowed the adjutant's second horse as well as his groom. A quarter of a mile on the way I realised that I had forgotten my box-respirator; the only solution of the difficulty was to take the groom's, and send him back to remain in possession of mine until I returned; and all that morning and afternoon I was haunted by the fear that I might perhaps be compelled to put on the borrowed article.

The reconnoitring party consisted of Major Mallaby-Kelby, Major Veasey, Major Bullivant, young Beale of A Battery, and Kelly and Wood of D Battery, who loaded themselves with a No. 4 Director, the tripod instrument with which lines of fire are laid out.

When we approached the highest point along the main road leading east, Major Mallaby-Kelby sent back word that the road was under observation; we must come along in couples, two hundred yards between each couple. The Boche was sending over some of the high-bursting shells which he uses so much for ranging purposes, but we were not greatly troubled. We dipped into a slippery shell-scarred track that wound through a hummocky copse, swung southwards along a sunken road, and then made due east again, drawing nearer a dense forest of stubby firs that stretched far as eye could see. This was the wood into which our infantry had pushed fighting patrols on Sept. 1. Every few yards we met grim reminders of the bloody fighting that had made the spot a memorable battle-ground. My horse shied at two huddled grey forms lying by the roadside - bayoneted Huns. I caught a glimpse of one dead German, half covered by bushes; his face had been blown away. Abandoned heaps of Boche ammunition; fresh gaping shell-holes; one ghastly litter of mutilated horses and men, and a waggon rolled into the ditch, revealed the hellish execution of our artillery. The major called a halt and said we would leave our horses there.

We struck north-east, away from the forest, and, reaching the cross-roads on top of the crest, gazed across the great wide valley that from the canal sloped up to the blue haze of heights still held by the enemy. Through the glasses one saw the yellows and greens of bracken and moss and grass in the middle distances. "We're getting into country now that hasn't seen much shelling," remarked the major with satisfaction. But the glasses also showed slopes seared and seamed with twisting trenches and tawny waggon tracks.

Our path lay along a road bordered by evenly-planted, broken and lifeless poplars. The major called out for us to advance in single file, at intervals of twenty-five yards. When high-velocity shells struck the ground a hundred yards short of the road and a hundred yards beyond it, we all of us dropped unquestioningly into the narrow freshly-dug trench that ran at the foot of the poplars. About five hundred yards on, to the left of the road, we passed a shell-blasted grove that hung above a melancholy rubbish-heap of broken bricks and shattered timber.

"Government Farm!" called Major Mallaby-Kelby, with an informative gesture.

Government Farm was a datum point that batteries had mercilessly pasted two days before.

"Government Farm!" repeated Major Bullivant, who walked behind Mallaby-Kelby.

"Government Farm!" echoed Major Veasey, with out-stretched arm; and I, in my turn, passed the word to Beale.

Young Beale was in exuberant spirits. He not only turned his head and shouted "Government Farm!" with a parade-ground volume of voice; he followed with the clarion demand of "Why don't you acknowledge orders?" to Kelly, who was so surprised that he nearly dropped the Director before responding with a grin, and thrusting out his arm in the way laid down in the gun-drill book for sergeants to acknowledge gunnery orders passed along the line of guns.

We came to another large wood that stretched down towards the canal, and, once more in a party, moved along the southern edge of it. An infantry captain, belonging to the Division we were now working under, stepped from beneath the trees and saluted. "We're reconnoitring for battery positions," said Major Mallaby-Kelby, answering the salute. "Can you tell me how the front line runs now?"

"We're sending two patrols through the wood to the canal now," replied the captain, "The Boche hadn't entirely cleared out three-quarters of an hour ago."

"We may as well go on," said Major Mallaby-Kelby, after three or four minutes further conversation. "The Boche must be over the canal by now… and we have to select battery positions as soon as possible. We don't want to bring the guns up in the dark." There was a general feeling for revolvers, and we entered the wood and followed a bridle-path. I could imagine that wood in the pleasant careless days of peace, a proper wood for picnics and nutting expeditions. Ripening blackberries even now loaded the bramble bushes, but the foul noxiousness of gas shells had made them uneatable. The heavy sickly smell of phosgene pervaded the close air; no birds fluttered and piped among the upper branches. The heavy steel helmet caused rills of sweat to run down the cheeks.

We forged ahead past a spacious glade where six tracks met. "There's a hut we could use for a mess," said Major Veasey. "Mark it up, Kelly; and look at that barrel, it would be big enough for you to sleep in." Snapped-off branches, and holes torn in the leaf-strewn ground, showed that the guns had not neglected this part of the wood; and in several places we noted narrow ruts a yard or so in length, caused by small-calibre projectiles. "Ricochet shots from whizz-bangs fired at very close range," commented Major Bullivant.

After certain hesitations as to the right track to follow, we reached the north-western edge of the wood. Major Mallaby-Kelby refused to allow us to leave cover, and we knelt hidden among the prickly bushes. "For heaven's sake don't show these white breeches, Veasey," laughed Major Bullivant.

A village nestled at the foot of the slope. Not a sign of life in it now, although the Boche was certainly in possession the day before. "There are some Boches in that trench near the top of the slope," said Major Veasey suddenly. "Can you see them? Eight degrees, two o'clock, from the farm chimney near the quarry." I looked hard and counted three steel helmets. "We could have some good shooting if we had the guns up," added the major regretfully. A Boche 5·9 was firing consistently and accurately into the valley beneath us. I say accurately, because the shells fell round and about one particular spot. "Don't see what he's aiming at," said Major Bullivant shortly. "He's doing no damage.... He can't be observing his fire."

There was a discussion as to whether an 18-pdr. battery placed near a long bank on the slope would be able to clear the wood at 3000 yards' range, and Major Mallaby-Kelby and Major Bullivant slipped out to inspect a possible position at the corner where the edge of the wood curved north-east. Then Major Mallaby-Kelby decided that it was time to return; and on the way back Major Veasey said he would be content to bring his 4·5 how. battery into the glade where the six tracks met. "Might as well make us trench mortars," growled Kelly to me. "We shan't be more than a thousand yards from the Boche."

Just before we came out of the wood Major Mallaby-Kelby called to me to chalk the sign of Brigade H.Q. on an elaborate hut that stood forty yards off the track - a four-roomed hut, new and clean. It was not pleasant, however, to find two dead Boche horses lying in the doorway.

An enemy bombardment started as we left the wood. Major Veasey and his party went off immediately towards where the horses were waiting. The other two majors, still seeking battery positions, bore away to the south, and I followed them. A 4·2 battery suddenly switched its fire on to the strip of ground we were crossing, and we ran hurriedly for shelter to a trench that lay handy. Shells whistled over our heads, and we panted and mopped our brows while taking a breather.

"No wonder he's shelling here," exclaimed Major Mallaby-Kelby. "The ——rd" [our companion Brigade] "have a battery here.... Look at those dead horses... three, five, seven - why, there are twelve of 'em."

"Yes, sir," I put in, "that happened yesterday when they were bringing up ammunition."

We moved up the trench, but we seemed to draw fire as if we had magnetic properties. "We'll move back again," remarked Major Mallaby-Kelby with energy, and he started off, Major Bullivant following.

We had gone about fifty yards when Major Bullivant turned swiftly, gave me a push, and muttered "Gas!" We ran back to where we had been before, and looked round for Major Mallaby-Kelby. "Damn it," he said abruptly when he came up, sneezing, "I forgot to bolt. I stood still getting my box-respirator on."

When the shelling died down we walked farther along the trench, which turned westwards. Excellent positions for the three 18-pdr. batteries were found not far from the trench; and returning again towards the wood for our horses, we chanced upon a deep dug-out that Major Mallaby-Kelby sent me down to explore. "Don't touch any wires or pegs," he said warningly; "the Hun may have left some booby-traps." The dug-out was thirty feet deep, and had only one entrance. But I found recesses with good wire beds, and a place for the telephonists. "We'll make that Headquarters," decided the major, and I chalked out our claim accordingly.

When we got back to the batteries we found that orders for the move had come in; the teams were up; and after a very welcome cup of tea the journey to the new positions was started. Wilde, the signalling officer, and myself led the way with the Headquarters' vehicles, and followed a beautifully hidden track that ran through the wood and came out a hundred yards from our selected dug-out. Three red glares lit up the sky behind the heights held by the Boche. "By Jove," said Wilde, "he must be going back; he's burning things."

My day's work was not yet ended. Our own infantry had been brought up again, and it was imperative that we should be in early communication with the ———rd Brigade, the Brigade commanded by the forceful young brigadier who had discussed artillery arrangements with the colonel for the operation in which Judd and Pottinger had done so well with their forward section. There was a shortage of telephone wire, and at 8.15 P.M. Wilde's line had not been laid. Major Mallaby-Kelby decided that the only alternative was for me to go and report to the brigadier, whose headquarters were not far from the road leading to Senate Farm. It was very dark, and the fact that the whole way was under Boche observation made it impossible for me to use my torch. Shells were falling about the cross-roads - and I have undertaken more agreeable walks. I went down into the Infantry brigade signal-hut first to find whether we had at last got a line through. We hadn't. When I asked for the General's mess, the signalling sergeant conducted me along a passage that in places was not three feet high. Climbing up a steep uneven stairway, I found myself at the top looking into the mess with only my head and shoulders exposed to view. The General was examining a map. His brigade-major, a V.C. captain with gentle eyes and a kindly charming manner; his staff captain, a brisk hard-bitten soldier, with a reputation for never letting the Brigade go hungry; the signal officer, the intelligence officer, and other junior members of the staff, were seated round the same table. "What about the ———nd Brigade?" I heard the General say, mentioning our Brigade.

"We haven't heard from them yet," observed the brigade-major.

"I'm from the ———nd Brigade," I said loudly.

There were startled ejaculations and a general looking round to the spot where the voice came from.

"Hallo, Jack-in-the-box!" exclaimed the brigadier, staring at my head and shoulders, "where did you come from?"

I explained, and the General, laughing, said, "Well, you deserve a drink for that.... Come out of your box and we'll give you some targets.... I didn't know any one could get in that way."

Before I went away the tactical situation was explained to me. I was given the points the Infantry would like us to fire upon during the night. Also I got my drink.

The last thing Major Mallaby-Kelby said before going off to sleep was, "Extraordinary long time since we met any civilians. Haven't seen any since July."

CHAPTER XII

THE MAJOR'S
LOST PIPE

S EPTEMBER 4: "A full mail-bag and a bottle of white wine are the best spirit revivers for war-worn fighting-men," said Major Mallaby-Kelby contentedly, gathering up his own big batch of letters from the one and sipping a glass of the other.

During two days Brigade Headquarters and the four batteries had received piles of belated letters and parcels, and there was joy in the land. I remember noting the large number of little, local, weekly papers - always a feature of the men's mail; and it struck me that here the countryman was vouchsafed a joy unknown to the Londoner. Both could read of world-doings and national affairs in the big London dailies; but the man from the shires, from the little country towns, from the far-off villages of the British Isles, could hug to himself the weekly that was like another letter from home - with its intimate, sometimes trivial, details of persons and places so familiar in the happy uneventful days before the war.

As for the white wine, that did not greatly interest the other members of Brigade Headquarters mess. But the diary contained the bald entry, "At 9.30 P.M. the whisky ran out," in the space headed Aug. 28; and none had come to us since. People at home are inclined to believe that the whisky scarcity, and the shortage of cakes and biscuits, and chocolate and tobacco, scarcely affected officers' messes in France. It is true that recognised brands of whisky appeared on the Expeditionary Force Canteens' price-list at from 76 to 80 francs a dozen, but there were days and days when none was to be bought, and no lime-juice and no bottled lemon-squash either. Many a fight in the September-October push was waged by non-teetotal officers, who had nothing with which to disguise the hideous taste of chlorinate of lime in the drinking water. Ah well!

There was also the serious matter of Major Mallaby-Kelby's pipe. It became a burning topic on Sept. 4. "I must have dropped it yesterday when we tumbled into that gas," he told me dolefully. "I mustn't lose that pipe. It was an original Dunhill, and is worth three or four pounds…. I'll offer a reward for it…. Will you come with me to look for it?" And he fixed his monocle and gazed at me compellingly.

"Does the offer of a reward refer to me, sir?" I inquired with all the brightness at my command. For answer the major commenced putting on his steel helmet and box-respirator.

It was fitting that I should go. I had accompanied the major on all his excursions, and my appearance over the horizon had become a sure warning to the batteries that the major was not far off. "Gunner Major and Gunner Minor" some one had christened us.

The major conducted the search with great verve. We encountered a gunner chopping wood, and he told him the story of the pipe. "I'll give twenty-five francs to any one who brings it to me," he concluded. The gunner saluted and continued to chop wood.

"Rather a big reward!" I remarked as we walked on.

"Do you think twenty-five too much? Shall I make it fifteen?"

"You've committed yourself now," I answered solemnly.

Our arrival at the trench in which we had sheltered the day before coincided with the whizz-phutt of a 4·2 dud. "I shall be sorry if I get you killed looking for my pipe," said the major cheerfully. We waited for the next shell, which exploded well behind us, and then hastened to the spot where our quest was really to commence. Four gunners belonging to the ——rd Brigade stood idly in the trench. The major stopped and looked down upon them. He addressed himself directly to a wall-faced, emotionless kind of man whose head and shoulders showed above the trench top.

"I was down here yesterday," began the major, "and lost my pipe. It was a very valuable pipe, a pipe I prize very much. I think it must be somewhere in this trench…."

The wall-faced man remained stolidly silent.

"I want to get it back again," went on the major; "and if any of you fellows find it and bring it to me - I'm Major Mallaby-Kelby, commanding the ——nd Brigade - I'll give a reward of twenty-five francs."

"Is this it, sir?" said the wall-faced man in matter-of-fact tones, whipping out of his pocket a thin-stemmed pipe with a shapely, beautifully-polished bowl.

"By Jove, that's it!" exclaimed the major, taken aback by the swift unexpectedness of the recovery. "Yes, by Jove, that's it," he continued, his face lighting up. He took the pipe and rubbed the bowl affectionately with the palm of his hand.

"Twenty-five francs reward!" I murmured softly.

"Yes, that's right," he said briskly, and began turning out his pockets. Three maps, a pocket-handkerchief, some ration biscuits, and a note-case with nothing in it. "You must lend me twenty-five francs," he declared masterfully.

The wall-faced gunner accepted the money without any sign of repressed emotion, and saluted smartly. The smiles of the other men broadened into grins as the major and myself set our faces homewards.

There were more serious matters to consider when we got back. D Battery had had two men killed by shell fire in the wood; the other batteries had had to send away a dozen men between them, overcome by gas; the Infantry brigadier wished to discuss fresh plans for hastening the enemy's departure from the neighbourhood of the canal.

In the afternoon I accompanied the major on a round of the batteries. Nests of Boche machine-gunners were still checking the advance of our infantry - they had fought heroically these fellows; but slowly, methodically, implacably the work of rooting them out was going on. Our farther advance was only a matter of hours now. "We're ordered not to risk too many casualties on this front," the Infantry brigadier had told the major. "The enemy will have to fall back when certain movements north and south of us are completed…. But we mustn't let him rest." Beale of A Battery had returned from the most crowded glorious experience of his young life. He had taken a gun forward to support two companies of the infantry who were striving to establish posts on the eastern side of the canal. Their progress was stayed by machine-guns and snipers, and the casualties were beginning to make the company commanders doubt if the operation was worth while. Beale reconnoitred with two platoon commanders and located the machine-guns, returned and brought his gun up, and from an open position fired over four hundred rounds; and afterwards went forward in front of the advanced posts to make sure that the machine-guns had been definitely put out of action. This brilliant effort enabled the infantry to move forward afterwards without a casualty. Dusty, flushed with the thrill of what he had been through, Beale knew that he had done fine work, and was frankly pleased by the kind things said about him.

The following day produced fresh excitements. Major Simpson had gone down to B Battery's waggon line to secure something like a night's rest - although I might say that after the spring of 1917 the Boche night-bombers saw to it that our waggon lines were no longer the havens of peace they used to be. Disaster followed. The Boche drenched the battery position with gas. Captain Denny, who had come up from the waggon line to relieve the major, was caught while working out the night-firing programme. Overbury, young Bushman, and another officer were also gassed; and eight men besides. C Battery were victims as well, and Henry and a number of the gunners had been removed to the Casualty Clearing Station.

And before lunch-time a briefly-worded order was received directing Major Mallaby-Kelby to report immediately to a Field Artillery Brigade of another Division. Orders are apt to arrive in this sudden peremptory fashion. Within an hour and a half the major had bidden good-bye to us and ridden off, a mess cart following with his kit. And Major Veasey came to reign in his stead.

Major Mallaby-Kelby left one souvenir, a bottle of the now famous white wine which had got mislaid - at least the cook explained it that way. The omission provided Brigade Headquarters with the wherewithal to drink the major's health.

At nine o'clock that night I stood with Major Veasey outside our headquarters dug-out. A mizzling rain descended. Five substantial fires were burning beyond the heights where the Boche lay. "What's the odds on the war ending by Christmas?" mused the major. "… I give it until next autumn," he added.

A battery of 60-pounders had come up close by. Their horses, blowing hard, had halted in front of our dug-out half an hour before, and the drivers were waiting orders to pull the guns the final three hundred yards into position. Two specks of lights showed that a couple of them were smoking cigarettes. "Look at those drivers," I said. "They've been here all this time and haven't dismounted yet."

The major stepped forward and spoke to one of the men. "Get off, lad, and give the old horse a rest. He needs it."

"Some of these fellows will never learn horse management though the war lasts ten years," he said resignedly as he went downstairs.

I remember our third and last night in that dug-out, because the air below had got so vitiated that candles would only burn with the feeblest of glimmers.

CHAPTER XIII

NURLU AND LIERAMONT

SEPTEMBER 6: The expected orders for the Brigade's farther advance arrived at 2 P.M., and by eight o'clock Wilde and myself had selected a new headquarters in a trench south of the wood. A tarpaulin and pit-prop mess had been devised: I had finished the Brigade's official War Diary for August; dinner was on the way; and we awaited the return of Major Veasey from a conference with the Infantry brigadier.

The major came out of the darkness saying, "We'll have dinner at once and then move immediately. There's a show to-morrow, and we must be over the canal before daybreak…. Heard the splendid news?… We've got right across the Drocourt Quéant line…. That's one reason why we are pushing here to-morrow."

We had a four-miles' march before us, and Manning and Meddings, our mess waiter and cook, farther down the trench, could be heard grumbling at the prospect of another packing-up, and a search in the dark for fresh quarters. "We always lose knives and forks and crockery when we move like this," Manning was saying in his heavy-dragoon voice.

"You and Wilde had better look for a headquarters somewhere near the cross-roads at Nurlu," the major told me. "The adjutant and myself will find where the batteries are and join you later."

There was a twenty minutes' delay because in the dark the G.S. waggon had missed us and vanished round the corner of the wood. As we moved off I felt a wet muzzle against my hand, and, stooping, perceived a dog that looked like a cross between an Airedale and a Belgian sheep-dog. "Hullo, little fellow!" I said, patting him. He wagged his tail and followed me.

The German shelling had died down, and we hoped for an uneventful journey. But night treks across ground that has been fought over usually test one's coolness and common-sense. The Boche had blown up the bridges over the canal, and descending the slope we had to leave the road and follow a track that led to an Engineers' bridge, so well hidden among trees that the enemy artillery had not discovered it. But it was a long time before our little column completed the crossing. A battery were ahead, and between them and us came a disjointed line of infantry waggons - horses floundering in the mud, men with torches searching for shell-holes and debris that had to be avoided. Only one vehicle was allowed on the bridge at a time, and a quarter to eleven came before the six mules scrambled the G.S. waggon over. The real difficulty, however, was to decide upon the track to take the other side of the canal. Maps were useless; these were tracks unknown to the topographers. Not one of them followed the general direction in which I believed Nurlu to be. I resolved to take the track that went south-east, and hoped to come upon one that would turn due east. Heavy shells, one every four minutes, rumbled high overhead, and crashed violently somewhere south of us. "They are shooting into Moislains," said Wilde. We trudged along hopefully.

The dog was still with us, running in small circles round me. "That must be the sheep-dog part of him," I said to Wilde. "He's a bit thin, but he seems a wiry little chap."

The looked-for track due east came when I began to think that we were drawing too near to where the big shells were falling. After half a mile we reached a metalled road; the track we had passed along went over and beyond it. The point to be decided now was whether to go straight on or to turn left along the road. Not a soul, not a single vehicle in sight; it was hard to believe that three Divisions were to make a big attack on the morrow. I halted the waggons on the road, and turned to Wilde. "Let's send Sergeant Starling (the signalling sergeant) to find where this track leads to. We'll walk up the road and find some one who can show it us on the map. There are bound to be dug-outs in this bank."

We walked for half a mile, meeting no one. The dog and an orderly accompanied us. In the distance my ear caught a familiar sound - the clip-clop of horses trotting. It came nearer and nearer. Then we saw a horseman, wearing the Artillery badge, leading a light draught horse.

"What battery do you belong to?" I asked, stopping him.

"B, sir."

"Where are you going now?"

"A shell came, sir, and hit our waggon. My traces were broke, and I'm going back to the waggon line, sir."

"Where is B Battery?"

"Up this road, sir, and I think you take a turning on the left, but I can't quite remember, sir; we had a bit of a mix-up."

"Bring up the waggons," I told the orderly. "We're on the right road. If Sergeant Starling isn't back, leave some one behind to bring him along."

Before long a jingling and a creaking told us that our carts were close at hand. We walked on, and, reaching a cross-roads, waited to shout for those behind to keep straight on. Half a minute afterwards I heard my name called. A single light shone out from a dug-out in the bank.

It was Garstin of C Battery who had hailed me. "Major Veasey is here with Major Bartlett," he said, coming towards us. The two majors were sitting in a dug-out no bigger than a trench-slit. "What do you think of my quarters?" smiled Major Bartlett. "Sorry I can't ask you to have a drink. Our mess cart hasn't arrived yet."

"We've found B and C, so far," interposed Major Veasey, puffing at his pipe, "and I must find the ———th Infantry Brigade before I finish to-night…. This road takes you direct to Nurlu, you know."

Wilde and I and the headquarters waggons resumed our march. We had reached a sunken portion of the road, when above us began the deep steady drone of Boche aeroplanes. We halted the waggons.

A wait, during which Lizzie, the big mare, whinnied, and we looked up and strained our ears to follow the path of the 'planes. Then, farther away than the whirring in the skies had led us to expect, came the ear-stabbing crack of the bombs. One! - two! - three! - four! - five! - six! in as quick succession as rifle-shots. "Damn 'em," said Wilde apprehensively. "I hope they don't get any of our horses."

We were quite near Nurlu now, and, leaving the waggons in the shelter of the sunken road, Wilde and I again forged ahead. An Army Field Brigade was forming its waggon lines in a field off the roadside amid sharp angry cries of "Keep those lights out!" Soon we approached another sunken road leading into the village. Through the hedge that rose above the bank I saw a black oblong hut. "Let's look at this place," I said.

In the darkness we made out a number of huts. A ring of sandbags showed where a tent had been pitched. Pushing away the blanket that covered the opening to a huge mined dug-out, we looked upon a row of sleeping engineers. "There are plenty of empty huts here," a corporal, half-awake, told us. It was past midnight. "This will do us for to-night," I said to Wilde.

A humming overhead reminded us that Boche 'planes still hovered near. As we came out of the dug-out a string of red lights floated downwards. A machine-gun spluttered, and a bullet pinged close to us. "What's he up to?" said Wilde, his eyes gleaming. We drew back. A bomb fell three hundred yards away; then another, and another. The ground shook; we thought of our waggons and horses in the road. The dog had dashed outside.

When the 'planes had passed, I sent the orderly to bring up the waggons. The horses went back to the other side of the canal; the men soon found cover for the night. Wilde and I made for the hut that we had noticed first of all. It was not very spacious - nor very clean: but it contained four wire beds to accommodate the major, the adjutant, Wilde, and myself. "Why, it's a guard-room," I called, shining my torch on a painted board affixed to the door.

So, for once in our lives, we slept in a guard-room. The little dog had curled himself up in a corner.

Sept. 7: Zero hour for the launching of the attack was 8 A.M., much later than usual. The village of Lieramont was the first objective, and afterwards the infantry were to push on and oust the Boche from

Guyencourt and Saulcourt. It was to be an attack on the grand scale, for the enemy had brought up one fresh Division and two others of known fighting capacity. He was likely to hold very stoutly to the high ground at Epéhy. Our A Battery was under orders to follow close on the heels of the infantry, to assist in wiping out machine-gun nests.

The camp in which we had settled overnight possessed at least three empty Nissen huts in good condition. The place had been captured from the British during the March retreat, and retaken not more than three days ago. Our guard-room sleeping quarters were not roomy enough for four simultaneous morning toilets; so I had my tin bowl and shaving articles taken over to one of the Nissen huts, and I stripped and managed a "bowl-bath" before breakfast. The dog, who had quite taken possession of me, stretched himself on the floor and kept an eye upon me.

The wily Boche had improved our Nissen huts. Trap-doors in the wooden floors and "funk-holes" down below showed how he feared our night-bombers. Jagged holes in the semicircular iron roofing proved the wisdom of his precautions.

By half-past eight a German 5·9 was planking shells over the camp, near enough for flying fragments to rattle against the roof and walls of the huts. Fifty rounds were fired in twenty minutes. The Boche gunners varied neither range nor direction; and no one was hurt. The shelling brought to light, however, a peculiarity of the dog. He chased away in the direction of each exploding shell, and tried also to pursue the pieces of metal that whizzed through the air. Nothing would hold him. When he returned, panting, it was to search for water; but after a short rest the shells lured him out again in vain excited quest.

Round his neck was a leather collar with a brass plate. The plate bore the name of a brigadier-general commanding an infantry brigade of a Division that had gone north. "No wonder he follows you," grinned Wilde. "He thinks you are a General…. It must be your voice, or the way you walk."

"More likely that I use the same polish for my leggings as the General," I retorted.

Major Veasey called me, and we started forth to see how the battle was progressing. The village of Lieramont had fallen very quickly, and Major Bullivant had already reported by mounted orderly that his battery had moved through the village, and come into action near the sugar factory.

"Oh, the leetle dawg!" said Major Veasey in wheedling tones, fondling the dog who frisked about him. Then he got his pipe going, and we strode through desolated Nurlu and made across rolling prairie land, broken by earthworks and shell-holes. A couple of heavy hows. were dropping shells on the grassy ridge that rose on our left - wasted shots, because no batteries were anywhere near. We stuck to the valley, and, passing a dressing station where a batch of walking cases were receiving attention, drew near to the conglomeration of tin huts, broken walls, and tumbled red roofs that stood for Lieramont. We stopped to talk to two wounded infantry officers on their way to a casualty clearing station. The advance had gone well, they said, except at Saulcourt, which was not yet cleared. They were young and fresh-coloured, imperturbable in manner, clear in their way of expressing themselves. One of them, jacketless, had his left forearm bandaged. Through a tear in his shirt sleeve I noticed the ugly purple scar of an old wound above the elbow. Odd parties of infantry and engineers stood about the streets. Plenty of wounded were coming through. I ran in to examine a house that looked like a possible headquarters of the future, and looked casually at a well that the Boche had blown in. The dog was still at my heels.

"Now we want to find the sugar factory to see how Bullivant is getting on," said the major, refilling his pipe. We pulled out maps and saw the factory plainly marked; and then followed a hard good-conditioned road that led over a hill.

We were getting now to a region where shells fell more freely. A mile to the north-east machine-gun duels were in progress. When we saw the wrecked factory with its queer-looking machinery - something like giant canisters - we pressed forward. No sign whatever of A Battery! I looked inside some tin huts: one had been used as a German mess, another as an officers' bath-house; flies swarmed upon old jam and meat tins; filth and empty bottles and stumps of candles, a discarded German uniform, torn Boche prints, and scattered picture periodicals. "There's no one here," mused Major Veasey. "I suppose the battery has moved forward again."

Beyond a tangled heap of broken machinery, that included a huge fly-wheel, bent and cracked, stood a big water-tank, raised aloft on massive iron standards. "We might be able to see something from up there," said the major. There was a certain amount of swarming to be done, and the major, giving up the contest, aided me to clamber up. Out of breath I stood up in the dusty waterless tank, and got out my binoculars. Towards where the crackle of machine-guns had been heard, I saw a bush-clad bank. Tucked up against it were horses and guns. Big Boche shells kept falling near, and the landscape was wreathed in smoke.

Before we got to the battery we met Major Bullivant, whose gestures alone were eloquent enough to describe most war scenes. A rippling sweep of his left arm indicated where two machine-gun nests on the bosky western slopes of Saulcourt held up our infantry; a swan-like curl of the right wrist, raised to the level of the shoulder, told where A Battery had been situated, less than a thousand yards from the enemy. "A company of the —— were faltering because of the deadliness of the machine-guns," he said. "… I got hold of a platoon commander and he took me far enough forward to detect their whereabouts…. We fired 200 rounds when I got back to the battery. My gunners popped them off in find style, although the Boche retaliated…. The infantry have gone on now…. I found two broken machine-guns and six dead Germans at the spots we fired at…. It's been quite a good morning's work."

He smiled an adieu and went off to join a company commander he had arranged to meet. When we reached the bank A Battery were about to move to a sunken road farther forward. Smallman, from South Africa, nicknamed "Buller," was in charge, and he pointed joyously to an abandoned Boche Red Cross waggon that the battery had "commandeered." Four mules had been harnessed to it; the battery waggon line was its destination.

"Gee-ho! they went off in a hurry from here," remarked Major Veasey, looking at a light engine and three trucks loaded with ammunition and corrugated iron that the enemy had failed to get away on the narrow-gauge line running past Saulcourt. "What we ought to do is to have a railway ride back. The line goes to Nurlu. That would be a new experience - and I'm tired enough."

"Yes, that would be better than the four-in-hand in the G.S. waggon that you took to the sports meeting," I added.

A Hun 5·9 was firing persistently on a spot 400 yards between Saulcourt and where we stood. For once in a way the dog neglected shells, and searched for bully-beef leavings among the tins thrown aside by the battery drivers. We were not absolutely safe. The Boche shells were fitted with instantaneous fuses, and after each burst bits of jagged iron flew off at right angles to points as far distant as 700 yards. As we turned to go a piece whistled over our heads and hit one of the Red Cross waggon lead-mules. The poor beast dropped and brought down his frightened, kicking, companion mule also. The drivers had released them by the time Major Veasey and I came up. The wounded mule found his feet, and was led a few yards away. A horrible tear, 8 inches long, showed a smashed jawbone and cheekbone; he moved his head from side to side in his pain. "I shall have to shoot him," said the major, loading his revolver. The mule stared dully as the major approached, but drew back sharply when he saw the revolver. The driver could not hold him properly, and the first bullet-hole was not the half-inch to an inch below the forelock that means instantaneous death. The poor animal fell, but got up again and staggered away. The major had to follow and shoot again.

We struck off in a more northerly direction on our way back to Nurlu, searching for the forward section of B Battery that had been told off to work in conjunction with a certain Infantry battalion. We met Wheater, who was commanding the section, and he told the major that he had not taken his two guns farther forward, because the battalion commander had gone off in a hurry without giving him instructions, without even telling him the line the infantry had reached.

"How long have you been here?" asked the major pointedly.

"Three hours, sir."

"Well, my dear fellow, you certainly should have taken your guns farther forward by now, battalion commander or no battalion commander. You've got a mounted orderly, and you could have sent him back to Brigade Headquarters, informing them of your new position. Then you could have got into touch with the infantry and asked them for targets. It's useless staying here."

The arrival on horseback of the major-general commanding the Division attacking in this portion of the front turned the conversation. Not long appointed to his present command, the General during the March retreat had been the senior Infantry brigadier in our own Division. He was a particularly able and resourceful soldier; his first demand was for information regarding the work done by our forward guns. The major told him that Wheater's section remained where it was because of the neglect of the battalion commander.

The General listened quietly, and cast a keen eye upon Wheater, "You can take your guns up in safety to Guyencourt, and you'll find plenty to shoot at there. Tell any one who wants to know that your instructions come direct from the Divisional commander.... And don't rely too much on battalion commanders. Very few battalion commanders know anything about artillery. It's a pity, but it's a fact." He responded with dignity to our salutes, and rode off, followed by his attendant staff officers and the grooms.

The major got more and more tired of the walking. It was half-past two now, and we were both pretty hungry. The dog seemed as frisky and energetic as when he chased the shells at breakfast-time. We passed a big dressing station; a wheeled stretcher stood outside. "As we didn't take a train ride, should I push you back in that, major?" I inquired with due seriousness. Major Veasey smiled, and we started on the last mile and a half.

There were prospects, we learned when we got back to Nurlu and read the reports received by the adjutant, of another move forward for the batteries.

"This looks like bringing the waggon lines over the canal," said the adjutant, showing the major the following wire from the staff captain:-

"Good spring at V 201 b 2.7. Water-cart filling-point being arranged. Approaches good for water-carts. Troughs now in order at V 202 c 8.5."

Another message of the same tenor, having to do with gun repairs, ran -

"No. 347 light shop moves to Moislains to-morrow. Will undertake quick repairs. Longer jobs will be sent back to Nos. 124 B—— and 192 F——."

A third telegram supplied a reminder that the spiteful Boche still had time to leave devilish traps for the unwary -

"Advanced guard ——th Division found small demolition charges in Nissen hut at W 123 b 8.9, and mined dug-out W 129 d 3.2."

"Yes," remarked Major Veasey, "we are certain to move again to-night. The wise man will take a lie down until tea-time." And he hied him to the wire bed in the guard-room.

*　　*　　*　　*　　*

At 8.15 that night Wilde and I, the Headquarters party, and the dog, having waited an hour and a half for the orderly that Major Veasey had promised to send back to guide us to a new headquarters, settled in some old German gun-pits, scooped out of a lofty chalk bank. Our march had brought us through Lieramont and beyond the shell-mauled cemetery where the Boche in his quest of safety had transformed the very vaults into dug-outs.

The horses were sent back to the waggon line and the drivers told to bring them up again at 6 A.M.; and I was arranging the relief of the orderly stationed on the roadside to look out for the major when the major's special war-whoop broke cheerily through the darkness. "The opening of the gun-pit faces the wrong way, and we have no protection from shells - but the tarpaulin will keep any rain out," was the best word I could find for our new quarters.

It was a moderately calm night. We four officers lay down side by side with just our valises to soften the ruggedness of the ground. Fitful flashes in front showed our own guns firing; high-velocity shells, bursting immediately behind us, made us ponder on the possibility of casualties before the night was out. But we were dog-tired, and slept well; and by 7 A.M. the dog no longer snuggled against my feet, and we were preparing for further departure.

"We come under the ———th Divisional Artillery at 7.30, and have to settle in Lieramont and await orders," explained Major Veasey. "They don't want our Brigade to push on…. They say that the infantry could have walked into Epéhy without trouble, but they were too fagged. The latest report is that the Boche is back there again."

Our chief aim when we walked back towards Lieramont was to secure decent quarters before troops coming up should flood the village. Our first discovery was a Nissen hut in a dank field on the eastern outskirts. It wanted a good deal of tidying up, but 'twould serve. We were ravenous for breakfast, and the cook got his wood-fire going very quickly. There were tables and chairs to be found, and the dog and I crossed the road, russet-red with the bricks from broken houses that had been used to repair it, on a journey of exploration. Built close to a high hedge was an extra large Nissen hut, painted with the Red Cross sign. Inside twenty wire beds in tiers; dozens of rolls of German lint and quantities of cotton-wool littered the floor. Outside, five yards from the door, lay the body of a British officer. A brown blanket covered all but his puttees and a pair of neat, well-made brown boots.

Through an opening in the hedge we came upon more Nissen huts. One of them was divided by a partition, and would do for a mess and for officers' sleeping quarters. Another large building could accommodate the men, and I found also a cook-house and an office. I used chalk freely in "staking-out" our claim, and hurried back to the major in a fever of fear lest some one else should come before we could install ourselves.

There were three incidents by which I shall remember our one night's stay in Lieramont. First, the men's cook discovered a German officer's silver-edged iron cross. One of the servants, a noted searcher after unconsidered trifles, had found a Boche officer's overcoat in one of the huts. He went through the pockets and threw the coat away. The cook, coming after him, picked up the coat, and, "Blow me," said he, "if this didn't fall out."

Also, while Major Veasey, Major Simpson, and Major Bullivant were standing talking, a British soldier, pushing a bicycle, passed along the road. Following him, sometimes breaking into a run to keep up, came a plump, soft-faced German boy in infantry uniform, the youngest German I had seen in France. "Why, he's only a kid," said Major Veasey. "He can't be more than sixteen."

"Was ist ihr regiment?" called Major Bullivant. I took it that the major was asking the youngster to what regiment he belonged.

The British private and his prisoner stopped. The boy Boche smiled sheepishly, yet rather pleasantly, and said something which I didn't understand, and don't believe Major Bullivant did either.

There was a half-minute pause. Then the practical British private moved on, calling simply, "Come on, Tich!" The phrase, "He followed like a lamb," became appropriate.

And I remember one further episode, not so agreeable. Major Veasey and myself had been to call on the Divisional Artillery, under whose orders we were now working. When we returned the dead British officer still lay outside the Red Cross hut. But the neat brown boots had been removed.

"By God, that's a ghoulish bit of work," said the major, angry disgust in his face. "The man who did that is a cur."

CHAPTER XIV

THE FIGHT FOR RONSSOY

SEPTEMBER 16: The first autumn tints were spreading over field and tree, and the tempestuous rains of the last few days had chilled the air; but the weather had righted itself now, and would prove no bar to the next advance, which it was whispered would take place on the 18th. The American offensive at St Mihiel on the 12th had undoubtedly keyed-up our men, and any one supposed to know anything at all was being button-holed for fore-casts of the extent of the Allies' giant thrust up to the time of the winter rains.

There had been a four days' withdrawal of our Brigade to more peaceful areas behind the line, and, praise the Saints! we had again come under our own Divisional Artillery.

The colonel had returned, and, as usual, the first day or so after coming off leave, appeared preoccupied and reserved. Still there was no one like our colonel; and, in the serene atmosphere of his wise unquestioned leadership, petty bickerings, minor personal troubles, and the half-jesting, half-bitter railings against higher authority, had faded away. He brought the news that the medical board in England would not permit the C.R.A. to return to France; and the appointment of C.R.A. had gone to the colonel of our companion Field Artillery Brigade, now the senior Field Artillery officer in the Division - a popular honour, because, though we thought there could be no colonel so good as ours, - we should not have been such a good Brigade had we admitted any other belief, - we all knew Colonel —— to be a talented and experienced gunner, and a brave man, with great charm of manner. Besides, it kept the appointment in the family, so to speak. We wanted no outsider from another Division. "You must all congratulate General —— when you meet him," said our colonel gently.

The four days behind the line had been interesting in their way, despite the rain-storms. We had hot baths and slept in pyjamas once more. Some of the younger officers and a few of the N.C.O.'s had made a long lorry trip to Abbeville to replace worn-out clothes. Major Bullivant and the adjutant had borrowed a car to search for almost forgotten mess luxuries; and coming back had given a lift to a *curé*, who in the dark put his foot in the egg-box, smashing twenty of the eggs. There had been the booby-trap in the blown-up dug-out. A chair that almost asked to be taken stood half-embedded in earth near the doorway. I was about to haul it away to the mess when I perceived a wire beneath it, and drew back. Afterwards some sappers attached more wire, and, from a safe distance, listened to a small explosion that would have meant extreme danger to any one standing near. Also there had been the dead horse that lay unpleasantly near our mess. Major Veasey, "Swiffy," the doctor, our rollicking interpreter M. Phineas, and myself all took turns at digging a hole for its burial; and there was plenty of laughter, because old Phineas refused to go near the horse without swathing his face in a scarf, and when wielding the pick raised it full-stretch above his head before bringing it, with slow dignity, to earth - for all the world like a church-bell-ringer. Two nights in succession German night-bombers had defied our anti-aircraft guns and brought cruel death to horses camped alongside the canal. On the second night we had witnessed a glorious revenge. Our search-lights had concentrated upon a Gotha, and they refused to let it escape their glare. Then suddenly from up above came the putt-puttr-putt of machine-guns. Red and blue lights floated down; the swift streakings of inflammatory bullets clove the cobalt sky; with ecstasy we realised that one of our airmen was in close combat with the invader. When the enemy 'plane crashed to earth, a blazing holocaust, cheers burst from hundreds of tent-dwellers who had come out to view the spectacle.

And now on the 16th of September we had pitched tents a mile south of Lieramont, which we had left on the 9th, on the confines of a wood that stretched down to a road and fringed it for three parts of a mile to the village of Templeux la Fosse. Wilde and the adjutant had departed in high spirits, and their best clothes, to catch the leave train, and I was doing adjutant. Hubbard, a new officer from D Battery, who before getting his commission had been a signalling sergeant, filled Wilde's shoes. I had ridden into Templeux la Fosse to conduct a polite argument with the officer of a Division newly arrived from Palestine on the matter of watering arrangements. His point was that his Division had reached the area first and got the pumps into working order, and his instructions were to reserve the troughs for the horses of his own Division. I argued that if our horses did not water in Templeux they would have to do a seven-mile journey three times a day to the next nearest *abreuvoir*. "And you can't claim the exclusive use of a watering-point unless Corps grants special permission," I concluded.

"But Corps haven't instructed you to water here," he persisted.

"Neither have they told us *not* to come here," I countered.

We parted, agreeing to refer the whole matter to Corps. Corps, I might add, ruled that we should be allowed to water 200 horses per hour at certain hours, and that the other Division should police the performance.

I had returned in time to administer the distribution of fifty-nine remounts come from the base to replace battery horses killed by bombs and shell-fire, or evacuated by "Swiffy," our veterinary officer, to the Mobile Veterinary Section, as a result of the hard-going and watering difficulties since the advance started on August 8th.

I was talking to the staff captain about the ammunition dumps he had arranged for the coming battle, when the brigade clerk handed me a buff slip just arrived from the Casualty Clearing Station. It stated simply that 2nd Lieut. Garstin had died as the result of gun-shot wounds. Poor boy! a handsome well-mannered youngster, who had come out to France practically from school.

I finished talking to the staff captain and walked to the colonel's tent. I told him of Garstin's death.

"Wounded last night taking up ammunition, wasn't he?" said the colonel gravely.

"Yes, sir. He had finished the job and was coming back towards Lieramont. Two of the men were wounded as well."

The colonel pulled out the note-book in which he kept his list of the officers in the Brigade.

"That leaves C Battery very short of officers. You'd better transfer - let me see - M'Whirter from 'B.'… And ask the staff captain if we can have an officer from the D.A.C."

A little later I sent out the following wire to B and C Batteries:-

"2nd Lieut. J. M'Whirter will be attached to C Battery on receipt of this message. 2nd Lieut. F.E.R. Collinge of No. 1 Section D.A.C. will join B Battery to-day."

The night bristled with excitements. No. 1 Section of the D.A.C., with two hundred horses, were camped a hundred yards from us, and at 9 P.M. I was in their mess, talking books of the day, horses, and stage gossip. A lull in the conversation was broken by the low unmistakable drone of an enemy aeroplane. It sounded right overhead. "What's happened to our anti-aircraft people?" said Major Brown, starting up from the table. "How's he got through as far as this without any one shooting at him?"

We waited in silence. I wondered what had become of the dog, who had followed me, but had remained outside the trench-cover mess.

The first bomb crashed near enough to put out the candles and rattle the glasses on the table. "That fell over there," said the padre, pointing to behind the wood. "No, it was on this side, not far from my horses," put in Major Brown quickly.

Three more bombs shook the ground beneath us. Then we heard more distant explosions.

Outside we saw torch flashings in the D.A.C. horse lines, and heard hurrying to and fro. "Swiffy" also had run down to give his aid.

So serious had been the loss of horses through bombing during the summer of 1918 that after each fatal raid an official report had to be forwarded and a formal inquiry held to decide whether full precautions for the safety of the horses had been taken. At 9.30 P.M. I received this note from Major Brown:-

"The following casualties occurred to animals of this Section by hostile bombs at 7 P.M. on 16th inst. -
"Map location D 230, c. 97: killed, 7; wounded, 11."

Half an hour later a message from C Battery, who were a mile and a half away along the valley, informed me that their casualties in horses and mules numbered 19.

At two in the morning I was aroused by a furious beating of wind and rain upon the tent. Hubbard, already in receipt of wet on his side of the tent, was up fastening the entrance-flap, which had torn loose. Sharp flashes of lightning and heavy thunder accompanied the squall when it reached its height. "I hope the pegs hold," shouted Hubbard, and we waited while the tent-sides strained and the pole wavered. The dog growled, and a scuffling behind us was followed by the appearance, at the back of the tent, of the colonel's head and shoulders. In his pyjamas, drenched and shivering with cold, he struggled inside. "My tent's down," he called sharply. "Houston's got my kit into his bivouac.... You two fellows hop outside and hammer in the pegs.... Let's save this tent if we can.... And some one lend me a towel for a rub down!"

Wrapped in rain-coats, Hubbard and myself faced the skirling rain. When we slipped inside again the colonel had dried himself. I lent him a blanket and my British warm, and he settled himself contentedly on the ground, refusing to occupy either camp-bed.

"The annoying part," he said, with the boyish ring in his voice that made his laugh so attractive, "is that my tent was much better put up than yours."

The wind still blew when we got up in the morning. A valiant tale came from "Swiffy," the doctor, and M. Phineas. They occupied a tent 'twixt a bank and a hedge, nearer to the D.A.C.M. Phineas had held up the pole with folds of wet canvas alternately choking him or whirling round him, while "Swiffy" yelled for him to kneel upon the tent bottom to keep it fast, and expected him to fetch a servant at the same time. The doctor, enfolded by the wanton canvas in another state compartment of the blown-about tent, was cut off from communication with the other two, and fought the battle on his own.

The struggle to keep the tents from collapsing was crowned at 6 A.M. by the urgent and peremptory order from Division: "All tents in the Divisional forward area are to be struck before dawn."

It was an order that breathed an understanding fear of the inquisitive eyes of enemy aerial observers. But if the G.S.O. who issued the order really knew ——

* * * * *

Under cover of the darkness the Brigade moved up 6000 yards to secret positions for the morrow's battle. We were behind our own infantry once again, and it was to be a big advance. We had come over forty miles since August 8 in a series of three-to eight-mile leaps; for the third time the battalions had been brought up to something like strength, and they were full of fight. In the mud and slime of the Somme and Flanders in 1916 and 1917, when each advance was on a narrow front and ceased after a one-day effort, I always marvelled at the patient, fatalistic heroism of the infantry. A man went "over the top" understanding that, however brilliant the attack, the exultant glory of continuous chase of a fleeing, broken enemy would not be his; and that, should he escape wounds or death, it would not be long before he went "over the top" again, and yet again. But this open fighting had changed all that. It showed results for his grit and endurance to the humblest "infanteer." And remember, it was the civilian soldier - unversed in war, save actual war - who accepted and pushed home the glorious opportunities of achievement that these wondrous days offered.

The colonel and I mounted our horses at eight o'clock, saw C and D Batteries begin their march, and called upon the new C.R.A. in his hut-headquarters at Lieramont. He was genuinely pleased at being congratulated upon his appointment, and, I remember, produced for me a Havana, come straight from London. Both the General and the brigade-major had good things to say of the dog, who was now definitely known as "Ernest" - chiefly because I had said "Hullo" to call him so many times that inevitably one recalled Mr. Frank Tinney and his mode of addressing his stage assistant.

From Lieramont the colonel and myself rode eastwards two miles and a half. The road was crowded with waggons and horses, returning in orderly fashion from delivering ammunition. In the distance guns boomed. When we got to the *pavé* the colonel said we would walk across country the rest of the way. Our horses had only been gone a couple of minutes when the colonel suddenly halted and exclaimed, "I've let Laneridge go back with my steel helmet."

"Should we wait a few minutes on the road, sir?" I responded quickly; "Laneridge is likely to come back and try to catch you…. Of course he doesn't know where our headquarters will be."

For answer the colonel stood in the centre of the road and shouted with studied clearness - "Laneridge!… Laneridge!"

We tried a joint call, and repeated it; but there was no sound of returning hoofs.

One curious result followed. An infantry soldier, who had passed us, came back and, in a north-country accent, asked, "Beg pardon, sir, but did you call me? - my name's Laneridge, sir."

"No," said the colonel, "I was calling my groom."

The man passed on. "That's a really striking coincidence," remarked the colonel. "Laneridge is not a common name."

After waiting five minutes we continued our walk, and crossing a valley dotted with abandoned gun-pits and shallow dug-outs, came to a shrub-covered bank from which a battery was pulling out its guns.

"Our headquarters will be here," said the colonel succinctly. "Hubbard has been sorting things out. There are dug-outs along the bank, and I expect we shall find something in the trench down there."

Hubbard had indeed found a place for the mess in the trench, while he pointed to a cubby-hole in the bank that would do for the colonel, and to another shelter, a yard high from roof to floor, in which he and I could lie down. The telephone lines to the batteries and to Div. Art. were laid. He was ready for the battle.

Zero hour was at 5.20 A.M. The battery commanders had received the operation orders during the afternoon. I reported our arrival to the brigade-major; and not worrying much about some hostile 'planes that seemed to be dropping bombs in the neighbourhood of the front line, we turned in.

At 1.30 A.M. the telephone near my head buzzed. I heard the colonel say, "Are you troubled by gas?"

"Haven't noticed any, sir."

"You had better have your box-respirator ready. It seems to be coming in a cloud down the valley."

I dozed off again, but half an hour later the uneasy movements of "Ernest" roused me. I sneezed several times, and felt a burning in the throat. This was undoubtedly gas. Hubbard I found to be a heavy sleeper, but by punching hard enough I made him open his eyes, and we put on our box-respirators. It was half an hour before the gas sergeant reported that the air had cleared. We slept once more. Half an hour before zero time the gas rattle sounded again, and indeed we were wearing our respirators, when at 5.20 the usual sudden crackle and rumble all along the front announced the opening of the barrage. Judged by the quickness with which he put down a retaliatory barrage, the enemy was prepared for our attack. Nothing could now hold "Ernest." He dashed tirelessly north, south, east, west, towards whichever point of the compass he heard a gun firing or a shell exploding. "I'm sure that dog's mad," commented the colonel when we breakfasted at 7 A.M. "I watched him from my dug-out for three-quarters of an hour after the barrage started. He passed the opening eighty times, then I got tired of counting. He seems to take a marvellous interest in shells…. It's a pity the staff captain can't use him for ammunition returns."

While we were conducting a settled defence of the line, or registering our guns for a battle, no one visited the "O.P.'s," or the front line, more than the colonel. Many and many a morning, with a couple of sandwiches and a slab of chocolate in his pocket, he tramped to the O.P. and stayed there until dark, criticising the shooting of the batteries and finding fresh targets for their fire. But during a set battle he did all his work on the telephone, in touch with Divisional artillery one way, and with the batteries, the F.O.O.'s, and the infantry the other. There is never much news during the first hour, or even until the full artillery programme has been completed. By that time the Brigade expects definite reports as to whether the infantry have reached their objectives, and upon what new points they require artillery assistance for consolidating positions, or for repelling counter-attacks.

But on this occasion the first message reached Brigade at 5.50 A.M. C Battery reported that immediately the barrage opened the Boche retaliated upon them with 5.9's. They had had six killed and ten wounded. The killed included the sergeant who so splendidly commanded C's forward sniping-gun on that bewildering, nerve-testing March 21st.

I spoke to the other batteries. D Battery, and B, who had horses handy to move forward when the first objective was taken, had been little troubled, but A had had their mess smashed in, and three of the servants wounded. I rang up "Buller," who was doing liaison with the ———th Infantry Brigade, and he said it was understood that two companies of the ——— had lost their way, but generally the attack proceeded well.

The uncertainty lasted until 11 A.M., when the colonel completed a telephone conversation with the brigade-major. The Division on our left had not gained its first objective because of exceedingly stout opposition on the part of a German corps, who had gained a fine fighting reputation during the past two weeks. The ———th south of our Division had done very well, capturing and advancing beyond the village of Templeux le Guerard. Our Divisional infantry had cleared Ronssoy after tough fighting, but their farther progress was checked because of the hold-up on the left. Reserve battalions of the Division chiefly affected by this resistance were to attack as soon as possible.

"The Australians have done extraordinarily well down south," the colonel told me. "They simply marched through with their tanks, capturing guns and prisoners wholesale, and are on their most distant objective."

Then he rang up Major Simpson. "Don't take your battery forward until you get definite orders from the Brigade," he said. "The enemy still hold the high ground north of us."

Major Bullivant, always keen on making an early reconnaissance during a set battle, rang up at noon to say that he had been as far as a high wood, a mile and a half in front of his battery. "I got a very long view from there," he went on, "and saw no sign at all of any Boche...."

The colonel, putting on his pince-nez, studied his map and asked the major for the exact position. "Yes," he observed, "that's on the 140 contour, and you must have seen as far as —— copse."

His next remark revealed how his mind was working. "Did you notice any tracks from the wood towards the batteries?... Two tracks!... but my map shows a line of barbed wire running across.... Good!... there is a useable track as far as 19 c, and by striking east before you come to the cross tracks it is possible to find an opening in the wire.... Good, Bullivant.... I expect I shall move the batteries that way.... No, no orders to move yet!"

At 1.15 P.M., after further talks with the brigade-major, the colonel told me to send out this message to the four batteries:-

> "Brigade will advance as soon as possible to position in F 20, or if that locality is full up, in F 21 c. Prepare to advance, and report to Brigade commander at F 20 c 4, 2."

The colonel's horses had been ordered up from the waggon line. "Hubbard and I will go on," he told me, "and Hubbard can commence laying out lines to the batteries' new positions. You will remain here to keep in touch with Division. I shall be back before we move, and batteries are not to go forward until orders are issued from here."

He returned at 4 P.M. and told me to send out orders for an immediate advance to the positions chosen. I was returning from the signallers' dug-out when a young major belonging to the ——s passed, followed by a sergeant. The major looked pale and worn, but walked quickly. There are moments when personal acquaintance with members of other branches of the Service possesses a very direct value. I did not know Major —— very well, but a habit contracted through frequent visits to the Infantry made me call out "Any news?"

"Our Brigade's doing a clearing-up attack at five o'clock," he answered without stopping.

"We don't know anything about that," I said, catching him up. "How long is it since orders were issued?"

"I've only just left the General," he replied, still walking ahead.

"Can you spare two minutes to explain the scheme to the colonel," I pressed. "Our batteries are just about to move up."

"I hardly have time to get to the battalion," he answered with a frown of dissent.

"Two minutes!" I pleaded - and succeeded. We hurried to the mess. There was a quick, clear exchange of words between the major and the colonel. The major sped away as the colonel thanked him. "Telephone at once to the batteries to prevent them moving!" said the colonel, turning to me.

Before five minutes had passed, the colonel, after a telephone talk with the brigadier-general, had arranged a short barrage programme for the batteries.

"There's usefulness in your being a gossip, you see," he smiled, a quarter of an hour later.

The orders for the batteries to advance still held good, and immediately the barrage ceased they pulled out. By 6 P.M. the colonel had ridden forward again. My instructions were to remain until the divisional signalling officer had laid a line to the new Brigade Headquarters. At eight o'clock, followed by "Ernest" and the Brigade signallers who had stayed with me, I rode through St Emilie and dipped into a cul-de-sac valley crowded with the field batteries of another Division. Our way took us toward and across gorse-clad, wild-looking uplands. Night approached. Just as we halted at a spot where two puddly, churned-up sunken roads crossed, guns behind and on either side of us belched forth flame and rasping sound. Eighteen-pounder shells screamed swiftly over us; the whole countryside spurted flashes. One of the horses plunged with nervousness. "It's an S.O.S. call, sir," said a driver who had put his horse under a bank, raising his voice against the din. "Ernest," his little body quivering with excitement, was already racing backwards and forwards. I told my groom to take my horse into the sunken road, and started to look for the colonel and the headquarters party. A sticky walk up the track to the left took me within a couple of hundred yards of the village of Ronssoy, where most of the Boche shells were falling. No signs of Headquarters up there. After a lot of shouting to persuade the dog to keep near me, I turned back and went through the mud again, past the cross-roads junction, and along a still slimier, water-logged cart-track. I found every one on Headquarters digging shelters in the side of the road. The servants had rigged up a corrugated-iron habitation for the colonel. The brigade clerks, the signallers, and the cooks had dug hard, and made use of trench-covers, with the swift resource that long experience of trench-life had developed into a kind of second nature. Hubbard had arranged an "elephant," raised on two rows of ancient sandbags, for himself and me to snuggle under.

"I've sent out S.O.S. lines to the batteries," said the colonel, who was sitting on a box in a long-disused gun-pit. "We'll turn this place into a mess to-morrow."

The firing died down. I sent some one to tell the groom to take the horses back to the waggon line which was being established at the headquarters position we had just left. The cook prepared us a simple meal. By 10 P.M. the brigade-major had telephoned instructions for the night-firing with which the batteries were to busy themselves. Our night was disturbed by the swish-plop of gas shells, but none came near enough seriously to disquiet us.

CHAPTER XV
"ERNEST" IS LOST

S EPTEMBER 19: That morning Bob Pottinger reported at Brigade Headquarters, smiling all over his face. An extra leave warrant had come in, and it was his turn to go. For weeks past every one had known of his eagerness to get home, in order to conduct certain matrimonial projects to the "Yes or No" stage. Leave to England was going nicely now. Dumble, young Beale, Judd, and Hetherington were away, and the men were going at the rate of five per day. Officers had to be five months in France since their last leave - mostly it ran to seven; the men's qualification was twelve months. Happy is the army that is attacking! Only when the enemy has full possession of the initiative is leave entirely cut off.

Of the 5 P.M. attack carried out the night before by the ———th Brigade, all that we knew was that unexpectedly large numbers of the enemy had been met. The fighting had been fierce, and the Boche still held some of the ground the Brigade had set out to take. Right through the night our guns had been busy firing protective bursts.

The mystery of the Boche's unlooked-for strength was explained by a Divisional wire that reached us about 8 A.M. It stated that a prisoner captured by the ———th Brigade said that at 7 A.M. on the 18th, following urgent orders resulting from the British offensive at 5.20, a whole Boche division came by bus from Maretz, fourteen miles back. Their mission was to make a counter-attack that would win back the original line. They deployed at Bony, near the canal, and completed their march in readiness for an attack at 6 P.M. But the 5 P.M. thrust by our ———th Brigade completely surprised them, and in fact broke up their offensive. The prisoner also reported that many casualties had been caused by our artillery fire.

The brigade-major, telephoning at 9 A.M., told us further details about the main offensive of the day before. The hold-up on our left had continued until late in the evening, in spite of renewed attacks on a big scale. "The German Alpine Corps have some of the stiffest fighters we have run against for a long time," he went on. "On the outskirts of Epéhy one post was held by three officers and forty-five men until 7.45 P.M. When they surrendered there were only seventeen not wounded."

The sunken road we were occupying led towards the red-brick, modern-looking village of Templeux-le-Guerard. A German encampment, quite a large one, containing several roomy huts newly built and well fitted up, stood outside the eastern edge of the village. The colonel had just pointed out that any amount of material for the improvement of our Headquarters was to be had for the fetching, and I had despatched the wheeler and a party of servants and signallers to the German encampment when the telephone bell rang.

It was the brigade-major again. "We're doing another attack," he said cheerfully, "to finish the work started last evening.... I want you to open on line F 10 c 2.0 to F 16 b 0.8.... Dwell there till 11.20.... Then creep 1100 yards in a north-easterly direction - 100 yards each four minutes - to F 11 a 4.0 to F 11 d 2.5.... Dwell twenty minutes.... Then creep 100 yards each four minutes to F 11 b 1.3 to F 11 d 8.7.... 4·5 hows. on Sart Farm.... Open at Rapid Rate on start-line for first four minutes.... Then go to Normal Rate for the creep, and Slow on final protective barrage.... Is that clear?... Right!... Good-bye."

I had repeated the map co-ordinates as the brigade-major gave them, and had written them down; and the colonel, coming in to the mess, followed the telephone conversation on his map. I handed him my note-book, and for five minutes he worked in his rapid silent way, with his ivory pocket-rule and scale for measuring map co-ordinates. Then he told the telephonist on duty to get him each battery in turn; and the Brigade was soon a stage nearer in its preparations for supporting the Infantry brigade selected to make the attack.

Ten minutes later the brigade-major again rang up to say that the how. battery was required to fire smoke-shells on certain points.

Before the fight began the colonel made a tour of the batteries. The party sent to the German camp returned with forms and tables, and plenty of corrugated iron and boards; and it was while I was detailing a party of them to dig a sleeping-place for the colonel farther into the bank that a group of officers, headed by a red-tabbed staff captain, came along. Even if I had not recognised him from his portraits - or because two winters before the war he and I stayed in the same hotel at Nice - there was no doubt as to his identity. Name and title appeared written in indelible pencil on his box-respirator. He told me he was looking for a headquarters for his brigade, and he had heard that the sunken road was a likely spot. "I don't know how long we shall be here," I replied, "but we intend to carry out as many improvements as possible. It will be a decent place to take over when we leave." And I indicated the digging party. "Ernest," as usual, was extremely affable, and received any amount of petting and patting from the visiting officers. Just as they departed the assistant brigade clerk came to me with a batch of men's leave warrants. I went into the mess, and was occupied signing the warrants and other documents for ten minutes or so. When I came out there was no sign of "Ernest." Ten minutes later the attack started and the air was fluttered with the swish and scream of shells.

An hour passed. The colonel returned. We lunched. Afterwards the colonel removed his jacket, did a bit of sawing, and directed the wheeler and his party in the task of boarding-in our gun-pit mess, so as to leave it no longer exposed to wind and rain on two sides. Hubbard, who was proud of his strength, climbed on top and pulled and shifted the three six-inch girders to more suitable positions. I took a turn with pick and shovel in the improvement of the colonel's dug-out. The dog had not come back. One of the orderlies thought he had seen him running along with the officers who had called before lunch.

About half-past three the brigade-major called for our 18-pounders to drive off another Boche wave with a half-hour's shower of shrapnel; he also wanted our how. battery to devote itself to Sart Farm and Holland Post, which forward observers reported to be little strongholds of enemy trench-mortars and machine-guns. Still no sign of "Ernest." The mess-cart arrived at five o'clock, and as a last resource I scribbled a note to the doctor, who was as fond of the dog as any of us, describing the titled staff captain, and urging him to scour the countryside until he struck a trail that would lead to "Ernest's" recovery.

At 7.30 P.M. an S.O.S. call, telephoned by Drysdale, who was doing liaison with the ——th Infantry Brigade, showed how desperately the Boche was contesting the occupation of the strong points on this portion of the front, although a Corps Intelligence Summary, delivered about the same time, told us that 60 officers and 2315 other ranks, wounded and unwounded, had passed through the Corps prisoners of war cages since 6 A.M. the day before, and that the strength of the average Hun infantry company had been reduced to 60 rifles.

As the colonel, Hubbard, and myself sat down to dinner, the following message was handed to me:-

"Wire has been laid out to O.P. at F 16 c 42 by B and C Batteries. The contours on the small paper 1/20,000 map are not correct in this neighbourhood. New zero line was registered on Tombois Farm."

"Yes, I've already warned the batteries that the special maps are not reliable," commented the colonel.

The end of the day found our infantry in possession of most of the strong points they had striven to seize, but at a heavy cost. And all through the night our batteries poured forth fierce deadly fire to harass and nullify Hun efforts to loosen our grip.

It was the same sort of warfare next day. The fighting was carried out yard by yard. There was a certain post, Doleful Post, very valuable to the Boche because it dominated the immediate neighbourhood. It was our batteries' business to make it hellishly uncomfortable for him. At 10 A.M. the colonel, after a talk with Division, ordered the Brigade to bring harassing fire to bear during the next twenty-four hours upon Doleful Post and the valley running north-east from it. The three 18-pdr. batteries were to work in two-hour shifts, firing 50 rounds an hour;

the 4·5 how. battery was to fire 15 rounds per hour continuously. Next day the infantry were to storm the post, and thus secure a jumping-off spot for another forward leap.

With a more or less settled programme laid down - for twenty-four hours at any rate - the colonel, Hubbard, and I devoted some thought to the building of our headquarters. "It looks as if we were in for a spell of trench warfare without the protection we were accustomed to in trench-warfare days," observed the colonel. "There are no mined dug-outs to hide in." The cook, a Scottish miner, had contrived a kind of two-storied habitation in his little stretch of the bank; and he and Manning and my servant felt themselves moderately safe. The colonel's home - heavy "elephant" roof and wooden walls stuffed well into the bank - being complete, the wheeler, the servants, Hubbard, and myself put backs and forearms into the task of fashioning a similar shelter for Hubbard and me. I, of course, could not stray far from the telephone. The staff captain wanted to talk about new ammunition dumps and gun-repairing workshops. Major Bullivant inquired whether he couldn't be selected for the next gunnery course at Shoeburyness. Major Veasey thought it time another captain relieved Drysdale as liaison officer with the Infantry Brigade. And all the time there were routine papers and returns to be looked through and signed.

"There's something that will do for the September War Diary," said the colonel, putting in front of me a letter sent to him by the brigadier-general commanding one of our Infantry brigades. It ran:-

"I am anxious that you and your officers and men should know how grateful I and my battalion commanders are to you for the excellent barrage you gave us yesterday morning (Sept. 18) under such very difficult circumstances. They all realise that with the moving of batteries, getting up the ammunition, and the frequent barrages you are called upon to provide, besides the harassing and the normal shooting, a very great strain is placed on your Brigade. And the success we had yesterday was largely made possible by the splendid work of your people."

About eleven o'clock the doctor, who had ridden from the waggon line, came in gaily singing "Hail! hail! the gang's all here," to a tune from the "Pirates of Penzance." "I've located 'Ernest,'" he shouted triumphantly when he saw me.

"Splendid," I answered, smiling in return. "Have you got him at the waggon line?"

"No; I saw him as I was coming up here. He was trotting along with a captain who was going towards that village with the factory, over there."

"Was he a staff captain, with a Military Cross and another ribbon?" I asked.... "Didn't you tell him it was our dog?"

"That's so. I told him that, and 'Ernest' came and jumped around when he saw me; but the captain said it couldn't be our dog, because a brigadier-general's name was on the collar, and he wasn't going to let him go; his colonel wanted him. Besides," added the doctor plaintively, "'Ernest' wouldn't follow me."

"His colonel!" I repeated, puzzled. "Didn't he say 'his General'? A staff captain is on a brigadier-general's staff.... His colonel?... Are you sure he was a staff captain? Was he wearing red?"

"I didn't see any red," replied the doctor. "He was walking behind a waggon that had a pile of wood and iron on it. It looked as if they were moving."

My face fell. "Did you notice his regiment? Was he a gunner or an infantryman, or what?" I asked quickly.

"Well, I can't say that I did. I don't know all your regiments."

The colonel joined us. "Laneridge has brought my mare up," he remarked pleasantly. "You'd like a little exercise, perhaps. When the doctor has finished his sick parade you take my mare and see if the dog can be found."

The doctor and I rode across country, and scoured the village he had pointed to, but there was no trace of "Ernest." We spoke to a couple of military policemen, told them all about our loss, saw that they inscribed particulars in their note-books, and then continued our inquiries among some heavy gunners, who had pulled into a garden near the sugar factory. I even narrated the story to an Irish A.P.M., who was standing in the street conversing with a motoring staff officer. "I've been in this village fully an hour and haven't seen a dog such as you describe," said the A.P.M. "And I'm sure I should have noticed him…. I'm fond of dogs, and I notice them all…. I'll help you any way I can…. Give me full particulars, and I'll pass them round to my police."

He listened while I tried to obtain further clues from the doctor as to the branch of the service to which the captain, seen that morning with "Ernest," belonged. The doctor, his cap tilted backwards, a long dark cigar protruding at an angle of 45 degrees from the corner of his mouth, did his best, but it was no good. "I'm sorry - I don't know your regiments well enough," he said at last.

It was at this point that the doctor's groom - in the building trade before the war - entered into the conversation. He had heard everything that had been said since the quest began, but this was the first remark he had made.

"The officer the medical officer spoke to this morning, sir, was in the —— Pioneers," he said to me.

"Why didn't you tell us that before?" asked the doctor impatiently.

"Sorry, sir, you didn't ask me," was the toneless reply.

The doctor looked unutterable things, and the lighted end of his cigar described three or four irregular circles. "Gosh!" he pronounced briskly. "We gotta put more pep into looking for this dog, or the war'll end before we find him."

A high-velocity shell bursting on the near side of the factory helped to decide us. The A.P.M. said that a party of the Pioneers had marched down the street half an hour ago. The doctor and I bade him good-bye, went through the village, and were directed to a lane alongside a railway embankment. In one among a row of wooden huts, where the Headquarters of the reserve infantry brigade were quartered, we found the colonel of the Pioneers finishing lunch. He and our colonel were old friends, and immediately I explained the object of my visit he became sympathetic. "Yes," he laughed, "we have your dog - at least our A Company have him. I believe they found him wandering on the other side of the valley…. Stop and have some lunch, and I'll send for him."

"No, thank you, sir…. I shall have to be getting back."

A subaltern went off to fetch the dog. The doctor left to pick up the horses and to return to the waggon line. The colonel invited me to have a drink. But there was disappointment when the subaltern returned. "I'm afraid the dog has gone again, sir - about half an hour ago."

"Really!" said the colonel.

"Yes, sir; he was in A Company's mess when two Gunner officers passed, and he went after them."

"He knows your badge, at any rate," remarked the colonel to me with twinkling eyes. "I'm sorry you've had your journey for nothing. But we'll keep a look-out and send him back if he returns to us."

"I'm going to have another search round the village before I go back, sir," I responded determinedly. "We're getting warmer."

Turning from the lane into the road that led into the village, I noticed a groom who had been waiting with his two horses since the first time I passed the spot. At first he thought he hadn't seen a dog that looked like a cross between an Airedale and a Belgian sheep-dog. Then he fancied he had. Yes, he believed it had passed that way with an R.A.M.C. major. "But those men near that ambulance car will tell you, sir. They were playing with the dog I saw, about half an hour ago."

Yes, I was really on the trail now. "That's right, sir," remarked the R.A.M.C. sergeant when he had helped two walking wounded into the ambulance car. "I remember the dog, and saw the name on the collar…. He followed our major about twenty minutes ago. He's gone across that valley to Brigade Headquarters…. I don't think he'll be long."

"What's it like up there?" asked one of the ambulance men of a slight, fagged-looking lance-corporal of the Fusiliers, who had been hit in the shoulder.

"Hot!" replied the Fusilier. "One dropped near Battalion Headquarters and killed our sergeant…. I think there are five more of our lot coming along."

There were two more places to be filled before the ambulance car moved off. Another Fusilier, wounded in the knee, hobbled up, assisted by two men of the same regiment, one of them with his head bandaged.

"Hullo, Jim!" called the lance-corporal from the ambulance. "I wondered if you'd come along too. Did you see Tom?"

"No," responded the man hit in the ankle.

The ambulance moved off. An empty one took its place. It was a quarter to two, but I was resolved to wait now until the R.A.M.C. major returned. Three shells came over and dropped near the railway. More walking wounded filled places in the ambulance.

The major, with "Ernest" at his heels, came back at a quarter-past two. "Ernest" certainly knew me again. He leapt up and licked my hand, and looked up while the major listened to my story. "Well, I should have kept him - or tried to do so," he said. "He's a taking little fellow, and I've always had a dog until a few weeks ago.... But" - with a pleasant smile - "I think you've earned your right to him.... I've never seen a dog so excited by shells.... Well, good-bye!"

He walked away, and "Ernest" started after him. I stood still in the centre of the road. The dog turned his head as if to see whether I meant to follow. Then he came back, and quietly lay down at my feet.

We had a joyous walk home. There were shells to scamper after, wire to scramble through, old trenches to explore. The return of "Ernest" brought a deep content to our mess.

*   *   *   *   *

Sept. 21: The attack which started at 5.40 A.M. was carried out by two of our Divisional Infantry brigades; a brigade of another Division attacked simultaneously. The object was to close with the main enemy positions in the Hindenburg Line. Tanks were put in to break down the opposition - sure to be met by the brigades on the left and right; and every officer in the Division knew that if the final objectives could be held the Boche would be compelled to withdraw large forces to the far side of the canal. The attack was planned with extraordinary attention to detail. Battalions were ordered not to attempt to push on beyond the final objective; trench mortars were to be moved up to cover the consolidation of the final positions; the reconnaissance work had been specially thorough. Our batteries had horses and limbers in readiness for a quick rushing up of the guns.

The earlier part of the operation went well enough, but by 8 A.M. we knew that our two Infantry brigades were having to go all out. The Boche machine-gunners were firing with exemplary coolness and precision. At 8.30 the brigade-major telephoned that every gun we possessed must fire bursts on certain hostile battery positions. The colonel and I didn't leave the mess that morning; the telephone was rarely out of use. At half-past ten Major Bartlett, who had gone forward to an infantry post to see what was happening, got a message back to say that, harassed by heavy machine-gun and rifle fire, our infantry were coming back. Aeroplane calls for artillery fire on hostile batteries were twice responded to by our batteries. Drysdale, doing liaison with the ——rd Infantry Brigade, reported that two battalions had had severe losses. A buff slip from the Casualty Clearing Station informed us that the lead driver of our brigade telephone cart had died in hospital overnight: he had been hit just after leaving the Headquarters position the previous evening, and was the second Headquarters driver to be killed since Sept. 1. The only relief during a morning of excitement and some gloom was the arrival of three big cigars, sent by the doctor for the colonel, Hubbard, and myself. As the colonel didn't smoke cigars, the only solution was for Hubbard and myself to toss for the remaining one. Hubbard won.

At one o'clock it became clear that our infantry could not hope to do more than consolidate upon their first objective. There was no prospect of the batteries moving forward, and at 1.30 the colonel told me to send out this message to all batteries -

"Gun limbers and firing battery waggons need not be kept within 2000 yards of gun positions any longer to-day."

Major Veasey called on us at tea-time, and the talk ran on the possibilities of the next few days' fighting. "The Boche seems bent on holding out here as long as he can," said the major. "I think he's fighting a rear-guard action on a very big scale," said the colonel thoughtfully.

"Our air reports indicate much movement in his back areas.... And most of his artillery fire is from long range now."

"Let's hope it continues in that way," went on the major, filling his pipe. "If only he'd stop his beastly gas shells it wouldn't be so bad. It's not clean war. I'd vote willingly for an armistice on gas shells."

"Are you improving your accommodation at the battery?" asked the colonel. "We're likely to be here a few days, and we must make as much protection as we can."

"We've got quite a decent dug-out in the bank to sleep in," answered Major Veasey, getting up to go, "but our mess is rather in the open - under a tarpaulin. However, it's quite a pleasant mess. Bullivant and Simpson came to dine last night, and we played bridge till eleven."

I had sent out the S.O.S. lines to batteries, and we had sat down to dinner a little earlier than usual, owing to the desirability of showing as little light as possible, when the telephone bell rang. I put the receiver to my ear.

A strong decided voice spoke. "Is that the adjutant, sir?... I'm Sergeant —— of D Battery, sir.... Major Veasey has been badly wounded."

"Major Veasey wounded," I repeated, and the colonel and Hubbard put down knives and forks and listened.

"Yes, sir,... a gas shell came into the mess. Mr. Kelly and Mr. Wood have been wounded as well.... We've got them away to the hospital, sir.... Mr. Kelly got it in the face, sir.... I'm afraid he's blinded."

"How was Major Veasey wounded?"

"In the arm and foot, sir.... Mr. Wood was not so bad."

"There's no other officer at D Battery, sir," I said to the colonel, who was already turning up the list of officers in his note-book.

"Tell him that the senior sergeant will take command until an officer arrives," replied the colonel promptly, "and then get on to Drysdale at the infantry. I'll speak to him.... I don't like the idea of Veasey being wounded by a gas shell," he added quickly. Depression descended upon all three of us.

The colonel told Captain Drysdale to inform the Infantry brigadier what had happened, and to obtain his immediate permission to go to the battery, about half a mile away. "You've got a subaltern at the waggon line…. Get him up," advised the colonel, "the sergeant-major can carry on there…. Tell the General that another officer will arrive as soon as possible to do liaison."

The colonel looked again at his note-book. "We're frightfully down in officers," he said at last. "I'll ask Colonel —— of the ——rd if he can spare some one to take on to-night."

"I hope Veasey and Kelly are not badly wounded," he said later, lighting a cigarette. "And I'm glad it didn't come last night, when there were three battery commanders at the bridge party. That would have been catastrophe."

That night the Boche rained gas shells all round our quarters in the sunken road. Hubbard and myself and "Ernest" were not allowed much sleep in our right little, tight little hut. One shell dropped within twenty yards of us; thrice fairly heavy shell splinters played an unnerving tattoo upon our thick iron roof; once we were forced to wear our box-respirators for half an hour.

At 11.30 P.M. the colonel telephoned from his hut to ours to tell me that new orders had come in from the brigade-major. "We are putting down a barrage from midnight till 12.15 A.M.," he said. "You needn't worry. I've sent out orders to the batteries…. Our infantry are making an assault at 12.15 on Doleful Post. It ought to startle the Hun. He won't expect anything at that hour."

CHAPTER XVI

THE DECISIVE DAYS

SEPTEMBER 22: It was as the colonel expected. The Boche took our hurricane bombardment from midnight to 12.15 A.M. to be an unusually intense burst of night-firing; and when our guns "lifted" some six hundred yards, our infantry swept forward, and in a few minutes captured two posts over which many lives had been unavailingly expended during the two preceding days. Sixty prisoners also were added to their bag.

But the enemy was only surprised - not done with. This was ground that had been a leaping-off place for his mighty rush in March 1918. Close behind lay country that had not been trod by Allied troops since the 1914 invasion. He counter-attacked fiercely, and at 5.10 A.M. a signaller roused me with the message.

"Our attack succeeded in capturing Duncan and Doleful Posts, but failed on the rest of the front. S.O.S. line will be brought back to the line it was on after 12 midnight. Bursts of harassing fire will be put down on the S.O.S. lines and on approaches in rear from now onwards. About three bursts per hour. Heavy artillery is asked to conform."

I telephoned to the batteries to alter their S.O.S. lines, and told the colonel what had been done. Then I sought sleep again.

After breakfast the brigade-major telephoned that the Division immediately north of us was about to attempt the capture of a strong point that had become a wasps' nest of machine-gunners. "We have to hold Duncan Post and Doleful Post at all costs," he added. All through the morning messages from Division artillery and from the liaison officer told the same tale: fierce sallies and desperate counter-attacks between small parties of the opposing infantry, who in places held trench slits and rough earthworks within a mashie shot of each other. About noon the Germans loosed off a terrible burst of fire on a 500-yards' front. "Every Boche gun for miles round seemed to be pulverising that awful bit," "Buller," who had gone forward to observe, told me afterwards. "My two telephonists hid behind a brick wall that received two direct hits, and I lay for a quarter of an hour in a shell-hole without daring to move. Then half a dozen of their aeroplanes came over in close formation and tried to find our infantry with their machine-guns.... I got the wind up properly." Our batteries answered three S.O.S. calls between 10 A.M. and 1 o'clock; and, simultaneously with a news message from Division stating that British cavalry had reached Nazareth and crossed the Jordan, that 18,000 prisoners and 160 guns had been captured, and that Liman von Sanders had escaped by the skin of his teeth, came a report from young Beale that Germans could be seen massing for a big effort.

I passed this information to the brigade-major, and our guns, and the heavies behind them, fired harder than ever. Then for an hour until 3 o'clock we got a respite. A couple of pioneers, lent to us by the colonel, who had shown himself so sympathetic in the matter of the lost dog, worked stolidly with plane and saw and foot-rule, improving our gun-pit mess by more expert carpentering than we could hope to possess. The colonel tore the wrapper of the latest copy of an automobile journal, posted to him weekly, and devoted himself to an article on spring-loaded starters. I read a type-written document from the staff captain that related to the collection, "as opportunity offers," of two field guns captured from the enemy two days before.

But at 3.35 the situation became electric again. The clear high-pitched voice of young Beale sounded over the line that by a miracle had not yet been smashed by shell-fire. "Germans in large numbers are coming over the ridge south of Tombois Farm," he said.

I got through to the brigade-major, and he instructed me to order our guns to search back 1000 yards from that portion of our front.

"Don't tell the batteries to 'search back,'" broke in the colonel, who had heard me telephoning. "It's a confusing expression. Tell them to 'search east,' or 'north-east' in this case."

By a quarter to four the telephone wires were buzzing feverishly. More S.O.S. rockets had gone up. The enemy had launched a very heavy counter-attack. Our over-worked gunners left their tea, and tons of metal screamed through the air. Within an hour Drysdale sent us most inspiring news.

"The infantry are awfully pleased with our S.O.S. barrage," he said briskly. "As a matter of fact, that burst you ordered at 3.40 was more useful still,… caught the Germans as they came out to attack…. They were stopped about 150 yards from our line…. They had to go back through our barrage…. It was a great sight…. The dead can be seen in heaps…. Over twenty Boche ran through our barrage and gave themselves up."

Drysdale had more good news for us twenty minutes later. Two companies of a battalion not attacked - they were to the right of the place to which the enemy advanced - saw what was happening, dashed forward along a winding communication trench, and seized a position that hitherto they had found impregnable. They got a hundred prisoners out of the affair.

Two more S.O.S. calls went up before dinner-time, but a day of tremendous heavy fighting ended with our men in glorious possession of some of the hardest-won ground in the history of the Division.

"If we can hold on where we are until really fresh troops relieve us we shall be over the Hindenburg Line in three days," said the colonel happily, as he selected targets for the night-firing programme.

He had written "From receipt of this message S.O.S. lines will be as follows ——" when he stopped. "Can't we shorten this preliminary verbiage?" he asked quizzically. "Castle made this opening phrase a sort of tradition when he was adjutant."

"What about 'Henceforth S.O.S. lines will be'?" I replied, tilting my wooden stool backwards.

"That will do!" said the colonel.

And "henceforth" it became after that.

For two more days we carried on this most tiring of all kinds of fighting: for the infantry, hourly scraps with a watchful plucky foe; for the gunners, perpetual readiness to fire protective bursts should the enemy suddenly seek to shake our grip on this most fateful stretch of front; in addition to day and night programmes of "crashes" that allowed the gun detachments no rest, and at the same time demanded unceasing care in "laying" and loading and firing the guns. And with the opposing infantry so close to each other, and the front line changing backwards and forwards from hour to hour, absolute accuracy was never more necessary. The Brigade had had no proper rest since the early days of August. The men had been given no opportunity for baths or change of clothing. Our casualties had not been heavy, but they were draining us steadily, and reinforcements stepped into this strenuous hectic fighting with no chance of the training and testing under actual war conditions that make a period of quiet warfare so valuable. And yet it was this portion of "the fifty days," this exhausting, remorseless, unyielding struggling that really led to the Boche's final downfall. It forced him to abandon the Hindenburg Line - the beginning of the very end.

I was going to write that it was astonishing how uncomplainingly, how placidly each one of us went on with his ordinary routine duties during this time. But, after all, it wasn't astonishing. The moments were too occupied for weariness of soul; our minds rioted with the thought, "He's getting done! Let's get on with it! Let's finish him." And if at times one reflected on the barrenness, the wastefulness of war, there still remained the satisfying of the instinct to do one's work well. The pioneers had done their very best, and made quite a house of our mess, even finding glass to put in the windows. I don't know that the old wheeler understood me when I emphasised this thoroughness of the pioneers by adding, "You see, we British always build for posterity"; but before we went away he began to take a pride in keeping those windows clean.

On Sept. 25 we heard without much pleasure that we had come under another Divisional Artillery, and were to retire to our waggon lines by nightfall. "I'd rather stay here a few days longer and then go out for a proper rest," said the colonel, taking appreciative stock of the habitations that had arisen since our occupation. "I'm afraid this order means a shift to another part of the line." And it was so. Our Brigade was to side-step north, and the colonel and the battery commanders went off after lunch to reconnoitre positions. An Australian Field Artillery brigade came to "take-over" from us, and I yarned with their colonel and adjutant and intelligence officer while waiting for our colonel to return. I told them that it was ages since I had seen a 'Sydney Bulletin.'

"I used to get mine regularly," said their adjutant, "but it hasn't come for ten weeks now. I expect some skrim-shanker at the post-office or at the base is pinching it…. I'm going to tell my people to wrap it up in the 'War Cry' before posting it. I know one chap who's had that done for over a year. No one thinks of pinching it then."

One of the Australian batteries was late getting in, and it was half-past seven before the colonel and I, waiting for the relief to be complete, got away. The Boche guns had been quiet all the afternoon. But - how often it happens when one has been delayed! - shells fell about the track we intended to take when we mounted our horses, and we had to side-track to be out of danger. When we arrived at Headquarters waggon lines it was too late to dine in daylight; and as Hun bombers were on the war-path, our dinner was a blind-man's-buff affair.

The colonel had been told that we should be required to fight a battle at our new positions on the 27th, and already the batteries had commenced to take up ammunition. But when - the Hun aeroplanes having passed by and candles being permissible in our tents - the brigade clerk produced an order requiring us to have two guns per battery in action that very night, I considered joylessly the prospect of a long move in the dark.

"They expect us to move up to-night, sir," I told the colonel, handing him the order brought by a motor-cyclist despatch-bearer about eight o'clock.

"Oh!" said the colonel - and the "Oh!" was a *chef-d'oeuvre* of irony.

Then he wrote a masterly little note, perfect in its correctness, and yet instinct with the power and knowledge of a commander who had a mind of his own. He wrote as follows, and told me to hand the message to the returning despatch-rider:-

"Ref. your B.M. 85 dated 25th Sept., I regret that I shall not be able to move one section per battery into action to-night.

"I was late in returning from my reconnaissance owing to delay in fixing position for my Brigade Headquarters; did not get the order until eight o'clock, and by that time batteries had started moving ammunition up to the positions. All available guides had gone up with the ammunition waggons.

"My batteries will be prepared to fire a barrage by dawn on 27th Sept.

"In confirmation of my telephone conversation with B.M. to-day positions selected are as follows:-"

The message closed with the map co-ordinates of the positions chosen for our four batteries, and with a request for the map location of the Divisional Artillery Headquarters, to which the note was sent.

Next day, the 26th, was a day of busy preparation. We learned that, for the first time, we should be in active co-operation with an American Division. The infantry of the British Division we were working under had been told off to protect the left flank of the American Division. The object of the attack was the capture of the last dominating strong-posts that guarded a section of the Hindenburg Line, immediately north of the section for which our own Divisional infantry had battled since Sept. 19. The enemy was to be surprised. Our guns, when placed in position, had to remain silent until they began the barrage on the 27th. That morning, therefore, topographical experts busied themselves ascertaining exact map locations of the batteries' positions so as to ensure accurate shooting by the map. The point was emphasised by the colonel, who wrote to all batteries:-

"Battery Commanders are reminded that as barrages on morning of 27th will be fired without previous registration of guns.

"THE LINE LAID OUT MUST NOT BE ENTIRELY DEPENDENT ON COMPASS BEARING. Check it by measuring angles to points which can be identified on the map. All calculations to be made by two officers working separately, who will then check each other.

"Every precaution must be taken not to attract the attention of the enemy to batteries moving forward into action. Nothing to be taken up in daylight, except in the event of *very* bad visibility."

The colonel rode over to see the C.R.A. of the Division to whom our Brigade had been loaned. After lunch he held a battery commanders' conference in his tent, and explained the morrow's barrage scheme. "Ernest," the dog, spent a delighted frolicsome hour chasing a Rugby football that some Australians near our waggon lines brought out for practice. Hubbard went on to the new positions to lay out his telephone lines. I occupied myself completing returns for the staff captain.

By five o'clock I had joined the colonel and Hubbard at the new positions. Our only possible mess was a roofless gun-pit not far from a road. The colonel and Hubbard were covering it with scrap-heap sheets of rusty iron, and a tarpaulin that was not sufficiently expansive. Further down the road was a dug-out into which two could squeeze. The colonel said Hubbard and I had better occupy it. He preferred to sleep in the gun-pit, and already had gathered up a few armfuls of grasses and heather to lie upon. Manning and the cook had discovered a hole of their own, and the two clerks and the orderlies had cramped themselves into a tiny bivouac.

The final fastening-down of the gun-pit roof was enlivened by heavy enemy shelling of a battery four hundred yards north-east of us. Several splinters whistled past, and one flying piece of iron, four inches long and an inch wide, missed my head by about a foot and buried itself in the earthen floor of the mess. "That's the narrowest escape you've had for some time," smiled the colonel.

Ten minutes later the brigade clerk brought me the evening's batch of Divisional messages and routine orders. This was the first one I glanced at:-

"Wire by return name of war-tired captain or subaltern, if any, available for temporary duty for administration and training of R.A. malaria convalescents. Very urgent."

CHAPTER XVII

WITH THE AMERICANS

SEPTEMBER 27: Our meetings with the Americans had so far been pretty casual. We had seen parties of them in June and July, training in the Contay area, north of the Albert-Amiens road; and one day during that period I accompanied our colonel and the colonel of our companion brigade on a motor trip to the coast, and we passed some thousands of them hard at work getting fit, and training with almost fervid enthusiasm. It used to be a joke of mine that on one occasion my horse shied because an Australian private saluted me. No one could make a friendly jest of like kind against the American soldiers. When first they arrived in France no troops were more punctilious in practising the outward and visible evidences of discipline. Fit, with the perfect fitness of the man from 23 to 28, not a weed amongst them, intelligent-looking, splendidly eager to learn, they were much akin in physique and general qualities to our own immortal "First Hundred Thousand." I came across colonels and majors of the New York and Illinois Divisions getting experience in the line with our brigadiers and colonels. I have seen U.S. Army N.C.O.'s out in the field receiving instruction from picked N.C.O.'s of our army in the art of shouting orders. Their officers and men undertook this training with a certain shy solemnity that I myself thought very attractive. I am doing no lip-service to a "wish is father to the thought" sentiment when I say that a manly modesty in respect to military achievements characterised all the fighting American soldiers that I met.

They were not long in tumbling into the humours of life at the front. I remember an episode told with much enjoyment by a major of the regular U.S. Army, who spent a liaison fortnight with our Division.

There is a word that appears at least once a day on orders sent out from the "Q" or administrative branch of the British Army. It is the word "Return": "Return of Personnel," "Casualty Returns," "Ammunition Returns," &c., all to do with the compilation of reports. The American Division to which the major belonged had been included among the units of a British Corps. When, in course of time, the Division was transferred elsewhere Corps Q branch wired, "Return wanted of all tents and trench shelters in your possession." Next day the American Division received a second message: "Re my 0546/8023, hasten return of tents and trench shelters."

The day following the Corps people were startled by the steady arrival of scores of tents and trench shelters. The wires hummed furiously, and the Corps staff captain shouted his hardest, explaining over a long-distance telephone that "Hasten return" did not mean "Send back as quickly as possible."

"And we thought we had got a proper move on sending back those tents," concluded the American major who told me the story.

And now we were in action with these virile ardent fellows. Two of their Divisions took part in the great battle which at 5.30 A.M. opened on a 35-mile front - ten days of bloody victorious fighting, by which three armies shattered the last and strongest of the enemy's fully-prepared positions, and struck a vital blow at his main communications.

` The first news on Sept. 27th was of the best. On our part of the front the Americans had swept forward, seized the two ruined farms that were their earliest objectives, and surged to the top of a knoll that had formed a superb point of vantage for the Boche observers. By 7.30 A.M. the Brigade was told to warn F.O.O.'s that our bombers would throw red flares outside the trenches along which they were advancing to indicate their position.

But again there was to be no walk-over. The Boche counter-attack was delivered on the Americans' left flank. We were ordered to fire a two-hours' bombardment upon certain points towards which the enemy was pouring his troops; and the colonel told me to instruct our two F.O.O.'s to keep a particular look-out for hostile movement.

By 11 A.M. Division issued instructions for all gun dumps to be made up that night to 500 rounds per gun. "Stiff fighting ahead," commented the colonel.

At three o'clock Dumble, who was commanding A Battery, Major Bullivant having gone on leave, reported that the Americans were withdrawing from the knoll to trenches four hundred yards in rear, where they were reorganising their position.

That settled the fighting for the day, although there was speedy indication of the Boche's continued liveliness: a plane came over, and by a daring manoeuvre set fire to three of our "sausage" balloons, the observers having to tumble out with their parachutes. All this time I had remained glued to the telephone for the receipt of news and the passing of orders. There was opportunity now to give thought to the fortifying of our headquarters. Hubbard, who prided himself on his biceps, had engaged in a brisk discussion with the officers of a near-by Artillery brigade headquarters regarding the dug-out that he and myself and "Ernest" had occupied the night before. Originally it had been arranged that we should share quarters with them, dug-outs in a neighbouring bank having been allotted for their overflow of signallers. But at the last moment an Infantry brigade headquarters had "commandeered" part of their accommodation, and they gave up the dug-out that Hubbard and I had slept in, with the intimation that they would want it on the morrow. As Hubbard had discovered that they were in possession of four good dug-outs on the opposite side of the road, he said we ought to be allowed to retain our solitary one. But no! they stuck to their rights, and during the morning's battle a stream of protesting officers came to interview Hubbard. Their orderly officer was suave but anxious; their signalling officer admitted the previous arrangement to share quarters; Hubbard remained firm, and said that if the Infantry brigade had upset their arrangements, they themselves had upset ours. I was too busy to enter at length into the argument, but I agreed to send a waggon and horses to fetch material if they chose to build a new place. When their adjutant came over and began to use sarcasm, I referred the matter to our colonel, who decided, "Their

Division has sent us here. The dug-out is in our area. There is no other accommodation. We shall keep it."

"Will you come over and see our colonel, sir?" asked the adjutant persuasively.

"Certainly not," replied the colonel with some asperity.

The next arrivals were a gas officer and a tall ebullient Irish doctor, who said that the dug-out had been prepared for them. Hubbard conveyed our colonel's decision, and ten minutes later his servant brought news that the doctor's servant had been into the dug-out and replaced our kit by the doctor's.

Hubbard, smiling happily, slipped out of our gun-pit mess, and the next item of news from this bit of front informed me that our valises had been replaced and the doctor's kit put outside. Hubbard told me he had informed the doctor and the gas officer that, our colonel having made his decision, he was prepared to repeat the performance every time they invaded the dug-out. "And I was ready to throw them after their kit if necessary," he added, expanding his chest.

The upshot of it all was that our horses fetched fresh material, and we helped to find the doctor and the gas officer a home.

The battle continued next day, our infantry nibbling their way into the Boche defences and allowing him no rest. The artillery work was not so strenuous as on the previous day, and Hubbard and I decided to dig a dug-out for the colonel. It was bonny exercise for me. "I think every adjutant ought to have a pit to dig in - adjutants get too little exercise," I told the colonel. After which Hubbard, crouching with his pick, offered practical tuition in the science of underpinning. We sweated hard and enjoyed our lunch. Judd and young Beale reported back from leave, and Beale caused a sensation by confessing that he had got married. A Corps wire informed every unit that Lance-Corporal Kleinberg-Hermann, "5 ft. 8, fair hair, eyes blue, scar above nose, one false tooth in front, dressed German uniform," and Meyer Hans, "6 ft., fair hair, brown eyes, thin face, wears glasses, speaks English and French fluently, dressed German uniform," had escaped from a prisoners of war camp. The mail brought a letter from which the colonel learnt that a long-time friend, a lieut.-colonel in the Garrison Artillery, had been killed. He had lunched with us one day in June, a bright-eyed, grizzled veteran, with a whimsical humour. India had made him look older than his years. "They found his body in No Man's Land," said the colonel softly. "They couldn't get to it for two days."

At half-past nine that night we learned that our own Divisional infantry were coming up in front of us again. There was to be another big attack, to complete the work begun by the Americans, and at zero hour we should pass under the command of our Divisional artillery. At four in the morning the telephone near my pillow woke me up, and Major Bartlett reported that the Boche had started a barrage. "I don't think he suspects anything," said the major. "It's only ordinary counter-preparation." In any case it didn't affect our attack, which started with splendid zest. The Boche plunked a few gas shells near us; but by 9.15 the brigade-major told me that the Americans and our own infantry had advanced a thousand yards and were on their first objective. "I smell victory to-day," said the colonel, looking at his map. By half-past ten Major Bartlett's battery had moved forward two thousand yards, and the major had joined a battalion commander so as to keep pace with the onward rush of the infantry.

Good news tumbled in. At 10.50 the intelligence officer of our companion Artillery brigade rang up to tell me that their liaison officer had seen our troops entering the southern end of a well-known village that lay along the canal.

"Ring up A and B at once," interjected the colonel, "and tell them to stop their bursts of fire, otherwise they will be firing on our own people. Tell our liaison officer with the ——th Infantry Brigade that we are no longer firing on the village…. And increase the how. battery's range by 1000 yards."

Five minutes later the brigade-major let us know that the Corps on our left had cleared a vastly important ridge, but their most northerly Division was held up by machine-gun fire. When the situation was eased they would advance upon the canal. Our D Battery was now firing at maximum range, and at 11.20 the colonel ordered them to move up alongside C.

The exhilarating swiftness of the success infected every one. Drysdale rang up to know whether we hadn't any fresh targets for D Battery. "I'm sure we've cleared out every Boche in the quarry you gave us," he said. The staff captain told us he was bringing forward his ammunition dumps. The old wheeler was observed to smile. Even the telephone seemed to be working better than for months past. In restraint of over-eagerness, complaints of short shooting filtered in from the infantry, but I established the fact that our batteries were not the sinners.

By tea-time all the batteries had advanced, and the colonel, "Ernest," and myself were walking at the head of the headquarters waggon and mess carts through a village that a fortnight before had been a hotbed of Germany's hardest fighting infantry.

The longer the time spent in the fighting area, the stronger that secret spasm of apprehension when a shift forward to new positions had to be made. The ordinary honest-souled member of His Majesty's forces will admit that to be a true saying. The average healthy-minded recruit coming to the Western Front since July 1916 marvelled for his first six months on the thousands of hostile shells that he saw hitting nothing in particular, and maiming and killing nobody. If he survived a couple of years he lost all curiosity about shells that did no harm; he had learned that in the forward areas there was never real safety, the fatal shell might come at the most unexpected moment, in the most unlooked-for spot: it might be one solitary missile of death, it might accompany a hideous drove that beat down the earth all around, and drenched a whole area with sickening scorching fumes; he might not show it, but he had learned to fear.

But on this move-up we were agog with the day's fine news. We were in the mood to calculate on the extent of the enemy's retirement: for the moment his long-range guns had ceased to fire. We talked seriously of the war ending by Christmas. We laughed when I opened the first Divisional message delivered at our new Headquarters: "Divisional Cinema will open at Lieramont to-morrow. Performances twice daily,

3 P.M. and 6 P.M." "That looks as if our infantry are moving out," I said.

We had taken over a bank and some shallow, aged dug-outs, occupied the night before by our C Battery; and as there was a chill in the air that foretold rain, and banks of sombre clouds were lining up in the western sky, we unloaded our carts and set to work getting our belongings under cover while it was still light. "There's no pit for you to dig in," the colonel told me quizzingly, "but you can occupy yourself filling these ammunition boxes with earth; they'll make walls for the mess." Hubbard had been looking for something heavy to carry; he brought an enormous beam from the broad-gauge railway that lay a hundred yards west of us. The colonel immediately claimed it for the mess roof. "We'll fix it centre-wise on the ammunition boxes to support the tarpaulin," he decided. "Old Fritz has done his dirtiest along the railway," said Hubbard cheerfully. "He's taken a bit out of every rail; and he's blown a mine a quarter of a mile down there that's giving the sappers something to think about. They told me they want to have trains running in two days."

Meanwhile the signallers had been cleaning out the deep shaft they were to work in; the cooks and the clerks had selected their own rabbit-hutches; and I had picked a semi-detached dug-out in which were wire beds for the colonel, Hubbard, and myself. True, a shell had made a hole in one corner of the iron roof, and the place was of such antiquity that rats could be heard squeaking in the vicinity of my bed-head, but I hoped that a map-board fixed behind my pillow would protect me from unpleasantness.

The colonel was suspicious of the S.O.S. line issued to us by Division that night. The ordinary rules of gunnery provide that the angle of sight to be put on the guns can be calculated from the difference between the height of the ground on which the battery stands and the height at the target. More often than not ridges intervene between the gun and the target, and the height and position of these ridges sometimes cause complications in the reckoning of the angle of sight, particularly if a high ridge is situated close to the object to be shot at. Without going into full explanation, I hope I may be understood when I say that the correct angle of sight, calculated from the map difference in height between battery and target, occasionally fails to ensure that the curve described by the shell in its flight will finish sufficiently high in the air for the shell to clear the final crest. When that happens shells fall on the wrong side of the ridge, and our own infantry are endangered. It is a point to which brigade-majors and brigade commanders naturally give close attention.

The colonel looked at his map, shook his head, said, "I don't like that ridge," and got out his ruler and made calculations. Then he talked over the telephone to the brigade-major. "Yes, I know that theoretically, by every ordinary test, we should be safe in shooting there, and I know what you want to shoot at…. But there's a risk, and I should prefer to be on the safe side…. Will you speak to the General about it?"

The colonel gained his point, and at 10.20 P.M. issued a further order to the batteries:-

"Previous S.O.S. line is cancelled, as it is found that the hillside is so steep that our troops in Tino Support Trench may be hit.

"Complaints of short shooting have been frequent all day. Henceforth S.O.S. will be as follows…."

"I'll write out those recommendations for honours and awards before turning in," he said, a quarter of an hour later, searching through the box in which confidential papers were kept. "Now, what was it I wanted to know? - oh, I remember. Ring up Drysdale, and ask him whether the corporal he put in is named Marchman or Marshman. His writing is not very clear…. If he's gone to bed, say I'm sorry to disturb him, but these things want to be got in as soon as possible."

It was a quiet night as far as shell-fire was concerned, but a furious rain-storm permitted us very little sleep, and played havoc with the mess. Our documents remained safe, though most of them were saturated with water. In the morning it was cold enough to make one rub one's hands and stamp the feet. There was plenty of exercise awaiting us in the enlarging and rebuilding of the mess. We made it a very secure affair this time. "What about a fire, sir?" inquired Hubbard.

"Good idea," said the colonel. He and Hubbard used pick and shovel to fashion a vertical, triangular niche in the side of the bank. The staff-sergeant fitter returned with a ten-foot stove-pipe that he had found in the neighbouring village; and before ten o'clock our first mess fire since the end of April was crackling merrily and burning up spare ammunition boxes.

The colonel went off to tour the batteries, saying, "I'll leave you to fight the battle." The brigade-major's first telephone talk at 10.35 A.M. left no doubt that we were pushing home all the advantages gained the day before. "I want one good burst on —— Trench," he said. "After that cease firing this side of the canal until I tell you to go on." The news an hour later was that our Divisional Infantry patrols were working methodically through Vendhuile, the village on the canal bank, which the Americans had entered the day before. Next "Buller," who was with the Infantry brigade, called up, and said that the mopping-up in the village had been most successful: our fellows were thrusting for the canal bridge, and had yet to encounter any large enemy forces. At twenty to one the brigade-major told me that our people were moving steadily to the other side of the canal. "We're properly over the Hindenburg Line this time," he wound up.

The Brigadier-General C.R.A. came to see us during the afternoon, and we learned for the first time that on the previous day the Americans had fought their way right through Vendhuile, but, on account of their impetuosity, had lost touch with their supports. "They fought magnificently, but didn't mop-up as they went along," explained the General. "The Boche tried the trick he used to play on us. He hid until the first wave had gone by, and then came up with his machine-guns and fired into their backs.... It's a great pity.... I'm afraid that six hundred of them who crossed the canal have been wiped out."

"I hear that our infantry go out for a proper rest as soon as this is over," he added. "They brought them up again to complete the smashing of the Hindenburg Line, because they didn't want to draw upon the three absolutely fresh Divisions they were keeping to chase the Hun immediately he yielded the Hindenburg Line. Our infantry must have fought themselves to a standstill these last three weeks."

"Any news about us?" inquired the colonel.

"No; I'm afraid the gunners will have to carry on as usual…. The horses seem to be surviving the ordeal very well…."

At 4.25 P.M. - I particularly remember noting the time - we were told by Division that Bulgaria's surrender was unconditional. "That will be cheering news for the batteries," observed the colonel. "I'd send that out." The brigade-major also informed us that British cavalry were reported to be at Roulers, north-east of Ypres - but that wasn't official. "Anyhow," said the colonel, his face glowing, "it shows the right spirit. Yes, I think the war will be over by Christmas after all."

"It would be great to be home by Christmas, sir," put in Hubbard.

"Yes," responded the colonel in the same vein, "but it wouldn't be so bad even out here…. I don't think any of us would really mind staying another six months if we had no 5·9's to worry us." And he settled down to writing his daily letter home.

October came in with every one joyously expectant. The enemy still struggled to hold the most valuable high ground on the far side of the canal, but there was little doubt that he purposed a monster withdrawal - and our batteries did their best to quicken his decision. The brigade-major departed for a Senior Staff Course in England, and Major "Pat" of our sister brigade, a highly efficient and extremely popular officer, who, with no previous knowledge of soldiering, had won deserved distinction, filled his place. Major "Pat" was a disciple of cheering news for the batteries. "This has just come in by the wireless," he telephoned to me on October 2nd. "Turkey surrendered - British ships sailing through the Dardanelles - Lille being evacuated - British bluejackets landed at Ostend."

"Is that official?" I asked wonderingly.

He laughed. "No, I didn't say that…. It's a wireless report."

"Not waggon line?" I went on.

He laughed again. "No, I'll let you know when it becomes official."

Formal intimation was to hand that Dumble, Judd, Bob Pottinger, young Beale, Stenson, and Tincler had been awarded the Military Cross, and Major Veasey the D.S.O. Drysdale was happy because, after many times of asking, he had got back from headquarters, Patrick, the black charger that he had ridden early in 1916.

The tide of success rolled on. A swift little attack on the morning of October 3rd took the infantry we were supporting, now that our own battalions had withdrawn for a fortnight's rest, on to valuable high ground east of the canal. "They met with such little opposition that our barrage became merely an escort," was the way in which Beadle, who was doing F.O.O., described the advance. Surrendering Germans poured back in such numbers that dozens of them walked unattended to the prisoners of war cages. "I saw one lot come down," a D.A.C. officer told me. "All that the sentry had to do was to point to the cage with a 'This-way-in' gesture, and in they marched."

One wee cloud blurred the high-spirited light-heartedness of those days. We lost "Ernest," who had marched forward with us and been our pet since Sept. 6th. The colonel and Hubbard took him up the line; the little fellow didn't seem anxious to leave me that morning, but I thought that a run would do him good, and he had followed the colonel a couple of days before. "I'm sorry, but we've lost 'Ernest,'" was the colonel's bluntly told news when he returned. "He disappeared when I was calling on B Battery…. They said he went over the hill with an infantry officer, who had made much of him…. It's curious, because he stuck to us when I went to see the infantry at Brigade Headquarters, although every one in their very long dug-out fussed over him."

There was poor chance of the dog finding his way back to us in that country of many tracks, amid the coming to and fro of thousands of all kinds of troops. We never saw or heard of him again. The loss of him dispirited all of us a bit; and I suppose I felt it more than most: he had been a splendid little companion for nearly a month.

The adjutant and Wilde returned from leave on Oct. 3rd, full of the bright times to be spent in London. "People in England think the war's all over. They don't realise that pursuing the Boche means fighting him as well," burst forth the adjutant. "By Gad," he went on, "we had a narrow escape the day we went on leave. I never saw anything like it in my life. You remember the factory at Moislains, near the place where we were out for three or four days at the beginning of last month. Well, Wilde and I caught a leave bus that went that way on the road to Amiens. The bus had to pull up about five hundred yards short of the factory, because there was a lot of infantry in front of us.... And just at that moment a Boche mine blew up.... Made an awful mess.... About eleven men killed.... We had taken the place three weeks before, and the mine had remained undiscovered all that time.... We must all of us have passed over that spot many times. You remember they made a Red Cross Station of the factory.... A most extraordinary thing!"

The Boche fire had died away almost entirely; it was manifest that the Brigade would have to move forward. I could go on leave now that the adjutant was back - Beadle and myself were the only two officers in the Brigade who had gone through the March retreat and not yet been on leave to England; but I was keen on another trip forward with the colonel, and on the morning of the 4th Wilde and I joined him on a prospecting ride, looking for new positions for the batteries.

It was a journey that quickened all one's powers of observation. We went forward a full five miles, over yellow churned wastes that four days before had been crowded battlefields; past shell-pocked stretches that had been made so by our own guns. At first we trotted along a straight road that a short time before had been seamed with Boche trenches and barbed wire. The colonel's mare was fresh and ready to shy at heaps of stones and puddles. "She's got plenty of spirit still," said the colonel, "but she's not the mare she was before the hit in the neck at Commenchon. However, I know her limitations, and she's all right providing I spare her going uphill."

Just outside the half-mile long village of Ronssoy he pointed to a clump of broken bricks and shattered beams. "That's the farm that D Battery insisted was Gillemont Farm, when we were at Cliffe Post on September 19," he explained. "The day I was with him at the 'O.P.,' Wood couldn't understand why he was unable to see his shells fall. He telephoned to the battery to check the range they were firing at, and then decided that the map was wrong. When I told him to examine his map more closely he spotted the 140 contour between this place and Gillemont Farm. It made Gillemont Farm invisible from the 'O.P.' Of course Gillemont Farm is 2000 yards beyond this place."

We reached a battered cross-roads 1200 yards due south of Duncan Post, that cockpit of the bitter hand-to-hand fighting of Sept. 19th and 20th. A couple of captured Boche 4·2's - the dreaded high-velocity gun - stood tucked behind a low grassless bank, their curved, muddy, camouflaged shields blending with the brown desolation of the landscape. Two American soldiers saluted the colonel gravely - lean, tanned, straight-eyed young fellows. For the first time I noticed that the Americans were wearing puttees like our men, instead of the canvas gaiters which they sported when first in France. Their tin hats and box-respirators have always been the same make as ours.

The colonel stopped to look at his map. "We'll turn north-east here and cross the canal at Bony," he said. We rode round newly-dug shell-slits, and through gaps in the tangled, rusted barbed wire; at one spot we passed eighteen American dead, laid out in two neat rows, ready for removal to the cemetery that the U.S. Army had established in the neighbourhood; we went within twenty yards of a disabled tank that a land mine had rendered *hors de combat*; we came across another tank lumbered half-way across a road. "Tanks always seem to take it into their heads to collapse on a main road and interrupt traffic," muttered the colonel sardonically.

There were twelve hundred yards of a straight sunken road for us to ride through before we reached Bony. That road was a veritable gallery of German dead. They lay in twos and threes, in queer horrible postures, along its whole unkempt length, some of them with blackened decomposed faces and hands, most of them newly killed, for this was a road that connected the outer defences of the Hindenburg Line with the network of wire and trenches that formed the Hindenburg Line itself. "Best sight I've seen since the war," said Wilde with satisfaction. And if the colonel and myself made no remark we showed no disagreement. Pity for dead Boche finds no place in the average decent-minded man's composition. Half a dozen of our armoured cars, wheels off, half-burned, or their steering apparatus smashed, lay on the entrenched and wired outskirts of Bony, part of the Hindenburg Line proper. In the village itself we found Red Cross cars filling up with wounded; Boche prisoners were being used as stretcher-bearers; groups of waiting infantry stood in the main street; runners flitted to and fro.

"We'll leave our horses here," said the colonel; and the grooms guided them to the shelter of a high solid wall. The colonel, Wilde, and I ascended the main street, making eastward. A couple of 5·9's dropped close to the northern edge of the village as we came out of it. We met a party of prisoners headed by two officers - one short, fat, nervous, dark, bespectacled; the other bearded, lanky, nonchalant, and of good carriage. He carried a gold-nobbed Malacca cane. Neither officer looked at us as we passed. The tall one reminded me of an officer among the first party of Boche prisoners I saw in France in August 1916. His arrogant, disdainful air had roused in me a gust of anger that made me glad I was in the war.

We went through a garden transformed into a dust-bin, and dipped down a hummocky slope that rose again to a chalky ridge. Shells were screaming overhead in quick succession now, and we walked fast, making for a white boulder that looked as if it would offer shielded observation and protection. We found ourselves near the top of one of the giant air-shafts that connected with the canal tunnel. Tufts of smoke spouted up at regular intervals on the steep slope behind the village below us. "We're in time to see a barrage," remarked the colonel, pulling out his binoculars. "Our people are trying to secure the heights. I didn't know that Gouy was quite clear of Boche. There was fighting there yesterday."

"There are some Boche in a trench near that farm on the left," he added a minute later, after sweeping the hills opposite with his glasses. "Can you see them?"

I made out what did appear to be three grey tin-helmeted figures, but I could see nothing of our infantry. The shelling went on, but time pressed, and the colonel, packing up his glasses, led us eastwards again, down to a light-railway junction, and through a quaint little ravine lined with willow-trees. Many German dead lay here. One young soldier, who had died with his head thrown back resting against a green bank, his blue eyes open to the sky, wore a strangely perfect expression of peace and rest. Up another ascending sunken road. The Boche guns seemed to have switched, and half a dozen shells skimmed the top of the road, causing us to wait. We looked again at the fight being waged on the slopes behind the village. Our barrage had lifted, but we saw no sign of advancing infantry.

The colonel turned to me suddenly and said, "I'm going to select positions about a thousand yards south of where we are at this moment - along the valley. Wilde will come with me. You go back and pick up the horses, and meet us at Quennemont Farm. I expect we shall be there almost as soon as you."

I followed the direct road to return to Bony. A few shells dropped on either side of the road, which was obviously a hunting-ground for the Boche gunners. At least a dozen British dead lay at intervals huddled against the sides of the road. One of them looked to be an artillery officer, judged by his field-boots and spurs. But the top part of him was covered by a rain-proof coat, and I saw no cap.

Quennemont Farm was a farm only in name. There was no wall more than three feet high left standing; the whole place was shapeless, stark, blasted into nothingness. In the very centre of the mournful chaos lay three disembowelled horses and an overturned Boche ammunition waggon. The shells were still on the shelves. They were Yellow Cross, the deadliest of the Boche mustard-gas shell.

I went on leave next morning, and got a motor-car lift from Peronne as far as Amiens. Before reaching Villers-Bretonneux, of glorious, fearful memories, we passed through Warfusee-Abancourt, a shell of its former self, a brick heap, a monument of devastation. An aged man and a slim white-faced girl were standing by the farm cart that had brought them there, the first civilians I had seen since August. The place was deserted save for them. In sad bereavement they looked at the cruel desolation around them.

"My God," said my companion, interpreting my inmost thought, "what a home-coming!"

CHAPTER XVIII

A LAST DAY
AT THE O.P.

WHEN, ON OCTOBER 21, I returned to France, the war had made a very big stride towards its end. Cambrai had been regained, and Le Cateau - "Lee Katoo," the men insisted on calling it - taken. Ostend was ours, Lille was ours; over Palestine we had cast our mantle. Our own Division, still hard at it, had gone forward twenty-four miles during my fortnight's leave in England. Stories of their doings trickled towards me when I broke the journey at Amiens on my way back to the lines. I met an Infantry captain bound for England.

"It's been all open fighting this last fortnight - cavalry, and forced marches, and all that - and I don't want to hear any more talk of the new Armies not being able to carry out a war of movement," he said chirpily. "The men have been magnificent. The old Boche is done now; but we're making no mistakes - we're after him all the while.

"Dam funny, you know, some of the things that are happening up there. The Boche has left a lot of coal dumps behind, and every one's after it. There's a 2000-ton pile at Le Cateau, and it was disappearing so rapidly that they put a guard on it. I was walking with my colonel the other day, and we came across an Australian shovelling coal from this dump into a G.S. waggon. A sentry, with fixed bayonet, was marching up an' down.

"The colonel stopped when we came to the sentry, and asked him what he was supposed to be doing.

"'Guarding the coal dump, sir.'

"'But what is this Australian doing? Has he any authority to draw coal? Did he show you a chit?'

"'No, sir,' replied the sentry. 'I thought, as he had a Government waggon, it would be all right.'

"'Upon my Sam!' said the colonel, astonished. Then he tackled the Australian.

"'What authority have you for taking away this coal?' he asked.

"The Australian stood up and said, 'I don't want any authority - I bally well fought for it,' and went on with his shovelling.

"Frankly, the colonel didn't know what to say; but he has a sense of humour. 'Extraordinary fellows!' he said to me as we walked off.

"Then we came across an American who was 'scrounging' or something in an empty house. He jumped to attention when he saw the colonel, and saluted very smartly. But what do you think? He saluted with a bowler hat on, - found it in the house, I expect.... I tell you, it was an eye-opening day for the colonel."

I lorry-hopped to the village that I had been told was Divisional Headquarters; but they had moved the day before, seven miles farther forward. There were nearly 200 civilians here. I saw a few faded, ancient men in worn corduroys and blue-peaked caps; a bent old crone, in a blue apron, hobbled with a water-bucket past a corner shop - a grocer's - shuttered, sluttish from want of paint; three tiny children, standing in doorways, wore a strangely old expression. There was a pathetically furtive air about all these people. For four years they had been under the Boche. Of actual, death-bringing, frightening war they had seen not more than five days. The battle had swept over and beyond them, carrying with it the feared and hated German, and the main fighting force of the pursuing British as well. But it was too soon yet for them to forget, or to throw off a sort of lurking dread that even now the Boche might return.

I got a lift in another lorry along a road crumbling under the unusual amount of traffic that weighed upon it. Our advance had been so swift that the war scars on the countryside had not entirely blighted its normal characteristics. Here were shell-holes, but no long succession of abandoned gun-positions, few horse-tracks, fewer trenches, and no barbed wire. The villages we went through had escaped obliterating shell fire. I learned that our attacks had been planned thus-wise. Near a bleak cross-roads I saw Collinge of B Battery, and got off the lorry to talk to him.

"Brigade Headquarters are at Bousies, about six miles from here," he said. "I'm going that way. The batteries are all in Bousies."

"What sort of a time have you had?" I inquired.

"Oh, most exciting! Shan't forget the day we crossed the Le Cateau river. We were the advance Brigade. The Engineers were supposed to put bridges across for us; the material came up all right, but the pioneers who were to do the work missed the way. The sapper officer who had brought the material wanted to wait till the proper people arrived, but the Boche was shelling and machine-gunning like mad, and the colonel said that bridge-building must be got on with at once. The colonel was great that day. Old Johns of D Battery kept buzzing along with suggestions, but the colonel put his foot down, and said, 'It's the sapper officer's work; let him do it.' And the bridges were really well put up. All the guns got across safely, although C Battery had a team knocked out."

I walked by Collinge's side through a village of sloping roofs, single-storied red-brick houses, and mud-clogged streets. It was the village which our two brigades of artillery occupied when the Armistice was signed, where the King came to see us, and M. le Maire, in his excitement, gave His Majesty that typically French, shall I say? clasp of intimacy and brotherliness, a left-handed handshake.

"Curious thing happened on that rise," remarked Collinge when we were in open country again. "The colonel and the adjutant were with an infantry General and his Staff officers, reconnoitring. The General had a little bitch something like a whippet. She downed a hare, and though it brought them into view of the Boche, the General, the colonel, and the others chased after them like mad. I believe the colonel won the race - but the adjutant will tell you all about it."

Away on the left a lone tree acted as a landmark for a sunken road. "Brigade tried to make a headquarters there," went on Collinge, "but a signaller got knocked out, and the Boche began using the tree as a datum point; so the colonel ordered a shift." Twenty rough wooden crosses rose mournful and remote in a wide, moist mangel-field. "The cavalry got it badly there," said Collinge. "A 4·2 gun turned on them from close range, and did frightful execution." We were near to a cross-road, marked balefully by a two-storied house, cut in half so that the interior was opened to view like a doll's house, and by other shell-mauled buildings. "The batteries came into action under that bank," he continued, pointing his cane towards a valley riddled with shell-holes. "That's where Dumble did so well. Came along with the cavalry an hour and a half before any Horse Artillery battery, and brought his guns up in line, like F.A.T.... See that cemetery on the top of the hill?... the Boche made it in August 1914; lot of the old Army buried there, and it's been jolly well looked after. The colonel walked round and looked at every grave one day; he said he'd never seen a better cared-for cemetery.... We had an 'O.P.' there for the Richemont River fight. The Boche shelled it like blazes some days.... And we saw great sights up that *pavé* road there, over the dip. They held a big conference there; all sorts of Generals turned up.... Staff cars that looked like offices, with the maps and operation orders pinned up inside; and when our battery went by, the road was so packed with traffic that infantry were marching along in fours on either side of the road."

We reached the outskirts of Le Cateau, descending a steep *pavé* road. "They shelled this place like stink yesterday," Collinge told me. "Headquarters were in one of those little houses on the left for one night, and their waggon line is there now, so you'll be able to get a horse.... I heard that Major Bartlett had both his chargers killed yesterday when C Battery came through.... Isn't that one of them, that black horse lying under the trees?"

I looked and saw many horses lying dead on both sides of the road, and thought little of it. That was war. Then all my senses were strung up to attention: a small bay horse lay stretched out on the pathway, his head near the kerb. There was a shapeliness of the legs and a fineness of the mud-checkered coat that seemed familiar. I stepped over to look. Yes, it was my own horse "Tommy," that old Castle, our ex-adjutant, had given me - old Castle's "handy little horse." A gaping hole in the head told all that needed to be told. I found "Swiffy" and the doctor in the workman's cottage that had become Brigade waggon-line headquarters. Yes, "Tommy" had been killed the day before. My groom, Morgan, was riding him. The Boche were sending over shrapnel, high in the air, and one bullet had found its billet. Poor little horse! Spirited, but easy to handle, always in condition, always well-mannered. Ah, well! we had had many good days together. Poor little horse!

*   *   *   *   *

I want always to remember Bousies, the village of gardens and hedgerows and autumn tints where we saw the war out, and lay under shell fire for the last time; whence we fought our final battle on November 4th, when young Hearn of A Battery was killed by machine-gun bullets at 70 yards' range, and Major Bullivant, with a smashed arm and a crippled thigh, huddled under a wall until Dumble found him - the concluding fight that brought me a strange war trophy in a golfing-iron found in a hamlet that the Boche had sprawled upon for four full years…. And the name punched on the iron was that of an Oxford Street firm.

Collinge and I rode into Bousies in the wan light of an October afternoon. At a cross-roads that the Boche had blown up - "They didn't do it well enough; the guns got round by that side track, and we were only held up ten minutes," said Collinge - Brigade Headquarters' sign-board had been planted in a hedge. My way lay up a slushy tree-bordered lane; Collinge bade me good-bye, and rode on down the winding street.

There were the usual welcoming smiles. Manning gave me a "Had a good leave, sir?" in his deep-sea voice, and Wilde came out to show where my horse could be stabled. "It's a top-hole farm, and after the next move we'll bring Headquarters waggon line up here…. The colonel says you can have his second charger now that you've lost 'Tommy.' He's taking on Major Veasey's mare, the one with the cold back that bucks a bit. She's a nice creature if she's given plenty of work."

"How is the colonel?" I asked.

"Oh, he's in great form; says the war may end any minute. Major Simpson and Major Drysdale are both away on leave, and the colonel's been up a good deal seeing the batteries register…. We got a shock when we came into this place yesterday. A 4·2 hit the men's cook-house, that small building near the gate…. But they haven't been troublesome since."

The end wall of the long-fronted narrow farmhouse loomed up gauntly beside the pillared entrance to the rectangular courtyard. A weather-vane in the form of a tin trotting horse flaunted itself on the topmost point. This end wall rose to such height because, though the farmhouse was one-storied, its steep-sloping roof enclosed an attic big enough to give sixty men sleeping room. Just below the weather-vane was a hole poked out by the Boche for observation purposes. Our adjutant used to climb up to it twice daily as a sort of constitutional. Some one had left in this perch a bound volume of a Romanist weekly, with highly dramatic, fearfully coloured illustrations. As the house contained some twenty of these volumes, I presumed that they betrayed the religious leanings of the farm's absent owner. A row of decently ventilated stables faced the farmhouse, while at the end of the courtyard, opposite to the entrance gates, stood an enormous high-doored barn. The entrance-hall of the house gave, on the left, to two connecting stone-flagged rooms, one of which Manning used as a kitchen - Meddings, our regular cook, was on leave. The other room, with its couple of spacious civilian beds, we used as a mess, and the colonel and the adjutant slept there. The only wall decorations were two "samplers" executed by a small daughter of the house, a school certificate in a plain frame, and a couple of gaudy-tinselled religious pictures. A pair of pot dogs on the mantelpiece were as stupidly ugly as some of our own mid-Victorian cottage treasures. And there were the usual glass-covered orange blossoms mounted on red plush and gilt leaves - the wedding custom traditional to the country districts of Northern France. The inner door of this room opened directly into the stable where our horses were stalled. An infantry colonel and his staff occupied the one large and the two small rooms to the right of the entrance-hall; but after dinner they left us to go forward, and my servant put down a mattress on the stone floor of one of the smaller rooms for me to sleep upon. Wilde took possession of the other little chamber. The large room, which contained a colossal oak wardrobe, became our mess after breakfast next day. The signallers had fixed their telephone exchange in the vaulted cellar beneath the house, and the servants and grooms crowded there as well when the Boche's night-shelling grew threatening.

After a long deprivation we had come into a country where cabbages and carrots, turnips and beetroot, were to be had for the picking; and there were so many plates and glasses to be borrowed from the farmhouse cupboards that I feared greatly that Manning would feel bound to rise to the unexampled occasion by exercising his well-known gift for smashing crockery. We dined pleasantly and well that night; and when the night-firing programme had been sent out to the batteries - the Boche was in force in the big thick forest that lay three thousand yards east of our farm - we settled down to a good hour's talk. Wilde told me of the German sniper they had found shot just before the advance to this village; the adjutant narrated the magnificent gallantry of an officer who had relinquished his job of Reconnaissance officer to the C.R.A. in order to join a battery, and had now gone home with his third wound since Zillebeke. "You remember how he came back in time for the August advance and got hit immediately and wouldn't let them send him back to England - you know we loaned him to the ——rd Brigade because they were short of officers. Well, he rolled up again about ten days ago, and got hit again in the Le Cateau attack. Major 'Pat' told me he was wonderful…. Lay in a shell-hole with his leg smashed - they poured blood out of his boots - and commanded his battery from there, blowing his whistle and all that, until they made him let himself be taken away." The colonel, who listened and at the same time wrote letters, said that the thing that pleased him most during the last few days was the patriotic instinct of some cows. When the Hun evacuated Le Cateau he took away with him all the able-bodied Frenchmen and all the cows. But his retreat became so rapid and so confused, that numbers of the men escaped. So did the cows: for three days they were dribbling back to their homesteads and pasturages.

All through the night the enemy shelled Bousies. He planted only two near us, but a splinter made a hole in the roof of the big barn and caught a mule on the shoulder.

The doctor came up from the waggon line next morning and accompanied me on a tour of the batteries. "If you follow the yellow wire you'll come to B Battery," said Wilde. "They are in the corner of a meadow. A Battery are not far away, across the stream." It was a golden autumn day, and our feet rustled through the fallen yellow leaves that carpeted a narrow lane bowered by high, luxuriant, winding hedges. "Why, this place must be a paradise in peace times," said the doctor, entranced by the sweet tranquillity of the spot. "It's like a lover's walk you see in pictures." We strode over fallen trees and followed the telephone wire across a strip of rich green. B Battery's guns were tucked beneath some stubby full-leaved trees that would hide them from the keenest-eyed aerial observer. "No sick, doctor," called Bob Pottinger from underneath the trench-cover roof of his three-foot hole in the ground. "We're improving the position and have no time to be ill." The doctor and I crossed a sticky water-logged field, and passed over the plank-bridge that spanned the slow vagrant stream. A battery had their mess in one of the low creeper-clad cottages lining the road. Their guns were thrust into the hedge that skirted the neat garden at the back.

Major Bullivant gave me welcome, and read extracts from Sir Douglas Haig's report on the Fifth Army Retreat - his 'Times' had just reached him. He asked the doctor whether it was too early for a whisky-and-soda, and showed us a Boche barometer, his latest war trophy. "We've lost quite a lot of men since you've been away," he told me. "Do you realise the Brigade has been only four days out of the line since August 1st? You've heard about young Beale being wounded, of course? I was on leave, and so was Beadle; and Tincler was sick, so there was only Dumble and Beale running the battery. Beale got hit when shifting the waggon line,… and it was rather fine of him. He knew old Dumble was up to his eyes that day, and told the sergeant-major not to tell Dumble what had happened to him, until the battle was over. Did you hear, too, about Manison, one of the new officers? Poor chap! Killed by a bomb dropped in daylight by one of our own aeroplanes as he was going to the O.P.

"The Boche hasn't done much night-bombing lately. I don't think he's got the 'planes. He gave us one terrible night, though, soon after we crossed the canal,... knocked out two of my guns and killed any number of horses. There were ammunition dumps going up all over the place that night;... he stopped us from doing our night firing.

"Have you heard the story of the old woman at S——?" he went on. "When the bombardment was going on the civilians went down into the cellars. The Germans hooked it, and the people came up from the cellars. But Boche snipers were still in the village, and our advance parties warned the inhabitants to keep below.... When, however, our troops came along in a body, one old woman rushed forward from under the church wall, in the square, you know.... She was excited, I expect.... A swine of a Boche in a house on the far side of the square shot her.... Our infantry surrounded that house."

"Well, I must quit," ejaculated the doctor suddenly. We went out and made for the village road again. A screaming swish, and a report that hurt the ears and shattered the windows in the front of the cottage. A Boche high-velocity shell had crashed a few yards away on the other side of the stream, and thrown up spouts of black slimy mud. The doctor and I scurried back to the shelter of the cottage wall. Another shell and another. A lieutenant-colonel of Infantry, on horseback, swung violently round the corner and joined us. Three more shells fell. Then silence. "These sudden bursts of fire are very disconcerting, aren't they?" remarked the colonel as he mounted and rode away.

"Say, now!" said the doctor to me. "I think we'll call back and have that whisky-and-soda Major Bullivant offered us before we resume our journey."

"We'll take a trip up to the 'O.P.' this morning," said the colonel to me at breakfast on October 28th. The wind was sufficiently drying to make walking pleasant, and to tingle the cheeks. The sun was a tonic; the turned-up earth smelt good. Our Headquarter horses had been put out to graze in the orchard - a Boche 4·2 had landed in it the night before - and they were frolicking mightily, Wilde's charger "Blackie" being especially industrious shooing off one of the mules from the colonel's mare. There was a swirling and a skelter of brown and yellow leaves at the gap in the lane where we struck across a vegetable garden. A square patch torn from a bed-sheet flew taut from the top of a clump of long hop-poles - the sign, before the village was freed, to warn our artillery observers that civilians lived in the cottage close by. Similar, now out-of-date, white flags swung to the breeze from many roof-tops in the village. "The extraordinary feature," the colonel mentioned, "was the number of Tricolours that the French had been able to hide from the Germans; they put them out when we came through." He nodded a pleasant good-day to a good looking young staff officer who stood on the steps of the house in the *pavé*-laid street where one of our infantry brigades had made their headquarters. The staff officer wore a pair of those full-below-the-knee "plus 4 at golf" breeches that the Gardee affects. "For myself, I wouldn't wear that kind of breeches unless I were actually on duty with the Guards," said the colonel rather sardonically - "they are so intensely ugly." A tiny piano tinkled at a corner house near the roofless church and the Grande Place. In two-foot letters on the walls in the square were painted, "Hommes" on some houses, "Femmes" on others: reminders of the Boche method of segregating the sexes before he evacuated the inhabitants he wanted to evacuate. Only five civilians remained in the village now - three old men and two feeble decrepit women, numbed and heart-sick with the war, but obstinate in clinging to their homesteads. Already some of our men were patching leaky, shrapnel-flicked roofs with biscuit-tins and strong strips of waterproof sheeting.

We passed through A Battery's garden at nine o'clock. "We won't disturb them," said the colonel. "Bullivant is a morning sleeper, and is certain not to be up after the night-firing." Round the corner, however, stood a new officer who looked smart and fresh, with brightly polished buttons and Sam Browne belt. He saluted in the nervously precise fashion of the newly-joined officer. The colonel answered the salute, but did not speak; and he and I worked our way - following the track of a Tank - through and between hedges and among fruit-trees that had not yet finished their season's output. We passed the huddled-up body of a shot British soldier lying behind a fallen tree-trunk. We were making for the quarry in which C and D Batteries were neighbours. On a ditch-bordered road we met ten refugees, sent back that morning from a hamlet a mile and a half away, not yet considered safe from the Boche. The men, seeing us, removed their hats and lowered them as far as the knee - the way in which the Boche had commanded them to proffer respect. One aged woman in a short blue skirt wore sabots, and British puttees in place of stockings.

There had been a mishap at D Battery in the early hours of the morning. Their five useable 4·5 howitzers had been placed in a perfect how. position against the bank of the quarry. In the excitement of night-firing a reinforcement gunner had failed to "engage the plungers," the muzzle had not been elevated, and the shell, instead of descending five thousand yards away, had hit the bank twelve yards in front. The explosion killed two of the four men working that particular how. and wounded a third, and knocked out the N.C.O. in charge of another how. forty yards distant. The colonel examined the howitzer, looked gravely severe, and said that an officers' inquiry would be held next day. He asked Major Bartlett of C Battery, who was housed in a toy-sized cottage in the centre of the quarry, how his 18-pdrs. were shooting; and mentioned that the infantry were apprehensive of short-shooting along a road close to our present front line, since it lay at an awkward angle for our guns. Major Bartlett, self-possessed, competent, answered in the way the colonel liked officers to answer - no "I thinks": his replies either plain "Yes" or "No." Major Bartlett gave chapter and verse of his battery-shooting during the two previous days, and said that every round had been observed fire.

Walking briskly - the colonel was the fittest man of forty-five I have known - we mounted a slope of turnip-fields and fresh-ploughed land. There was a plantation five hundred yards to right of us, and five hundred yards to left of us; into the bigger one on the left two 5·9's dropped as we came level with it. Splashes of newly thrown-up earth behind tree-clumps, against banks and alongside hedges, showed the short breast-high trenches, some six yards long, in which the infantry had fought a few days before. Fifteen hundred yards away the clustering trees of the great forest where the enemy lay broke darkly against the horizon. "You see that row of tall straight trees in front of the forest, to the right of the gabled house where the white flag is flying," said the colonel, pulling out his glasses - "that's the present front line." Three ponderous booms from that direction denoted trench mortars at work.

We descended the other side of the slope, keeping alongside a hedge that ran towards a red-roofed farm. In two separate places about three yards of the hedge had been cut away. "Boche soldiering!" remarked the colonel informatively. "Enabled him to look along both sides of the hedge and guard against surprise when our infantry were coming up."

"We may as well call at Battalion Headquarters," he added when we reached the farm. In a wide cellar, where breakfast had not yet been cleared away, we came upon a lieutenant-colonel, twenty-four years of age, receiving reports from his company commanders. Suave in manner, clear-eyed, not hasty in making judgments, he had learnt most things to be known about real war at Thiepval, Schwaben Redoubt, and other bloody places where the Division had made history; wounded again in the August advance, he had refused to be kept from these final phases. The colonel and he understood each other. There was the point whether liaison duties between infantry and artillery could be more usefully conducted in the swift-changing individual fighting of recent days from infantry brigade or from infantry battalion; there were conflicting statements by junior officers upon short-shooting, and they required sifting; a few words had to be said about the battalion's own stretch of front and its own methods of harassing the enemy. A few crisp questions and replies, all bearing upon realities, a smile or two, a consultation of maps, and another portion of the colonel's task for that day was completed.

We walked across more ploughed land towards a sunken road, where infantry could be seen congregated in that sort of *dolce far niente* which, on the part of infantry in support, is really rather deceptive.

A "ping-ping!" whisked past, and stung us to alertness.

"Hullo - machine-guns!" ejaculated the colonel, and we quickened our steps toward the sunken road.

A major and a subaltern of the machine-gunners clambered down the opposite bank.

"I believe I've spotted that fellow, sir," burst forth the major with some excitement. "I think he's in a house over there... might be a target for you... bullets have been coming from that way every now and again for two days.... I'll show you, if you like, sir."

The major and the colonel crept out on top of the bank, and made for a shell-hole forty yards in front. I followed them. The major pointed across the rolling grass lands to a two-storied grey house with a slate roof, fourteen hundred yards away. "I believe he's in there," he said with decision.

The colonel looked through his glasses.

The major spoke again. "Do you see the square piece removed from the church spire, sir?... That looks like an 'O.P.', doesn't it?"

The colonel opened his map and pointed to a tiny square patch. "I make that to be the house," he said. "Do you agree?"

"Yes, sir," replied the major. "We thought at first it was the house you see marked four hundred yards more south-east; but I believe that is really the one."

"I've got an 'O.P.' farther forward. I'm going up there now. We'll have a shot at the house," responded the colonel simply.

The major went back to the sunken road. The colonel and I walked straight ahead, each of us in all probability wondering whether the Boche machine-gunner was still on duty, and whether he would regard us as worthy targets. That, at any rate, was my own thought. We strode out over the heavy-going across a strip of ploughed land, and heard the whizz of machine-gun bullets once more, not far from the spot we had just left. We did not speak until we descended to a dip in the ground, and reached a brook that had to be jumped. We were absolutely by ourselves.

Up the slope, on the far side of the brook. More ploughed land. We were both breathing hard now.

Before we came to the crest of the slope the colonel stopped. "We're in view from the Boche front line from the top," he said sharply. "The 'O.P.' is a hole in the ground.... You had better follow me about twenty yards behind.... And keep low.... Make for the fifth telegraph-pole from the left that you will see from the top."

He moved off. I waited and then followed, my mind concentrated at first on the fifth telegraph-pole the colonel had spoken about. There was no shelling at this moment. A bird twittered in a hedge close by; the smell of grass and of clean earth rose strong and sweet. No signs or sound of war; only sunshine and trees and ——

The colonel's voice came sharp as whipcord. "Keep down! - keep down!" I bent almost double and walked fast at the same time. My mind turned to September 1916, when I walked along Pozières Ridge, just before the Courcellette fight, and was shouted at for not crouching down by my battery commander. But there were shells abroad that day.... I almost laughed to myself.

I tumbled after the colonel into the square hole that constituted the "O.P." - it had been a Boche trench-mortar emplacement. The sweat dripped down my face as I removed my tin hat; my hair was wet and tangled.

Johns, a subaltern of D Battery, was in the pit with a couple of telephonists. He was giving firing instructions to the battery.

"What are you firing at, Johns?" inquired the colonel, standing on a step cut in the side of the pit, and leaning his elbows on the parapet.

"Two hundred yards behind that road, sir - trench mortars suspected there, sir." He called, "All guns parallel!" down the telephone.

"Don't you keep your guns parallel when you aren't firing?" asked the colonel quickly. "Isn't that a battery order?"

Johns flushed and replied, "No, sir.... We left them as they were after night-firing."

"But don't you know that it is an Army order - that guns should be left parallel?"

"Y-e-es, sir."

"Why don't you obey it, then?"

"I thought battery commanders were allowed their choice. I ——"

The colonel cut poor Johns short. "It's an Army order, and has to be obeyed. Army orders are not made for nothing. The reason that order was made was because so many battery commanders were making their own choice in the matter. Consequently there was trouble and delay in 'handing over.' So the Army made a standard ruling."

Then, as was always the case, the colonel softened in manner, and told Johns to do his shooting just as if he were not looking on.

The new subaltern of A Battery suddenly lowered himself into the pit. The colonel brightened. "You see the grey house over there!... Can you see it?... Good!... An enemy machine-gun is believed to be there.... I want you to fire on that house.... There's the point on the map."

"Sorry, sir, my wire to the battery is not through yet - I've just been out on it."

The colonel looked at his watch. "It's half-past eleven now. Your line ought to be through by this time."

"Yes, sir; it's been through once, but it went half an hour ago. I expect my signallers back any minute."

"Very well! you can be working out your switch angle and your angle of sight while you wait."

Johns had now got his battery to work, and the sight of his shells bursting among the hedges and shrubs fired his Celtic enthusiasm and dissipated the nervousness he had felt in the colonel's presence. "Look at that! isn't that a fine burst?" he called, clutching my arm, - "and see that one. Isn't it a topper?"

An exclamation from the colonel, who had stood sphinx-like, his glasses directed upon the grey house, made every one turn. "I've spotted him," he called, his voice vibrating. "He's at the top-floor window nearest to us.... There he goes again.... I heard the 'ping' and saw dust come out of the window.... Now then, is that line through yet?"

The line wasn't through, and the excitement of the hunt being upon us, every one felt like cursing all telephone lines - they always did break down when they were most wanted. The five minutes before this line was reported to be through seemed an hour, and when the telephonist had laboriously to repeat the orders, each one of us itched to seize the telephone and shout ribald abuse at the man at the other end.

The first shell went into the trees behind the house. So did the round, three hundred yards shorter in range, by which it had been hoped to complete a plus and minus bracketing of the target. After a bold shortening of the range, the subaltern, directing the shooting of A Battery's guns, was about to order a wide deflection to the left, but the colonel stopped him. "Your line is all right," he said. "It looks as if you were too much to the right from the 'O.P.', but that's the deceptiveness of flank observation. The range is short, that's all. Give it another hundred yards and see what happens."

A direct hit resulted in twenty rounds, and there was jubilation in the "O.P." M'Whirter of C Battery turned up, also Captain Hopton of B, and preparations for a window-to-window searching and harrying of the Boche machine-gunners were eagerly planned. It was 2 P.M. now, and the colonel had forgotten all about lunch. "I think we can get back now," he said brightly. "Register on that house," he added, turning to the officers in the pit, "and you can give that machine-gunner a hot time whenever he dares to become troublesome."

We walked back to the sunken road in the highest of spirits, and after the major of the Machine-Gun Corps, who had watched the shooting, had thanked the colonel and expressed the view that the Boche machine-gunner might in future be reckoned among the down-and-outs, the colonel talked of other things besides gunnery.

I told him that though on my last leave to England I had noted a new seriousness running through the minds of people, I had not altogether found the humble unselfishness, the chastened spirit that many thinkers had prophesied as inevitable and necessary before the coming of victory.

"But what about the men who have been out here? Won't they be the people of England after the war - the real representative people?" returned the colonel, his eyes lighting up as he talked. "Theirs has been the chastening experience, at any rate. The man who comes through this must be the better man for it."

The conversation lost its seriousness when we discussed whether Army habits would weave themselves into the ordinary workaday world as a result of the war.

"Some of them would be good for us," said the colonel happily. "Here's one" - picking up a rifle and carrying it at the slope - "I'm going to carry this to the first salvage dump, and help to keep down taxation."

"It might be an interesting experiment to run Society on Active Service lines," I put in. "Fancy being made an Acting-Baronet and then a Temporary-Baronet before getting substantive rank. And the thought of an Acting-Duke paralyses one."

We laughed and walked on. Along the road leading back into the village we met a bombardier, who saluted the colonel with the direct glance and the half-smile that betokens previous acquaintance. The colonel stopped. "What's your name, Bombardier?" he demanded. The bombardier told him. "Weren't you in my battery?"

"Yes, sir," said the man, smiling, "when we first came to France.... I'd like to be back in the old Division, sir."

"I'll see what can be done," said the colonel, taking his name and number.

"I believe I remember him, because he often came before me as a prisoner," he told me, with a humorous look, as we continued our walk. "Very stout fellow, though."

It was a quarter-past three now, and the experiences of the day had sharpened the appetite. The colonel wasn't finished yet, however. He turned into the Infantry Brigade Headquarters, and spent a quarter of an hour with the brigadier general and his brigade-major discussing the artillery work that would be required for the next big advance. We discovered a lane we hadn't walked through before, and went that way to our farmhouse. It was four o'clock when we got back, and two batteries had prisoners waiting to go before the colonel. So lunch was entirely wiped off the day's programme, and at a quarter to five we sat down to tea and large quantities of buttered toast.

CHAPTER XIX
"THE COLONEL ———"

WE KNEW NOW that November 4th was the date fixed for the next battle. The C.R.A. had offered the Brigade two days at the waggon lines, as a rest before zero day. The colonel didn't want to leave our farm, but two nights at the waggon lines would mean respite from night-firing for the gunners; so he had asked the battery commanders to choose between moving out for the two days and remaining in the line. They had decided to stay.

It turned to rain on October 29th. Banks of watery, leaden-hued clouds rolled lumberingly from the south-west; beneath a slow depressing drizzle the orchard became a melancholy vista of dripping branches and sodden muddied grass. The colonel busied himself with a captured German director and angle-of-sight instrument, juggling with the working parts to fit them for use with our guns - he had the knack of handling intricate mechanical appliances. The adjutant curled himself up among leave-rosters and ammunition and horse returns; I began writing the Brigade Diary for October, and kept looking over the sandbag that replaced the broken panes in my window for first signs of finer weather.

The colonel and the adjutant played Wilde and myself at bridge that night - the first game in our mess since April. Then the colonel and I stayed up until midnight, talking and writing letters: he showed me a diminutive writing-pad that his small son had sent by that day's post. "That's a reminder that I owe him a letter," he smiled. "I must write him one…. He's just old enough now to understand that I was coming back to the war, the last time I said good-bye." The colonel said this with tender seriousness.

A moaning wind sprang up during the night, and, sleepless, I tossed and turned upon my straw mattress until past two o'clock. One 4·2 fell near enough to rattle the remaining window-panes. The wail through the air and the soft "plop" of the gas shells seemed attuned to the dirge-like soughing of the wind.

The morning broke calm and bright. There was the stuffiness of yesterday's day indoors to be shaken off. I meant to go out early. It was our unwritten rule to leave the colonel to himself at breakfast, and I drove pencil and ruler rapidly, collating the intelligence reports from the batteries. I looked into the mess again for my cap and cane before setting forth. The colonel was drinking tea and reading a magazine propped up against the sugar-basin. "I'm going round the batteries, sir," I said. "Is there anything you want me to tell them - or are you coming round yourself later?"

"No; not this morning. I shall call on the infantry about eleven - to talk about this next battle."

"Right, sir!"

He nodded, and I went out into the fresh cool air of a bracing autumn day.

I did my tour of the batteries, heard Beadle's jest about the new groom who breathed a surprised "Me an' all?" when told that he was expected to accompany his officer on a ride up to the battery; and, leaving A Battery's cottage at noon, crossed the brook by the little brick bridge that turned the road towards our Headquarters farm, six hundred yards away.

"The colonel rang up a few minutes ago to say that our notice-board at the bottom of the lane had been blown down. He wanted it put right, because the General is coming to see him this afternoon, and might miss the turning.... I've told Sergeant Starling.

"Colonel B—— came in about eleven o'clock," went on the adjutant. "He's going on leave and wanted to say good-bye to the colonel."

"Where is the colonel now," I asked, picking up some Divisional reports that had just arrived.

"He's with the Heavies - he's been to the Infantry. I told him Colonel B—— had called, and he said he'd go round and see him - their mess is in the village, isn't it?"

At twelve minutes past one the adjutant, Wilde, and myself sat down to lunch. "The colonel said he wouldn't be late - but we needn't wait," said the adjutant.

"No; we don't want to wait," agreed Wilde, who had been munching chocolate.

At a quarter-past one; "Crump!" "Crump!" "Crump!" - the swift, crashing arrival of three high-velocity shells.

"I'll bet that's not far from A Battery," called Wilde, jumping up; and then settled down again to his cold beef and pickles.

"First he's sent over to-day," said the adjutant. "He's been awfully quiet these last two days."

Manning had brought in the bread-and-butter and apple pudding that Meddings had made to celebrate his return from leave, when the door opened abruptly. Gillespie, the D.A. gas officer stood there. It was the habit to complain with mock-seriousness that Gillespie timed his visits with our meal-times. I had begun calling "Here he is again," when something drawn, something staring in his lean Scotch face, stopped me. I thought he was ill.

The adjutant and Wilde were gazing curiously at him. My eyes left his face. I noticed that his arms were pushed out level with his chest; he grasped an envelope between the thumb and forefinger of each hand. His lower jaw had fallen; his lips moved, and no sound came from them.

The three of us at the table rose to our feet. All our faculties were lashed to attention.

Gillespie made a sort of gulp. "I've got terrible news," he said at last.

I believe that one thought, and only one thought, circuited through the minds of the adjutant, Wilde, and myself: The colonel! - we knew! we knew!

"The colonel ——" went on Gillespie. His face twitched.

Wilde was first to speak. "Wounded?" he forced himself to ask, his eyes staring.

"Killed! - killed!" said Gillespie, his voice rising to a hoarse wail.

Then silence. Gillespie reached for a chair and sank into it.

I heard him, more master of himself, say labouringly, "Down at the bridge near A Battery… He and another colonel… both killed… they were standing talking… I was in A Battery mess… A direct hit, I should think."

The adjutant spoke in crushed awestruck tones. "It must have been Colonel B——."

I did not speak. I could not. I thought of the colonel as I had known him, better than any of the others: his gentleness, his honourableness, his desire to see good in everything, his quiet collected bravery, the clear alertness of his mind, the thoroughness with which he followed his calling of soldier; a man without a mean thought in his head; a true soldier who had received not half the honours his gifts deserved, yet grumbled not. Ah! no one passed over in the sharing out of honours and promotions could complain if he paused to think of the colonel.

I stared through the window at the bright sunlight. Dimly I became aware that Gillespie had laid the envelope upon the table, and heard him say he had found it lying in the roadway. I noticed the handwriting: the last letter the colonel had received from his wife. It must have been blown clean out of his jacket pocket; yet there it was, uninjured.

The adjutant's voice, low, solemn, but resolved - he had his work to do: "It is absolutely certain it was the colonel? There is no shadow of doubt? I shall have to report to 'Don Ack'!"

"No shadow of doubt," replied Gillespie hopelessly, moving his head from side to side.

Wilde came to me and asked if I would go with him to bring in the body. I shook my head. Life out here breeds a higher understanding of the mystic division between soul and body; one learns to contemplate the disfigured dead with a calmness that is not callousness. But this was different. How real a part he had played in my life these last two years! I wanted always to be able to recall him as I had known him alive - the slow wise smile, the crisp pleasant voice! I thought of that last note to his little son; I thought of the quiet affection in his voice when he spoke of keeping in touch with those who had shared the difficulties and the hardships of the life we had undergone. I recalled how he and I had carried a stretcher and searched for a dying officer at Zillebeke - the day I was wounded, - and how, when I was in hospital, he had written saying he was glad we had done our bit that day; I thought of his happy faith in a Christmas ending of the war. The hideous cruelty of it to be cut off at the very last, when all that he had given his best in skill and energy to achieve was in sight!

$$* \quad * \quad * \quad * \quad *$$

The shuffling tramp outside of men carrying a blanket-covered stretcher. They laid it tenderly on the flagstones beneath the sun-warmed wall of the house.

Wilde, his face grave, sad, desolate, walked through the mess to his room. I heard him rinsing his hands. A chill struck at my vitals.

$$* \quad * \quad * \quad * \quad *$$

It is finished. The colonel is dead. There is nothing more to write.

THE END